A Whole of The Whole

Bringing Back Uniqueness and Connectivity

Steve Patrick

Published by Steve Patrick

Salt Lake City, Utah

With much gratitude to:

Justin Pok • Cover Design
and final layout changes
required for printing

Dave Clark • Layout

Johannes Walter • Photo

Coffee Shops & Baristas
of Salt Lake City, Utah

All who allowed their glow to help me
see through my preconceptions

www.wholeofthewhole.com
www.lostinconcepts.com
www.passthroughbusinesses.com
www.lifeinfusedbusiness.com

ISBN (Paperback): 978-1-7322310-0-9

ISBN (Electronic Format): 978-1-7322310-1-6

To Maritza . . .

. . . with whom I first experienced

Grateful Being

Table of Contents

Part 2: Connectivity

Part 3: A Whole of the Whole

A Whole of The Whole

Bringing Back Uniqueness and Connectivity

Steve Patrick

Using words in such a way as to highlight
the Connectivity from which they come
rather than the separations to which they lead.

Author's Note – I Need to See for Myself

I often hear people say "I need to understand it for myself" or "I need to see for myself". All my life, I've felt that same need to know things *on* my own and *from* myself rather than take them on faith just because someone else says so.

I still feel that need.

Even though I've shifted away from needing to know things only in cognitive form, I still don't embrace the idea of "taking someone else's word for it" over my own experience. I want to know, not just believe.

What I've come to embrace is a different kind of knowing for myself. It's a way that underlies cognition and yet encompasses the noncognitive and the not known. It's a knowing that has brought peace, joy, and playfulness to a life that was rigidly right and good but incomplete and lacking. So much of what I'd accepted as "right and good" had been difficult for me to question because it had been so prevalent for so long.

I had confused "knowing for myself" with "thinking objectively" – and I believed all thinking had to be conceptual. My thinking objectively was highly restrictive because it was subject to the limitations of word-tools.

It turns out that most things that I thought were "right and good", the rules I had followed so rigidly, were arbitrary. I had accepted them as right simply because everything around me said so, not because I knew them for myself deep down.

I am uncovering what it is to know for myself deep down. I know you can too. Your uncovering will be uniquely yours. A version of knowing that does not copy or follow what we've been conditioned to accept, but one that forges new pathways of Being. Being that is uniquely me and uniquely you in Connectivity. Being that is me and is you as A Whole of The Whole.

Introduction

You Are the Source

In our world of how-to guides, it's easy to think that the primary source for what you want lies outside yourself. I spent much of my life trying to find an ideal job, perfect relationships, better ways to make more money, and an airtight philosophy for living.

If the ideas in this book catch your attention and pull at you, try them out. See if you discover something new for yourself. But ultimately anything new will come from *within yourself* – whenever something draws your attention, it's because there's already something inside you that recognizes it.

This book of narratives tells how I found the "new" by peeling off layers of *shoulds*, comparisons, *have-tos*, and pseudo certainties. These heavy overlays made it difficult for me and others to see what was ready to shine through, if only I would/could allow it.

Throughout my process, I needed – and still use – reminders to be patient and to allow myself to grow naturally. I've so often been pulled to look outside for advice, instruction, or guidance about my path. But every time I made the outside into a primary guide, it felt like I was trying to grab something and glue it onto myself – to force something to happen rather than to let it be nurtured. I've found that allowance, not force, is how I grow best.

I was a person of logic and reason who believed in an objective reality. Since the objective outside world was the key to my happiness, I thought I had to learn to mold that world to create what I wanted. I thought I had to be in control because I was independent and self-sufficient, and the outside world is objective.

Now I've uncovered a different reality for myself. I discovered what it is to "Be" – rather than to just think and feel and do, which for me meant *making* things happen.

I began to see that when I put my primary attention on thinking, feeling, and doing, I was looking outside myself for fulfillment. It was circular. Since I believed the outside determined my life experience, it was crucial that I put all my attention on it. For me, there was no whole self and no depth of Being. There was only a surface self that had to meet the expectations of objective reality – a surface reality I thought could make me happy.

Accepting concepts, logic, and reason as "bosses" made my mind cling to the outside world. I thought mind-as-boss took precedence over my body and other people and things near to me. After all, the mind is amazingly powerful. It made sense to believe it could make things happen and force them into place.

It turns out that my mind is powerful but not in the way I had thought. It is powerful as an interacting part of a whole self in an interconnected world. It is powerful as a very limited tool. Once I realized that allowance nurtured more expansive growth, and that force and willpower constricted this type of natural progress, my life experience became what I wanted: a grounded feeling of gratitude for myself and my surroundings. It was no longer a battleground demanding a win, a great achievement, or the careful categorizing of items into "right" and "wrong".

At long last, I found that the source of my knowing and growing was inside, not out. I hope you will find the same – that you are the source of yours.

Writing this Book

This book consists of narratives about finding my way to a better place. It's a journey that came through the discovery of ideas I'd not been aware of before: ideas that are less constricting and more open; ideas that point to possibilities instead of limits and boundaries. For me, they are ideas that breathe deeply with the flow of life.

As I practice these new, more open ideas, I feel as though shackles are being lifted off my shoulders. As I sense more and more release, I see more clearly the negative effects of those self-created chains.

It turns out that my shackles came from taking ideas too seriously, as absolutes rather than as one type of tool that can contribute to living. I have begun to free myself from rigid, tension-filled functioning by keeping in mind the limited nature of ideas, and by reminding myself that words are only tools – symbols that we create, well suited for some purposes but not for others.

This book describes how my misuse of word-tools was part of a seduction that lured me into an unwarranted sense of certainty. But the false certainty actually led to its opposite, self-doubt. I find that using words as absolutes brings me less certainty and security, not more, and that my sense of confidence increases as I view and use words as the limited, symbolic tools they are.

What words leave out makes them inadequate for certain jobs. Like any other tool, they are limited. But until I learned to see them only as tools, I was unaware of their limitations.

I was immersed in word-tools, like a fish in water, unable to see that anything else existed. As I opened up to see beyond cognition, I was surprised to find a sense of grounding that feels much better than confidence. As I move away from conceptual (word-based) certainty, I find a solid, grounded certainty of a different type.

Gradually I came to feel a sense of light playfulness with joyful peace as a background. Gradually the dominance of the ominous darkness, to which I was so accustomed, became less and less a part of my daily reality.

People say there is a first time for everything. This is a first book for me. At times, I felt doubt because I didn't know how it would turn out or even what section would come next. Yet with most sections, writing flowed out smoothly without struggle or thinking ahead.

What you see in this book is what came out of me when I was not constricted by taking my thoughts too seriously. It was written naturally, based on my experiences as I discovered what could happen when I placed my attention differently.

Terminology

I didn't write this book in a linear way. I wrote each section as it flowed out from wherever it came.

I roughly organized the sections into the three main parts. "Lost in Concepts" tells about feeling trapped by negativity in my mind. "Connectivity" describes experiencing less of these feelings of negativity as I began to allow and reduce the tension of those feelings. "A Whole of The Whole" points toward functioning as a whole-self, with an emphasis on the noncognitive – which is the source of the cognitive.

The journey of reading this book strikes me more like a treasure hunt than an instruction manual. I view it as material that may touch something in you, may serve as a catalyst for you, or may help you uncover a part of your core self that you may have sensed but haven't yet realized. Whenever I reread parts of this book – simply to remind myself and enjoy the insights – I find it continues to spur me toward uncovering parts of my core self that have not yet been fully realized.

Treasure hunts are meant to be fun. If you start reading a particular section and it's not fun, or if it doesn't tug at your desire to read more, I suggest you skip to any section with a title that sounds interesting.

If skipping around doesn't create an energy that pulls you to read more, I hope you will stop and do something else. I wish you enjoyment in living your life; not any feeling of compulsion that you should read this or any book.

I've found words to be approximations, not descriptions of "the truth". I see them as general indicators, at least as they apply to most life situations.

That is why I've occasionally used slashed sets of words to indicate a general *idea arena*. The slashed sets provide an array of words I view as essentially one and the same for the purpose of this book. One word may connect to your experience, another word to someone else's. There are times when it helps to be precise with words. But so much of the time, the limited nature of words doesn't warrant as much precision as we give them credit for.

With that in mind, I've included lists of what I view as essentially synonyms for the purposes of this book. Each word in a list belongs to the same general arena of meaning as the other words in that list. In any one section, I may have used one term rather than another. But I view that term as basically the same as the others in its listing.

- word ⇔ word-tool ⇔ concept ⇔ category ⇔ synthetic essential ⇔ language ⇔ symbol ⇔ label ⇔ name ⇔ snapshot ⇔ this-not-that-tool ⇔ cognitive ⇔ in-the-head ⇔ symbol system

- frozen reality ⇔ radar screen ⇔ surface self ⇔ perspective ⇔ point of view ⇔ opinion ⇔ ego ⇔ mind ⇔ conditioning ⇔ mind chatter

- experience ⇔ life ⇔ living that happens without words

- reality ⇔ Source ⇔ The Whole ⇔ Being ⇔ source self

Pop-Ins are groups of words that just came to me with no specific planning or intention. I felt surprise with each one. I would think, *Wow! That is amazing! I really like this!* Each one struck me as something I didn't create by myself.

I've listed some here because each carries a reminder I often use as I watch the tension produced by my mind chatter.

- Judge your experience, not people, events, situations, or circumstances

- Wow! I don't believe in right/wrong good/bad any longer!

- A Whole of The Whole

- *Enjoying knowing* is different from *enjoying knowing more than*

- Arm-in-arm

- Bringing back uniqueness and Connectivity

- Using words in such a way as to highlight the Connectivity from which they come rather than the separations to which they lead

- If there is only me, there is no me

Part 1: Lost in Concepts

What Is a Word?

So much of our lives involves using words. And for me they seem part of my world in the same way as houses, cars, trees, rocks, people, etc. It's easy to see them this way because they are such a large part of everything we do.

I wake up and yell "Bad dog!" because he pooped on the floor. Then, because I'm babysitting this dog while the owners are away, I worry, *What if I can't get the poop off of the carpet?* Then my mind moves to worries about my achy back, or whether I hurt my friend by something I said, or my boss's disappointment with my work. Words and the significance I put on them seem to be involved in every minute of my day.

I often feel like a fish in water. Word-based expressions and word-based inner thoughts are what my world is made of. What else is there in life except thoughts and communications made up of words? Well, there is also eating, sleeping, and bathing, but more often than not my mind is chattering about some worry, doubt, or hope even while I'm doing those potentially wordless activities.

My world is chock-full of word symbols that determine good/bad, right/wrong conclusions. These symbols also identify problems to be solved, worrisome outcomes, and other issues to be concerned about.

But what exactly is a word? Except for proper names such as Sam or Emily, every word comes from creating a category. Each word is a symbol we create as a shortcut for communicating a general category.

We see a variety of four-legged animals: a small brown fluffy one, then a large black one with a smooth fur, then a mid-sized white curly-haired one. By putting them all together into the same grouping, we create a concept. Then we assign a word to the concept/category; we give the whole grouping the name *dog* so that we can use it to think, write, and communicate.

We start with many different sizes and colors of actual dogs, and we end up with only one small word *dog*, which represents our choice to combine them all into one concept/category. We eventually learn that the word *dog* stands for a different concept than the words *cat* or *horse*. Words are a system of symbols we can speak or write in order to communicate.

Then we encounter other things that are round and roll across the floor. We eventually create another mental-grouping/category/concept and we call it *ball*. We learn that *dog* stands for a different mental grouping than *ball*. It's a bit like sorting things into piles.

We now have symbolic representations (words) of the kind of thing that barks and has four legs and the kind of the kind of thing that is round and rolls along the floor when we push it. Once we learn the category and the word that goes with it, we can quickly say *dog* when we see a barking, four-legged thing that we have never seen before. The differences in size, color, etc., no longer seem to matter because we know the concept and the word.

Words are very exclusive – they don't allow much flexibility. A dog cannot be a ball; a ball cannot be a dog. A word, as the symbol for a concept grouping, creates a world of differences with no overlap. It can't be both, it can be only one or the other. A word is a *this-not-that* categorization.

In using the words *dog* or *ball*, I leave out all the differences I first saw with my own eyes such as size, color, etc. I replace my experience of seeing the many different dogs and many different balls with shortcut tags we call *words*. I smooth over and minimize the importance of the uniqueness of each actual Being I experienced.

I forget that when I apply the one word *dog* to both very young dogs and to older ones, that I often misrepresent the full reality. When I say "Bad dog!" about what this three-month old puppy did on the living room floor, I omit relevant details, such as that it takes an average of six months to housetrain a puppy.

I also omit my part in this learning process. I may need to recognize that the puppy doesn't know what I'm saying when I tell him the proper place to poop. It may help to give this dog a small treat to develop an association that pooping outside is what I want and pooping inside is not. I've found that I am a master at using words in a way that pushes responsibility onto others, even small cute puppies.

The following quote illustrates how words leave out uniqueness.

> If I tell you to imagine a pink flower, you see a pink flower. I don't know what kind of flower it is; I don't know the shape or the size of this flower; I don't know exactly what shade of pink it is. But you do.[1]

One person might create a mental image of pink baby's breath, while another imagines a pink carnation or a pink rose. Different sizes, different shades of pink, different images; same word.

---

[1] Jody Whiteley, *Best Sleep Hypnosis Story Ever* (accessed November 3, 2017), https://www.youtube.com/?v=eu9RbDNaw-8, 7:26.

I find I easily forget that words are this-not-that tools – each word creates a separate bucket to indicate a general grouping. And in order to do that, the word leaves out details that make the reality of the experience unique. I forget that words carry only narrow slivers of a full context.

Words also leave out the surroundings in which we experience dogs. We see dogs running, sleeping, eating, playing – experiences that brought with them the interconnectedness these animals have with their environment. The word *dog* tells us nothing about the interconnectedness of the dog in the world.

In a sense, our word-tools are out of context because they leave out uniqueness and cannot carry the interconnectedness of the life experience from which we extracted them. That's why it's become so important to me to refer to words as only limited tools.

But the problem is not that words are limited tools. The problem is that I use them as if they weren't. I apply them to situations they are not suited for. I use them as absolutes as if they are truth-tellers, as I put judgmental labels on myself, other people, and puppies.

It's like trying to use a shovel as a scalpel. A shovel is a tool suited to digging a hole; a scalpel is suited to slicing skin during surgery. Each is a tool. But a shovel can't do the work of a scalpel. A shovel is a limited tool because it doesn't work for any of these other purposes.

As the limitations of word-tools became clearer to me, I learned to minimize their importance. Even now, I often remind myself of the full reality they leave out as reason to avoid taking them too seriously. This reduces the tension created by believing they are more than this-not-that buckets.

The *not* is something a word-tool grouping emphasizes. You are a woman not a man, dog, ball, etc. I am a man not a woman, flower, car, etc. Whatever anything is, as expressed through word-tools, includes a lot of "not".

Lost in Concepts

Every day, we are bombarded with what I call word-tools: symbols for the mental categories we call concepts. Why shouldn't we be immersed in them? After all, what else is there?

- What should I do?
- Why should I do it?
- How will I do it?
- What do I need to know, get, and manipulate in order to do it?

Goals, reasons, methods, knowledge, and resources – they are all concepts created by us. We are surrounded with concepts as they "guide" us through our days and affect our relationships with ourselves and others.

But what is a concept? Where does it come from? How often do we look beneath the surface of this world of words that masquerades as "everything"?

When we accumulate more and more concepts and then associate them based on logic and reason, we call it "knowledge" and come to feel that we know the truth. We feel we can be certain and gain security as long as we work within this structure, within the world of word-tool construction.

Widening my awareness, while allowing myself to consider reality outside my concept-based belief systems, led to sensing people and nature more deeply. It opened doors to questioning and to a vast potential that I hadn't known existed.

I began to see how firmly I had entrenched my certainty about knowing "the truth". I had been living almost completely within my own radar screen. (See "The Value of What I Don't Know" in Part 2: Connectivity.) Only my surface self existed – the one that deals with the goals, reasons, methods, knowledge, and resources of the world. I see now that I had closed out vast possibilities by regarding ideas as unquestionable because they were logical.

Why might I want to question my certainty? Because I keep running into person after person who appears to have a "the truth", a single, all-encompassing truth that is vastly different from mine. If we look, we find so many "the truths" that are different from those of my family, my friends, my community, my religion, my culture, etc. We all appear to think we know "the truth", and I for one often find myself spending lots of energy defending it.

How can there be so many versions of "the truth"?

I am trying to discover for myself, and to shine a light on, why so many "the truths" seem to exist in contradiction to one another. I view concepts and words as a part of understanding why we've formed these many opposing "the truths". It has to do with what concepts/words are, where they come from, and how their limitations contribute to the tendency to see them as everything.

As I have become more aware of the nature of our word-tools (concepts), I have come to know myself as a whole being and to feel the peace of Connectivity with other Beings and with the world around me. I have walked away, just a little, from a life dominated by the stress of having to constantly make sure something or someone is consistent with the this-not-that of a concept. (See "What Is a Word?")

I have walked, and continue to walk, toward a joyful flow of living in which I experience the color and vibrancy of life and the fullness of the moment, without as much of the resistance, tension, and defense I felt in the past.

Life feels different now. I found it by opening up to less-limiting concepts that were new to me. I looked within and weaved new concepts with daily experience of a state of awareness that is nonconceptual, a state that existed prior to words.

I know that you can experience this too, if you haven't already. I know it because you have the same inner state of awareness I have, an awareness that is the source of all types of knowing, cognitive and non-cognitive.

Feel Good Now

Who wouldn't want to feel good most of the time?

By this, I mean feeling good in a deeply beneficial way, not in the surface ways, such as the pleasures gained by overeating, illicit drugs, indiscriminate sex, extremely dangerous thrill seeking, etc. Pleasures that involve self-harm or harm to others is not what I mean by Feel Good Now.

Feel Good Now is a motto that's helped me shift attention away from negative thoughts/emotions and toward feeling just a little better. It's a shift from an inner state of tension/anxiety to one that is calm and more joyful. Feeling good means relaxed rather than tense, and at peace rather than filled with anxiety.

I first heard about Feel Good Now in Kevin Trudeau's *Your Wish Is Your Command* audio series. As I started applying it, I was surprised by how often I felt bad. It had become such a normal way of being that I hadn't noticed it until I started watching for it.

There was so much constant tension from blaming, resisting, and thinking I was superior. I felt so much fear, lack, loss, worry, and doubt. All this was accompanied by tension in my face, and I also noticed the strain during times I was labeling people as enemies. I began calling this *enemy mode* once I realized how frequently I fell into it.

I discovered these negatives fed on each other and multiplied into networks of badness. The scope of any one of them would expand to include an endless chain of interconnected word-tools: my wife divorced me because I have so many flaws, and that's also why I didn't get the promotion, and why people reject my social invitations; and that reminds me of being the last one chosen for a team in school, and of when my parents blamed me for something my brother did; etc.

To notice this rather than leave it operating underground gave me an exhilarating sense of a different kind of life.

It was great to feel tension in my face relax as I excused the driver who cut me off. I simply shifted my attention by reframing the situation. "This driver is, at the core, a human being just like me," I told myself. I realized that I too occasionally made other drivers uncomfortable when I changed lanes.

Using Feel Good Now was a huge awareness builder for me. I not only realized how tense I had been, I also felt more able to create better feelings, just by shifting attention from negative to positive.

It was as if I were turning on a mental/emotional monitor. I gradually saw that I could step back from being totally immersed in negative, judgmental thinking. The negativity I had thought was so real wasn't who I was anymore or what the world was – now I could disengage from it and shift to a better feeling place.

So the driver "who cut me off" could become the driver "who made me slow down". And it could also become the driver who was rushing to help his children, or who had a terrible fight with his spouse that morning, or whose best friend or mother had just had a heart attack.

If I then started worrying about getting to work on time and felt anxious as I imagined myself arriving late (because I had left my house at the last minute), I realized that it's okay for me to be late, and that I probably wouldn't be late anyway. I reminded myself again that the other driver is a person with needs and feelings like mine. I shifted my attention to look at a nearby tree, and my mind quieted just a bit and the tension lessened.

I practiced shifting attention a lot while driving to work. I'd be behind someone going half the speed limit and, just after my initial reaction of mentally calling him an idiot, I would make up a story that defended him. I'd excuse him by saying maybe he had a cake on the front seat, or maybe he was feeling bad about losing his job that morning, or maybe he was a new driver learning how to move this huge metal object down the road without crashing.

One of my favorite examples came out of working with other employees at the office. In my job I frequently met with different managers. There was a manager I'll call Jim who I needed to meet with. He was easily viewed as a "bad manager". He'd sent notice of a new procedure to thousands of customers without telling his service staff about the change. Jim's service staff had been surprised when they began receiving numerous calls and questions about something they knew nothing about. It's understandable that people labeled him as a "bad manager". And in my thoughts, I joined them by adopting this judgment along with them. At that time, flaw finding dominated my inner life.

As I prepared to meet with Jim, my boss suggested that I try choosing a different viewpoint. I realized that if I went to the meeting viewing Jim as a "bad manager", I would feel edgy, judgmental, closed, grumpy, etc. and I'd probably communicate some form of negativity toward him, even if only indirectly.

I wondered how I could change my view and asked myself what good things he'd done. By introducing the possibility, just by opening-up to the question, two positive experiences popped into my mind: (1) I had seen him lead meetings with his employees in which he covered all the points and requested and welcomed input from each individual; and (2) generally his positive, upbeat attitude had always contributed to generating feelings of comradery in me and in people throughout the company.

I held these positives in the foreground of my thoughts as I went to meet with Jim, and it felt good. The meeting went smoothly, we accomplished what we aimed for, and I enjoyed it! I had taken a tense and judgmental mind-set and shifted to a feel-good moment.

This surprising experience became a frequent reminder of the power of the Feel Good Now motto. It reminded me that I could shift focus away from a negative judgment toward an expanded view that brought the whole being of a person to the foreground.

It isn't that I pretended the flaws didn't exist; it's that I chose not to put my primary attention on them. Instead, I practiced placing positives in the foreground before I interacted with people. As a result, being around people felt better and was more productive. I saw that I behaved differently, and in a natural way, when I held positive thoughts in the foreground rather than negatives.

In his audio series, Kevin Trudeau warned about bringing to mind something from the past that felt good but was no longer available. "When I had" a romantic partner, or a better house, or a better job it felt so good. But now I don't have those, and thinking about them quickly slides me into feeling bad. So this was a warning for me about using Feel Good Now. If the positive I choose to shift attention to is a favorite from the past, and if I am not at peace about not having that same situation now, it backfires and makes me feel less good. If I bounce off of something good by sliding into lack or loss, I don't feel good.

So I remind myself that there are many feel-good options. Sometimes I shift attention to tonight's dinner with a friend. It feels good to look forward to it. Then it feels even better when I realize that if the dinner doesn't happen, I'll feel good watching a movie while I eat some of my favorite foods at home.

But Feel Good Now works best when I find something in this moment to enjoy or to just Be with, without a lot of thinking. I aim for positives about what I have now: the sight of those flowers, the warmth of the sun, the freshness in the air, or the eyes of the person I'm sitting across the desk from.

Feel Good Now was an introduction for me. It was a first recognition of the amount of judgment and nearly unnoticeable tension I'd been creating. And after being able to sense its results over and over again, I feel less like a victim of my surroundings and more in a Feel Good Now place. My ability to affect my inner world began to take form, while the feeling of being controlled by an unpleasant outer world gradually dissolved.

Objective Knowing

I had always believed the world was facts-based. I believed life was about knowing and learning the right ways of thinking about these facts. I believed if I knew the right facts, and put them together in the right ways, then what I knew would be the same as what others knew – well, if those "others" did the same. I thought that's what being objective meant.

I believed someone who went by intuition or used feeling as a guide was wrong and not worth listening to. They weren't using facts or integrating them in the right ways.

But, starting a few years before publication of this book, I began to sense something had gone wrong with these beliefs. I'd developed a vague discomfort about the claim that only one set of truths existed – an objective set of truths that everyone would see as true if only they all had the facts and integrated them correctly.

I put years of effort into studying objective philosophies. I identified with a group that claimed our objective ways of thinking were right; every other way of thinking was wrong. Our group alone knew the right ways, and we were superior to everyone who did not know. I had become proud of being uncompromising and firm in my knowledge partly because I had worked so hard at it, and partly because others who studied these objective philosophes thought the same.

Being right was like a closed case. Once I was certain of being right, there was nothing else to consider or to learn about that specific set of facts. They had been proven true, and hopefully more and more people would come to see this truth – the "truth" that I knew.

One of these truths was my belief in individuality. I thought every human being was a separate individual – "Just look, you can see the separateness," I would argue. I would have agreed that we are connected through business-related trading, but I believed our separateness was far more real than our interconnectedness. We are not our brother's keepers; and those who tried to be would be pulled down by moochers.

Being separate and right all the time is a tall order. It was a challenging way to live each moment, and I didn't fully notice the pressure it put on me and everyone around me. Tension, anxiety, and constriction became a way of life.

When I did notice a bit of these pressures, I concluded it was all worth it – it was just part of being committed to the truth. Yet still, I wondered.

When I began to shift my thinking toward Feel Good Now, questions started to arise. Does believing in "one truth for all" cause stress inside of me? Does it cause stress inside the people around me? If it does, is this stress really worth having?

I began to be suspicious that "one truth for all," which was how I viewed objectivity, didn't fit the reality of the vast variation and uniqueness across people and their experiences. And I began to see that it did cause stress inside me, over and over again.

The objectivity demands of being right all the time had created a mini-dictatorship inside me. If everything outside me depended on knowing and doing the right things, then the inside of me must reflect this too. I had to be able to back up my high standards. And this formed a circle – keeping a strict watch of correctness over myself justified my demands about what others should do. Judging was the right way to deal with myself and with others.

The need to meet these standards – to be one who knew the truth and to help others to know the same – was a tough road to walk. I had created an ideal self inside me that could never be satisfied. It was absolutely necessary to satisfy all the *shoulds* I had created. Being right had become more important than living life. And I thought it was right to apply these same ideal-self standards to everyone else.

While I imposed my standards on other people, and often hurt them by doing so, I did the same to myself. My life was restrained and obstructed through this whole process. I couldn't live freely and openly because I had to meet the objective standards of right and wrong I had set.

This book tells about my journey away from this closed, self-restraining way of living – away from viewing *have-to* and *should* as right and good. It tells about getting gradually more comfortable with not knowing for certain and with not needing to be objectively right all the time. And it tells about my journey toward a whole-self form of Being that has brought more spontaneity, playfulness, and joy than I'd ever imagined possible.

The Tyranny of the Should

I discovered an essay called "The Tyranny of the Should" about eight years ago. It helped me begin to notice that "shoulding on myself" is something I do constantly:

- I should be more efficient
- I should be more fun
- I should be more organized
- I should judge myself to make sure I am being what I should be.

(And, finally, I should end this list because it can go on forever!)

The essay is from psychoanalyst Karen Horney's book, *Neurosis and Human Growth*. As I became more aware of this type of dialogue, I saw that I had tried to live up to what Dr. Horney called the ideal self, and the ideal self is a master of *shoulding*. Taking my ideal self seriously led to a lifetime of self-criticism.

For the first time, I began to see the suffering created from measuring myself against an ideal. I realized that it was this "measuring" that caused the hatred I felt toward myself. Because no matter how well or how much I did, it was never enough; I always fell short of what could have been.

In me, the ideal self is a structure with preconceived images that can never be met because if I satisfy one image, there is always another higher image to reach for. It was as if I were trying to control myself, through evaluation and blame, in order to reach the good; and I ingrained it as a process of constant comparison to a standard. Since "there can always be improvement", the tyranny of the *should* never lets up.

This judging myself against ideals became a prime focus of my life. I thought it was a good thing. And I embraced it as good even though I suffered the punishment of disapproval and damnation from this tyrannical ideal self, who was always ready to push a *should* way of being or doing. Even though it caused mental anguish inside me, I still struggled hard to be a "good boy" who measured up to the ideals.

Isn't being good the most important thing in any life? And isn't disapproval and damnation the way to make it happen?

After watching the ideal self inside me for years, I discovered that creating "good" is not what *it* is ultimately interested in. My ideal self's prime function is to build up a pseudo me that feels superior because it holds and uses a set of ideals. I'm a "good boy" because I hold these ideals.

That's my word-dominated surface self – always pushed by fear of not measuring up to some conceptual idea of what I should be.

I saw more and more that this constant *shoulding* was a way to boost my ego, to offset a deep feeling of inadequacy. I strutted around feeling superior to people and to all of life, "because I hold high ideals".

Constantly judged against these types of standards, everyone, especially me, failed to measure up. Most of the time I felt bad, tense, and ready to cast stones at anyone who seemed to fall short. I suffered, and I made most people around me suffer too.

It surprises me now to realize that before I became aware of the *shoulding* function of my ideal self, I didn't know I was suffering.

I had been unaware of what it felt like to not suffer until I began watching for how this tyranny made me feel inside.

At the end of her essay "The Tyranny of the Should," Dr. Horney asks, "What does it do to a person when he recognizes that he cannot measure up to his inner dictates?"[2] Her answer lies in an essay that comes later in the same book: "Self-Hate and Self-Contempt."

I confirmed her findings by living the "Self-Hate and Self-Contempt" for most of my life.

Now I've found a different way to live.

---

[2] Karen Horney, *Neurosis and Human Growth,* Chapter 3: The Tyranny of the Should, page 85 (New York: W.W. Norton & Company, 1991).

Flaw Finding

Flaws are everywhere. Ask me to open my eyes, and I will find them. Actually, I don't even have to open my eyes to find something "wrong". I can hear them and think them too.

Show me something you think is perfect, and I can find a flaw in it. The perfection of a freshly painted room, a thoroughly cleaned floor, a cake made by a world-famous chef, a tree, a flower, a sunset – anything I see, hear, touch, or otherwise experience, I can find a flaw in it because I create the criteria by which I judge it.

One dot of the painted wall is less uniform; one part of the edge of the floor still has tiny smudge; I don't like cake that isn't perfectly moist; that tree blocks my view; that flower is drooping; the sun belongs above my head not low on the horizon where it blinds me so I can't see the road as I drive.

Once I noticed that I could find flaws in anything and everything, I realized that I could probably do the opposite. *Wow!,* I thought. *Maybe I should try that.*

So I tried it. I made it a practice to find positives in anything and everything. "Finding positives" may sound silly and like a worn-out cliché, but it led to one surprise after another. I noticed I could actually shift my perspective away from what first seemed like a flaw. It seemed like an amazing newfound ability that changed the feel of living.

I found I could always find something positive to redirect my attention to: the color of the paint on the wall, the fresh smell of the clean floor, the sweet taste of the cake, the beautiful shape of the tree, the fragrant scent of the flower, and the vibrant colors of the sunset.

For me this was major. I experienced my ability to redirect attention, to directly influence what it pointed to. Each day I found hundreds of chances to practice. As I practiced, I also became more aware of how continuous my flaw finding was. It seemed overwhelming at times to think I could change it. So I tried to focus on how it felt when I shifted toward positives, and it always felt better than the tension that went with the negative. Feeling good became like a new friend. And since flaw finding was so prevalent for me, it was a friend who was almost always available!

When I point my attention to flaws, I feel that life is flawed and that I am flawed. When I point it to positives, the transformation seems amazing. As I practiced watching my thoughts for flaws, and then shifting to positives, my daily life became like a bright adventure, and I began to feel grateful about simply being alive.

If someone were to ask me what one change will make them feel better about life, I would encourage them to notice how their own distaste, complaints, and flaw finding can be found anywhere and everywhere. It was significant for me to realize how all-encompassing flaw finding was. And I began to see that flaws are actually just illusions generated from my viewpoints. All of it created by my mind.

I still fall into flaw finding, especially when I'm having a bad day, which usually comes after I've judged, evaluated, or criticized myself. It's amazing to notice how strongly my flaw finding flows after I criticize, doubt, or feel bad about myself.

But despite the occasional bad day, I now experience hours and hours, even days, when I see and feel only positives all around me. This never happened for me years ago.

While studying objective philosophy, I took a course on definitions. We defined ten different words by looking directly at our own life experiences. It was a bit frustrating – we were not allowed to use a dictionary until we pulled-out/derived our own definition from our own life experiences.

Before this course, I viewed a definition in the same way I viewed a chair. They were just out there in the world. Chairs were in my house. Definitions were in a dictionary.

To me, they were just another part of reality like everything else. I would wake up, see my *room*, take a *shower*, walk outside and see a *tree*, go to *school,* sit in a *chair*, then look up a *definition* in the dictionary. Definitions were just one kind of "thing" encountered as I walked through life. The chair I sit in is made of wood; the definition is made of words. Simple, right?

The definitions course changed my viewpoint. It was the beginning of seeing the word-world a little differently.

The homework consisted of defining ten different words. For each word, we were required to describe in detail ten different real-life experiences of actual living that the word represented.

Here's an example. This description is from one of my real-life experiences that fits the word *party*.

> A friend invited me to her apartment to enjoy and get acquainted with others and to play games. All the guests brought food and drinks. It was on the day of her roommate's birthday. We talked, listened to music, and laughed with each

other. I talked to many people I'd never met before, including some of my friend's family.

I wrote similar descriptions for nine other parties I'd been to.

We also listed and discussed words that were similar to but different than *party*. These were called near-relative words.

For *party*, examples of near relatives were *meeting*, *awards banquet*, *funeral dinner*, and *dance*. My final definition was: A party is a social activity for enjoying friends or family.

Another concept we defined was *patience*. Here's an example of a recent experience I had with the concept *patience*:

> My friend and her husband were travelling for a couple of weeks and needed a sitter to stay with their new puppy. I happily agreed to take care of him. He was learning to use the lawn outside rather than the floors inside as a toilet. During the first few days he had about four to six accidents inside. On the fourth day, he left a pile of poop on the carpet that had somehow gotten smeared onto the adjoining wood floor.

> On that fourth day, I felt just a touch of irritation that came out of unrealistic wishes and expectations. I didn't want to show or express this irritation. He's a puppy who doesn't know; he's learning. I calmly put the puppy in his kennel so I could clean up without his playful interference. (He loves to chase and bite at the paper towels I use when I clean up his accidents.)

Examples of near relatives to *patience* were *self-discipline*, *self-control*, and *tolerance*. The final definition was: Patience is self-control consisting of calmly accepting the time and difficulties involved in the process of gaining something of value.

So for seven months and across ten different words, we students in the definitions course practiced pulling meaning out of the life sources from which the words came: our own firsthand life experiences. Then we practiced putting it all together to form definitions made up of word-tools.

In a way, I remained lost in concepts during and after this process. But at the same time I learned to give precedence to actual, real-life experience, rather than to word-based formulations. In some way, I had begun to ingrain the idea that everything "word" comes from life. Before words, there was just life.

Now wherever I went, I was a bit more alert to a way of knowing that didn't point me toward books or academia to find answers – a different kind of "knowing" that came out of life.

I used this in work situations over a period of more than fifteen years. As a human resource staff member writing job descriptions, I would go to the employee who was actually doing the work. I would observe the work firsthand as the employee explained how and why. At times, when I reviewed the descriptions with supervisors, they were surprised to read about parts of the work they had not been aware of and challenges and new developments not included in previous job descriptions.

As a regional supervisor of schools, I handled parent complaints about school directors. I talked firsthand to people involved to get the facts directly from the sources. That way I avoided jumping to conclusions based only on words I heard from a complaining parent.

While interviewing teacher candidates for the schools, it was common for candidates to give generalized answers to interview questions. At times, the words were so generalized they sounded like "blah, blah, blah" – empty of meaning like so much of my own talk. I learned to ask for real-life details, cutting through the word-stream abstractions to get to the actual life experience.

Going to the source, to the firsthand level of observable happenings, seemed different. It is common practice for many of us in families or organizations to discuss issues without including any of the people involved who deal with those issues firsthand. Talking directly to the source usually sheds light on current real-life situations.

This was part of my beginning to realize source. If I wanted a whole picture, I needed to remember that life experiences are the source. Life is the ultimate source of all books, all cognitive human knowledge, all definitions, and all words. I had entered the awareness that words do not exist in the same way as my chair, that tree, or that human being. Those are real. Words are tools we use as symbols for representing what is real.

Invulnerable Man Feels Compassion

I was married for sixteen years to a woman I loved and who loved me. During the last five years of our marriage, my rigid thinking became more separatist and elitist. I thought I had earned the right to feel superior to other people, including my wife, because "I knew philosophy" and had studied it diligently.

If you study hard, doesn't that mean you know more than others?

Since I knew the fundamental philosophical ideas that made the world work – objectivity, reason, logic, and productivity – I thought I could judge the value of any person by looking at them and hearing a few of their ideas. I made it a practice to judge people based on their ideas.

I also believed that those who voiced frustrations brought their problems on themselves. I thought that if they learned to "think like me," they would not complain about the world. I saw myself as an invulnerable, self-sufficient man who didn't need people. I felt no compassion for frustrated people in pain – they were just whiners. I knew the secrets of life, I had earned my knowledge through hard work, and the whiners were just lazy and stupid.

(Too bad I missed the fact that I too was whining and complaining when I talked about these "lazy, stupid people".)

In reality, my invulnerability was only on the surface; as I look back I see that I never felt it in a deep sense. I only felt superior, which I now view as word-based illusion. I had buried my deepest feelings under layers of "reasoning": Since I know how the world works, I'm superior to others, and I'm invulnerable to being hurt. I thought my superiority equaled feeling good. Doesn't it feel good to be smarter than other people?

Then my wife wanted a divorce. Hardly surprising now when I look back at the disconnected "superior" man she was married to. Suddenly, I didn't feel so good or so invulnerable and superior.

I felt the pain and suffering of a great loss – the loss of a partner/ companion I cared for and who cared for me. This pain lasted for about a year.

I remember driving to work one morning and being surprised by my own thought: Wow! *This* is the kind of pain people feel when they are hurting about a loss or something they feel is tragic.

It suddenly dawned on me that instead of looking down on them, I felt tenderness toward people who were in pain, something like empathy. I found that I wanted to comfort people who felt bad like this. During this period of my life I came to appreciate kindnesses from others, finding that it helped with the pain I was feeling.

This experience while driving to work never left me – it became what I call a *marker*, something meaningful I remember often. After years of shielding myself from vulnerability, weakness, and self-doubt, this was one of the first times I felt compassion and connection toward people. The separate, independent, superior guy had finally experienced compassion. The guy who had been stronger than all those "stupid, emotional people" was beginning to soften.

Posts in the Sand

I view word-tools as posts in the sand. I don't mean to imply concepts are totally unstable. I think of the sand as firm enough to hold the post, but only as a temporary placeholder. So, I aim to use words/concepts with awareness that they are temporary and moveable; they can be placed then replaced, or placed then discarded.

I feel a "pain in my back" and I remind myself that it's a sensation of this moment. When I hear my mind saying *The pain is getting worse*, I remember I'm freeze-framing something that moves.

I compare a past moment when I didn't feel the pain to this present one when I do. I draw a line that points up on the pain scale. Then I project a worst picture future, all from two points. I've forgotten that my word-tools are only snapshots of a moving flow of living that keeps changing. But if I freeze-frame that tiny slice of a sensation, I misrepresent the moving flow. Labeling my sensations only sensationalizes them. I have become like the evening news.

It's as if I placed a post in the ground and surrounded it in cement. I took a moment, put it with another moment, created a "pain-worse" post, then viewed it as "the truth" by putting cement in the post hole.

Using word-tools as posts in cement doesn't fit the ever-changing nature of my sensations. More than that, it doesn't fit the total flow of changeability I see everywhere around me. Viewing word-tools as posts in the sand fits the reality of my experience much better.

But when I'm lost in concepts, the post-in-cement analogy fits perfectly. When I've put them in cement, my posts hold up walls that keep out anything not fitting my firmly fixed, locked-in conceptions.

How about you? What fits your experience? When you are stuck in comparison, evaluation, judgment, doubt, worry, etc., does it feel like posts in cement?

Years ago, I was blind to the flow of sensations and the changeability of me and my surroundings. I saw it all as unchanging/permanent, partly because that was how I thought it should be. My structure of posts-in-cement, including what I thought should be, formed a fortress I called "the truth", all made of synthetic essentials which I now regard as highly limited representations of the reality of life.

Here's another analogy. Imagine word-tools as public parking places. Most public parking places are host to many different cars. One car comes, then leaves. Then another car comes. Public parking spaces are not meant to be permanent for one car. The purpose of a car is to move, and the purpose of a parking space is to temporarily hold that car. The same applies to word-tools.

Words/concepts freeze one moment of the complex, interconnected movement that is life and then put that moment into a neat little frame that can seem permanent. But, immediately after that, another moment is being lived. Updating my snapshot means that another word-tool now fits better. Since life changes, doesn't it make sense that a symbol representing it would also change?

So I often remind myself that words are temporary. They describe the sensation happening now, not a permanent aspect of reality. Life simply isn't permanent, but words carry a strong pull that makes it seem so.

I found how impermanent my thoughts were when I became aware of the *crazy thoughts* (see the next section) about my roommate not cleaning up her messes. Same with a man I saw at the gym and dance studio who I judged as gruff and unfriendly. Maybe he appeared that way a few times, but I did both of us a disservice when I froze those moments and formed a "mean guy" post which I put in cement. From then on, "mean guy" became the whole of him until I broke through that artificial wall by finally saying hello.

My labeling closed out the bigger picture of everything else about these people. Word-tools create a constricted perspective that is inapplicable to the complex whole of a person, sensation, or situation.

"He/she promised to marry me, love me forever, stay with me" etc. He/she probably meant it when they said it. It is real for us when we say it. But viewpoints, feelings, preferences, and situations change.

Who wants to be held to an artificial form of consistency just because we've formed a habit of using word-tools where they don't belong?

For most of my years I believed in being principled and making myself follow through whether I wanted to or not. Following through is part of doing the "right" thing, isn't it?

Being "true to my word" was more important than being genuine. Later I realized I was being genuine only to a moment in the past, not to the present moment and not to life as a whole. Being real about my life means taking into account the whole of it, including life's changeability.

I've been conditioned to think that if being genuine in this moment is different from some moment in the past, then I am being false to a previous one. But that narrow perspective is just one of the many ways I misuse word-tools as an excuse to blame. When I let my word take precedence over being true to what life has changed into now, I let a tiny sliver from the past take precedence over the reality of the continuous movement of the whole of life.

If someone promises to "marry me, love me forever, stay with me", why would I want to hold them to those words, sincere in the moment they were spoken but no longer a reality now that months or years have passed?

Using words as forces against the changeability of life is putting the frozen symbols of word-tools above, and against, reality. Who wants to be irrevocably tied to something that ceases to contribute to all the lives involved?

Why should words, well meant and hoped for at the time they were spoken, be used to shackle the lives of those who exchanged them? Expecting ourselves to be "true to our word" in this way ignores the wider context that our words are only symbols of an ever-changing reality. Just because a word makes it *appear* that we can freeze time doesn't mean the reality it represents stops.

Science too has shown that our word-truths aren't absolutes. What we once believed to be scientific truth is often later proven to be false. It was "real" only at one point in time and conditioned by one perspective. Scientists continue to find that what they think of as facts later lead to new observations and ever-changing explanations that undo what they initially believed would never change.

Blood types A, B, and O were believed to encompass all blood types until type AB was discovered. After that, Rh factor was discovered. Each discovery was tested against what actually worked to keep people alive, and each led to different decisions and better medical care. Each discovery moved posts from one place to another, in combination with adding new posts and totally removing others.

When I use words as if they describe unchanging absolutes, they become weapons of mass destruction, at least in terms of the negative energy I create inside and around me. Using words as posts-in-cement absolutes, without regard for their limitations, leads to a narrowing that closes my mind off from the wider view of what's real.

Once I became aware of the miniscule "knowing" that words/concepts carry, I was able to realize the damage I was inflicting by using words as if they were posts in cement. "I am right, other people are wrong." I wonder how many of us are caught in this illusion.

I am still realizing new layers of my own posts in cement. But each realization makes me feel just a little freer and a little more grateful to The Whole that is life. Viewing words as posts in the sand has been useful in pointing me away from creating weapons of mass destruction and the negative energy that accompanies them.

Crazy Thoughts

When I think of my childhood, the first idea that comes to mind is a minefield, such that any step might set off a hidden bomb. We kids never knew who would get blamed or yelled at. At any moment, for no reason we could figure, my mother or father would blow up like a bomb. And the bomb was usually aimed directly at one of us. At least that is the way I viewed it.

I remember Mother yelling at my brother for not drinking his orange juice one morning. I remember how furious she seemed as she blamed him, without stopping to find out the whole story. I'm not sure, but I think it was me or someone else who hadn't drunk the juice.

Another bomb was a time when my sister vomited in the car. My mother lost her temper and seemed enraged as she screamed at my sister. My aunt was also in the car. In my aunt's reaction, I saw something that wasn't a part of my usual world: a tender, caring outflow of understanding, affection, and empathy, rather than the blaming and punishment I was so used to. This contrast always stayed with me. And again, this is the way I viewed it.

But remembering this contrast didn't stop me from carrying forward my own raging and blaming. Even though I could look back and see my aunt's response as more constructive, I continued raging and blaming later in my life. My wife of more than sixteen years, whom I loved dearly, received plenty of raging and blaming from me.

A fish in water doesn't know what a non-water world would be like – water is life. For me, raging and blaming were life, just as they had been for my mother who had grown up with a violent, alcoholic father.

Neither I nor my mother had been able to stand back and notice what our minds were engulfed in. Even though my aunt had shown a different way, and even though I had wanted to avoid raging and blaming, I didn't find a way to reduce my reactivity until my late fifties.

I lived alone for many years during my fifties. Then, when I was about fifty-eight years old, I had a roommate for two-and-a-half years. Although we were not a couple, we were great companions. We went for walks, ate out, traveled, and spent holidays together. I describe it as "being married with no sex". Our companionship seemed to fill a transitional gap we each were experiencing at the time. It was during an experience with this roommate that I first gave the name *crazy thoughts* to my raging and blaming.

I had been feeling grumpy for a couple of days and finally decided to talk about what I viewed as her "being too messy". Although I had lost my temper with her before, this time I was intent on being calm.

I remember we were sitting on the floor in the kitchen. Just as I was about to bring up her "messy habits", she said something delightful that caught me off guard. All at once my grumpiness dissolved, and the idea of her needing to change her "messy habits" suddenly seemed crazy and unimportant. What I had planned to say immediately became ridiculous and unnecessary. And I saw clearly that my grumpiness about her "messiness" was inconsistent with my feelings of affection for her and with the whole picture of the respect we had shown each other.

The tension I had created inside my mind and body for three days had been a needless waste of energy. Except guess what? It was actually not a needless waste, because it led me to see that raging and blaming, whether expressed outside or only within myself, were disconnected from the whole picture of how I thought/felt about our companionship.

This roommate experience helped me see a wider picture of my raging and blaming toward my beloved ex-wife. Finally I saw what my mother hadn't been able to see when she was raging and blaming. Finally I saw how disconnected blaming could be. I labeled it *crazy thoughts*, and using that label helped me see more.

The next day after my crazy thoughts experience with my roommate I was shocked at how prevalent the crazy thoughts were. I had never before been aware of how frequently they were coming through my mind.

Time after time at the office where I worked I caught my mind cursing and berating other employees. And just as with my roommate, I began to see how insignificant these viewpoints were. These "observations" that I had previously thought of as "facts about people" became opinions of no importance.

This experience opened a window that shined light on a process that had dominated my thinking for most of my life. What had been unconscious before, had now been uncovered and made more visible: my mind streamed out crazy thoughts that didn't deserve serious consideration. Time after time I was surprised at how out-of-context and frequent the crazy thoughts were.

It was as if I had been a fish transformed into a flying fish – now suddenly I could fly out of and above the water I had been unconscious to before. The water had seemed to be all there was, the whole of reality. Now it didn't and wasn't.

For the first time, I started cautioning myself that my thoughts could not be trusted. I didn't think that I was crazy, and I didn't think that

I could *never* trust my thoughts. I just sensed that the mental movie that played most of the time was not reality and not reflective of the deep-down me, not my true feelings.

Since then, I've watched so many crazy thoughts about people I care about, respect, and feel affection for. Once I had negative thoughts about a beloved physical trainer who had helped me for years. I realized the negative thoughts were fictitious, and these words immediately popped-in my mind: *I* can *think it, but I don't.*

The "I don't" is the truth about me. The "I can think it" is the "something not real" that runs through my mind so easily. The "I can think it" points to my crazy thoughts; the "I don't" points to the deep-down me I've found to be so much more real, and so much more alive, than the mere surface self of my word-tool dominated cognitive mind.

Efficiency Monster

I went upstairs to get dirty laundry to put in the washer and to change into my gym clothes. I changed into gym clothes but forgot the laundry. Just as I was walking out the door to go to the gym, I remembered the laundry. *Arhg!* Now I was delayed! I went back upstairs, got the laundry, brought it downstairs, and put it in the washing machine. *Such a nuisance! I could have already been on my way to the gym! If only I had remembered to get the laundry when I was changing into my gym clothes!*

This is was one of so many instances when I've noticed the bad feelings created inside me by this self-blame and agitation toward life. Sensing the inner tension I can step back to watch the thoughts, as long as I don't regard the inner tension as worth having. If I regard the tension as worth it, my energy goes toward justifying the thoughts rather than watching.

In the past, I made efficiency into an absolute. It was a *should* that brought my energy to a negative place – *I should have remembered the laundry; since I forgot, I've wasted time again and that's time of my life that is gone forever; if I'd been efficient, I'd have gotten more done.*

Now, once I notice this negative energy, I have a choice about how I view it. Do I stand behind my feeling of regret by agreeing how unfortunate it is that I forgot the laundry? Do I cling to the belief that I need to try to be more efficient next time? Can I see that if I "try to be more efficient next time," I give strength to this absolute and invite it to continue?

Sure, I want to accept the "what's real" of feeling regret. But this can be done with a quick look. Once I've acknowledged the feeling, it's best if I avoid stewing over it and churning it around, which causes more negativity. I have a choice to either bless my efficiency *should* or question the very idea of it.

I've been plagued by this thought pattern most of my life but I wasn't aware of it until I was in my fifties. In the past, I viewed the tension and blaming as worthwhile because I was committed to the "high standards of getting more done with my time". As long as I held to that idea, I could not see that I was making myself into a slave of an efficiency mandate.

If I think of walking upstairs to get a shirt to wear, and while I'm there I also want to get my swimsuit from the towel rack in the upstairs bathroom, it's unquestionable that I should/must get both things at once. If I get the shirt and put it on but forget the swimsuit, I get tense as I walk back upstairs to get what I forgot. I hate it because I've wasted time. It's as if the cells in my body revolt because "This just didn't have to be. It's so stupid that I've wasted time and effort again!"

If I forget an item at the grocery store, if I struggle because I can't quickly get the pit out of a nectarine, if I choose a driving route where the traffic adds five minutes to my drive time – all these have been for me blameworthy, tension-producing experiences because they could have been more efficient.

A few years ago, I remember feeling shocked when I heard Alan Watts in an audio say: "There is no way of wasting time, because what is time for except to be wasted?"[3] Back then, that seemed crazy and wrong to me.

Finally, I gave this tension/blaming pattern the name *efficiency monster*. Here, word-tools helped as they gave me a label I could

---

[3] Alan Watts, *Out of Your Mind: Essential Listening from the Alan Watts Audio Archives,The Inevitable Ecstasy – This Is the Game* (track-section six) 07:59, (Boulder, CO: Sounds True, 2004).

use to remind myself of this pattern that caused me torment and unhappiness.

But at the same time, all my unquestioned efficiency monster *what ifs* and *only ifs*, all the measurements and comparisons, were made possible by me using word-tools in a way that hurt rather than helped.

Here's another one: *It would have been better if I'd switched the heat off five minutes ago. Now I'm a little too hot and I've needlessly increased my utilities bill.* Taking these words seriously and worrying – now that's a waste of time! And the tension produced inside is a waste of energy and of life.

My worship of efficiency, productivity, and getting more from life with less effort (profit) is a misuse of word-tools that brings me countless small moments of blame, pain, regret, and resistance to life. Each time I believe it's good to hold efficiency as an absolute, I am using words to narrow my focus rather than expand my view.

The inflexible this-not-that nature of word-tools supports my imperative for efficiency. Concepts/words are black and white in the way they function. And that always pulls me into an absolute right/wrong, mutually exclusive way of thinking.

Lost in the false importance of putting efficiency above life itself, I have thrown away moment after moment of potential enjoyment. But not because I could have "gotten more done".

Rather, I missed the moments of putting attention on the non-word world: enjoying the movement of my body as I walked up the stairs that second time; or the feel of my hand on the fabric of my shirt, swimsuit, or laundry; or my breathing as I moved my body to fetch these things.

Should I regret these moments of lost living? No, because without them I would never have come to see that my absolutist, rigid thinking was hurting me. Every moment is an opportunity to question whether I'm putting word-tools above life.

When "getting things done" is an unquestionable imperative, life takes a backseat. Instead of living fully in a state of gratitude, we let time become a vehicle for suffering, tension, and blame. That's what my efficiency monster feels like to me. Do you have one? If so, what does it feel like to you?

Overgeneralizing a Tool

Aren't things that are definite more important than the vague, spur-of-the-moment, or unplanned? My mind says yes.

I feel a pull to define what I will do ahead of time, and then to follow through as if those actions *have to happen*. For example, a plan for the day may include going to the coffee shop, to the grocery store, and to an appointment. Each step becomes part of a definite sequence. My mind grabs on firmly, saying these steps must happen because I've set them up as my plan. How will I ever get things done if I don't follow through with my plans?

As I'm driving to the grocery store, a call from my son comes in on my cell phone. I feel the compulsion to stick with my plan and get groceries even though he lives on the other side of the country and we talk only once or twice a month.

I must do what I said I was going to do! Right? Don't I need to complete my plan for the day? Isn't it right, good, and responsible to finish what I set out to do? All these thoughts and emotional pressures lurk in the background of my mind. It's as if these thoughts "know" that if they were in the foreground they would be noticed as ridiculous. So they stay back in the shadows, threatening that "if you don't do what has to be done, you won't be dependable and productive".

If I talk to my son for long, I won't be able to pick up groceries and get to my appointment in time. So I cut him short. I multitask and pick up groceries while only half-listening to what he says. Multitasking is good isn't it?

Yes, I told him that I love him as I ended the call. Yet it appeared that I loved my schedule more than my son. I allowed my *must-dos* and *shoulds* to dominate as I granted my plan the status of absolute. My son took second place to my misuse of a bunch of word-tools.

After I get groceries I realize I didn't really need anything I was picking up; I wasn't going to run out for a few days. But once I'd written it down, once I'd set an intention in motion, it all became frozen into a to-do list deemed more important than life itself.

I allowed thinking ahead, setting a plan, and writing the list to create a *have-to* situation where there was none. And I missed a chance to fully listen and *be* with my son on the phone.

Words, plans, goals, schedules, etc. can cause more problems than they solve. I often let artificially created "needs" crowd out the fuller reality of my living.

Words do that. They are so frozen and firm, so this-not-that, so definite and inflexible. For me, it's as if their level of importance becomes greater because of this rigid nature. They become like an authoritarian father around whom everyone jumps to do his bidding because he is so sure, so certain, so definite.

But I don't have to use word-tools this way. I don't have to obey my words or the thoughts I create from them. I don't have to take word-tools that seriously.

So I remind myself that every word is extracted as parts-per-million from a whole that cannot actually be broken into parts because of its web of interconnectivity. I remember that plans, along with everything else built from our words, are just utensils of communication like forks are utensils of eating. Regarding words as *have-to* absolutes is overgeneralizing their use.

Imagine overgeneralizing the use of a fork, carrying it everywhere to replace what you would have done with your hands. Try turning on the faucet, driving the car, washing the dishes, or typing on the computer. If I hold awareness of their limitations and don't overgeneralize my use of them, word-tools serve communication. Same with forks for the process of eating.

Viewing the world through lenses whose primary nature is this-not-that, creates the kind of rigidity I fell for: "either you follow your plan or you don't!" It's a misuse of tools that are best suited for things like "please pass the salt". As I shift to appreciating words for the simple communications they are fit for, I wean myself from overgeneralizing their use.

It's so easy to forget word-tool limitations because the overgeneralizing misuse is everywhere. It's as if we created a tool from life but have been conditioned to use that tool against life.

The definite nature of word-tools makes it easy to give them false importance, to forget that they are only symbols that point to but can't fully represent what is.

Slowing Down and Opening Up

I eat blueberries almost every day. In the past I would eat maybe three to five berries all at once in a handful. But just recently I began to see how it would feel to eat one at a time.

Today I noticed that in chewing one at a time I experience the flavor more fully. I found each batch of berries carries differences in flavor and freshness. Some berries are firm and sour, which is what I like best. Others are softer, not as sour, but have varying flavors which I've come to enjoy.

Previously I would throw soft ones down the drain without even trying them. But now that I eat one at a time I've come to appreciate textures and flavors in the soft berries too. (Well, all except the rare ones that taste spoiled after I bite into them.)

It's been fun to experience the different ways a blueberry can taste as I've put conscious attention on enjoying texture and flavor. It's felt good. It's as if the process of eating has *come alive* simply by being consciously attentive to what I'm doing in the moment.

Eating one berry at a time was challenging at first. But it brings good feelings to what was previously just "going through the motions". By slowing down just a little and experiencing the uniqueness of each berry I am *with life* more than when I unconsciously throw handfuls into my mouth.

I noticed the same kind of thing with muffins and coffee, but in a different way. I was in the habit of mentally labeling a muffin as I began to eat it, often thinking, *This muffin's dry*. When I clung to that label during the entire hour of coffee time, I felt negative about the muffin and sometimes stopped eating it.

Luckily I tried something different once. After I labeled the muffin as *dry*, I shifted my attention to other aspects such as the granular texture and flavor. I discovered that I could enjoy dry muffins once I opened up and shifted attention to these other qualities. But if I clung to my *dry* label, with all my attention on only the moistness, then I would end-up having a bad-muffin day.

Why should I eat anything without enjoying it? If I can expand my focus to include more than just the this-not-that of a dry muffin, why not do it? Why continue my habit of constricting experience by closing off possibilities when I eat blueberries, muffins, or anything else?

Word-tools do this. When I set up a word-based prejudice, I limit my experience through the labeling. I gain nothing from that labeling and I feel bad for no reason, ultimately because the words I chose could not carry the fullness of what the experience had to offer. The reality of the experience held much more than my words were allowing.

I've found my compulsion to label almost always hurts more than it helps. When I allow that compulsion, I allow word-tools to narrow and overshadow what I see and do. They actually take away from my experience of reality and life rather than add to it.

Slowing down and opening up has also increased awareness of the way word-tools support other life-limiting habits such as flaw finding. I continue to see more and more how word-tools take away from and close out the richness of experiencing life and its potential enjoyment.

Comparison Is the Devil

Just kidding. I don't really believe in devils. But my habit of comparison creates a lot of bad, devilish stuff inside.

Walking toward the coffee shop today, I saw a man going to his car. He smiled, and we greeted each other. As I watched him approach his shiny new-looking car, my mind chattered, *His car is nicer than mine*.

I noticed feeling a slight sense of discontent even though I like the car I have and don't want a different one. This type of comparison makes me feel small, even if just a little.

As I walked into the coffee shop I thought of the harmfulness of almost all the comparisons that cross my mind. Less-than, not enough, and lack are feelings that comparisons point my attention toward and they don't feel good.

In the coffee shop, I began chatting with a friendly acquaintance I'd talked to before. He proudly told me about his two sons in a way that was exciting and engaging. One son has a $40-million ten-year contract for consulting work. Another has an invention that may bring him millions. Even though I really liked hearing about their achievements, my mind muttered a wish based on comparison: *How easy life would be if I only I had that*.

Later that day I saw a woman and man on the street, hand-in-hand, laughing, flirting, and enjoying each other. And out comes another flash of comparison – they have an intimate relationship but I don't. Again my habitual comparison puts a damper on my feelings, shifting them to a slightly less good place.

A few years ago I began practicing Feel Good Now by shifting attention from things that felt tense, frightening, self-critical, etc., to things that felt just a little better. At first I thought I could Feel Good Now by putting attention on something I wanted that made me feel good. But more often than not I was surprised to find that a few minutes later I felt worse than when I'd started. The reason was comparison – I had slid down the slippery slope of longing for things I didn't have. I would think of positives I wanted, see that others had those positives, and end up feeling less good due to the comparison: "They have it, and I don't."

Now those feelings of not enough or lack are major watch points for me. When I catch a whiff of longing I bring in my reminder *Ahh, there's that feeling of lack that comes from comparison*. Then I remember that comparing is an ingrained habit, and I feel glad I was able to catch it and watch it without judging and blaming myself. Catching and watching reduces the constricted tension in my face. This more relaxed state leaves my energy free to shift attention toward something that feels just a little better.

In an interview, spiritual teacher Bentinho Massaro suggested that every instance of emotional suffering traces to a thought/feeling of lack.[4] This fits my experience of longing – something that always makes me feel small and/or less good because "poor little me" doesn't have that.

But here's what intrigued me even more about what Bentinho said. He went on to suggest that the thought/feeling of lack is not harmonious with the "what is" energetic vibrations of reality.

As I watch my own inner dialogue, I see that *lack* is a mental concept that I create through comparison made up of other word-tool products. It exists only in my mind. It is a "something missing"

[4] Tami Simon, *Waking Up: Over 30 Perspectives on Spiritual Awakening - What Does It Really Mean?*, Chapter 32, interview with Bentinho Massaro, 29:32 (Boulder, CO: Sounds True, 2015).

I create using imagination. It is as unreal as imagining a purple elephant falling down from the sky to squash me. Both the lack and the elephant falling make me feel bad if I believe them as real.

This may seem confusing. Of course lack exists: *I lack the job I want; my wife and I lack the house we want; my children lack the toys they want; my friend lacks the love relationship she wants; and my neighbor lacks the affectionate mother he would have liked.* Aren't these real?

All these gaps we call *wants* are created in the mind by using comparison. Or perhaps I should say they are created by misusing comparison.

The crazy thing is that there is no end to the lack I can create. Lack is just another form of Flaw Finding. I can find flaws in anything even the most perfect of things by creating a "something missing" and comparing it to a standard of perfection: standards based on what I prefer, or on what I think is wrong or right, or better or worse. Lack finding follows the same pattern, and it all starts with comparison.

I can choose to look at the world through a lack-finding lens, just as I can through a flaw-finding one. When I cling to a lens in this way I don't see anything clearly because the tint of the lens colors my world. My lack-tinted lens never lacks in creating comparisons. Everywhere I look, either I lack, or other people lack. Just as with flaw finding, lack finding is a view of life I choose to adopt.

That guy lacks the car I have; I lack the car that other guy has. And it's the same pattern with house, clothes, food, ability to travel, etc. Many of us believe it all comes down to lack of money because money can buy all those things. How often have I heard (and I have said it myself) the famous lack statement "If only I had the money"?

Lack can exist only in my mind and only through the imagination process of comparison. But this "they-have-I-don't-have" has no reference in reality; it exists only as a creation of my mind driven by where I point
my attention.

Flowers, water, people, toys, affection, cars, etc. – we can find these in life. They are real. We can point to them. I can point to a shiny new car, and then point to my thirteen-year old car. I can point to the man who makes $40 million. And, I can point to people who show and enjoy affection in their love relationship.

But when I then jump to create lack through the addition of an imagined, not real, comparison, it is just another variation of me misusing word-tools.

When I create a lack, I assume that an imaginary relationship created in my mind is "the truth" and has the same reality as flowers, water, people, etc. The comparison, the feeling of lack, is not harmonious with reality because it simply isn't real. When I hold comparison as if it's a reality, I emanate a self-made, self-destructive energy that takes away from life rather than contributes to it.

Superiority

I once asked a beloved friend how she would describe superiority. She said she thinks of superiority as "the fallacy of thinking you own the truth".

Superiority is a difficult issue for me. First of all, I often feel superior as I watch myself judge, compare, blame, criticize, and advise others, and as I brusquely take for granted so many things that support my life.

And second, I so often create the struggle of a "fight" against feeling superior; I resist it when I see it in myself. I call it "wrong" and try to reject this "bad thing I have in me". Then my reaction to blaming myself is to sometimes get caught in a circle of being superior about being superior: *This superiority is "bad", but since I'm smart enough to catch it, I'm pretty cool . . . yeah, I've "been there done that".*

Word-tools support me in a been-there-done-that type of attitude. Once I'm convinced that I know this thing because I've memorized the name of it in the form of a word, I dismiss any idea of fully experiencing it. The nature of word-tools is to foster superiority, making me think I own the truth because I can use the word.

Let me affirm again that I love words. I love all that I'm able to do with them. And at the same time I've found I can do a lot more with words when I embrace an awareness of their limitations. This includes realizing often they feed a know-it-all superiority that closes-off my living as a whole being.

In essence the word is no more than a label. I find that once I know the label for something, there seems to be nothing else to learn; I'm closed to anything new I might discover or experience.

I recently caught my internal voice saying, *Let me just get through hanging this laundry. This is only a "shirt", something I've seen a thousand times.* Then I realized that although I may have seen a shirt a thousand times, I've almost never taken the time to really look at it and feel it as I put it on a hanger. I realized that this is a different moment of my life, one that's not the same as the last time I hung this shirt.

But I miss those insights if I rush through the process with my mind in some other place. Since I view this as just a *shirt,* it's unnecessary to actually feel the cloth of it on my skin or be fully present in this process of hanging it. It's as if knowing the name makes it unnecessary to know the reality of what that name indicates. It's as if knowing the name makes it unnecessary to know life. This dismissive state of mind toward things in the world feeds my superiority.

I grew up surrounded by judgment and I embraced it, especially after I began studying objective philosophy, which I frequently used as a superiority tool. In believing there are objective right/wrongs, good/bads, etc., my superiority was reinforced in nearly everything I experienced. Reading a magazine, I criticized the grammar – I am superior. Then I would see flaws in the logic of the writing – I am superior. Walking past people, and labeling their body-shapes, hair, clothes, ways of walking, and talking, my labels pointing toward flaws again and again – I am superior.

Another way I sometimes still feel superior is when I catch people as they break a rule or social *should.* I compare their action to the rule, I criticize, and again – I am superior.

Superiority became a warning sign before I was aware of its full impact. It started with a vague discomfort as I would notice just a hint of it. As my awareness gradually grew, I identified it as a feeling I definitely wanted to watch for.

As I watched, I discovered that superiority *never* added to my life – it only fed my ego, my surface self. I eventually saw how it fueled defensiveness and a sense of feeling small in the world, which led to striking out and trying to squash people who seemed critical of me. Striking back became my endorsed reaction to consciously embracing superiority as a valid concept.

In his book *The Power of Now*, Eckhart Tolle refers to "the forcefully compulsive and deeply unconscious need to be right" as a form of violence.[5] I certainly used this need to be right as a form of violence . . . just ask my ex-wife.

Even though I have learned to recognize my compulsive need to be right as a form of violence, I aim to be gentle with it when it arises. I practice acknowledging and accepting it as I remind myself that there are less stressful ways of living. And I remind myself of The Value of What I Don't Know. (See the section by that title in Part 2: Connectivity.)

In other words, I acknowledge and accept the flow of judgmental, superiority thoughts without stimulating further growth of them. I find that if I do fall into criticizing myself, it sets the stage for an internal fight. It brings back to mind my enemy-mode functioning, the we-vs-them that's tied to the this-not-that nature of word-tools, all of which is intricately linked to my superiority thinking.

So I shift my attention to a context that is different from the objective right/wrong, good/bad that "I know so much about". I remind myself of the uselessness of blaming, flaw finding, and crazy thoughts. I remember the power of shifting my attention. And I tell myself again that comparison is the devil. Then I notice my breathing and bring to realization noncognitive ways of knowing, because in those there is no superiority.

---

[5] Eckhart Tolle, *The Power of Now,* Chapter Two: The Origin of Fear, page 44 (Novato, CA: New World Library and Namaste Publishing, 1999).

In his book *The Wisdom of Insecurity*, Alan Watts points out that there was a time in history when people experienced (saw) things first before they named them.[6] Now children more often name things before they fully experience them. So often we feel as though we "know all about it" just because we've memorized a word-symbol.

Who needs to actually experience living when it's so easy to use these powerful conceptual shortcuts? Why take time to get to know someone/something when I can just prance around with my words to show how much truth I own? *Liar, cheat, lazy, beautiful, best worker, strong.* Flaunting my words, I feel that I own more truth than other people. And that puts me above them and makes me better than they are.

So I often ask the following questions: Can I learn to look, hear, and smell without naming? Can I experience without describing in words? Can I live without justifying and judging? Can I keep in mind the limits of word-tools, knowing that they can serve without dominating? Can I learn to use noncognitive kinds of knowing?

To me superiority is a form of verbal overshadowing of life itself. When I filter experience through word-tools as if they provide the primary way of knowing, I put concepts over life. When I strut around with a been-there-done-that attitude, I don't realize how much I'm missing.

Word-tools are meant to contribute to, not detract from life. They are not meant as tools for the ego-puffing of superiority. They are not meant to support fallacies, including the fallacy that "I own the truth". Yet I've found they offer this support so well when I believe in the validity of being superior as I attempt to compensate for feelings of inadequacy.

---

[6] Alan Watts, *The Wisdom of Insecurity: A Message for an Age of Anxiety*, Chapter VI: The Marvelous Moment, page 101 (New York: Vintage Books, 1951).

Blaming Myself – Blaming Others (Externalizing the War Inside)

Today I was walking down the sidewalk, talking to a friend on my cell phone. From behind I heard a voice say "excuse me". It was a woman riding a bike. As I moved to the side so she could pass, I felt some tension. Then I thought/felt irritation toward the woman on the bike. It was as if I were blaming her, and I justified it by rationalizing that riding a bike on sidewalks in the city is illegal.

Shortly after finishing the call, I noticed a swirling of self-blame inside. It was like a voice inside me saying, *You shouldn't have been on your cell phone. You weren't paying attention as you walked on this public sidewalk. You could have caused a crash with that woman on the bike.*

Self-blame. I realized that the self-blame happened *before* the tension of irritation I felt toward the woman.

Here's another example.

> I frequently use a public restroom with a door that makes a loud bang if I don't catch it as it closes. Once when I didn't catch it, just after the bang, I watched my mind criticize the restaurant owner for failing to install bumper pads so the door would close without a loud bang. The owner had recently renovated the restroom to look stylish, so my mind continued by accusing him of putting appearance before quality, showiness over function.

Guess what came even before I started blaming the owner?

Self-blame. My stream of thought began with criticizing myself for failing to catch the door.

The pattern is: I attack myself; and then I attack someone or something outside myself.

I notice this so often now I'm beginning to wonder if I ever criticize or react negatively to the outside without first blaming myself in some way.

It's as if an attack directed outside is some kind of defense for an inside attack. Something in me seems to function as if blaming outside compensates for blaming inside. Maybe if I see the fault so I can clearly point to it on the outside, I won't have to see it, even in a vague way, on the inside.

Years ago I walked into a gym to work out and noticed a Zumba class with people dancing to a song I liked. I stopped to watch and noticed a girl moving to the music as if she had written the song, as if she felt it in every cell of her body. An attractive girl, totally into what she was doing, moving freely with no self-consciousness.

As the class ended and the girl walked out, I said to her, "You are a great dancer. I would pay to watch you dance!"

About five to ten minutes later a big muscly guy walked up to me and said in a threatening tone of voice, "That was my girlfriend you said that to! I want you to apologize to her!"

I looked at him silently. I remember being aware of his tension as I looked him straight in the eyes. After a silent pause I said calmly, "Where is she? I'll apologize."

He pointed, and I walked over to her and said, "I'm sorry about what I said. I didn't mean to offend you in any way." She seemed fine accepting my apology and I remember wondering if her boyfriend had felt more offended than she.

I apologized even though I didn't clearly understand what I was apologizing for. I was confused but I apologized without asking questions. Some part of me knew that reasons didn't matter in this situation. Only apologizing mattered.

When I had said "pay to watch you dance" I had been picturing this girl on a stage in a Broadway or Carnegie Hall type of musical production. Afterward, I wondered if the boyfriend or the girl had pictured a pole-dancing place or strip club.

As I think of it now, I'm surprised I was able to handle that situation without distorting it with word-tools or blaming. Typically I would have tried to make sense of it by saying, "I don't get it – why should I apologize?" Or I might have been a little confrontational and said, "Apologize for what?" This would fit my need of demanding cognitive/conceptual understanding before doing anything, and my argumentative "you better be able to prove it!" that I typically use to defend myself.

A couple of years ago I heard Byron Katie say, "Defense is the first act of war."[7] This shocked me when I first heard it because I thought actually starting a fight, the initial act of aggression, was the "first act of war".

At some point after that, I remembered the experience with the girl's boyfriend at the gym. I remembered the eye contact and silent pause that preceded my apology. And I understood that it takes two to make a war.

---

[7] Byron Katie, *Your Inner Awakening: The Work of Byron Katie: Four Questions That Will Transform Your Life*, read by the author, Chapter 3, 26:57 (New York: Simon & Schuster Audio, 2006).

The experience with the boyfriend, along with Byron Katie's statement, convinced me that a fight can exist only when two engage. What I had previously believed – that an aggressive "defense" is the natural consequence of initiated aggression – wasn't true.

Somehow at the gym I had chosen not to be the second party, not to complete the making of the war with the girl's threatening boyfriend. Somehow I did not blame myself, and so there was no need to defend. Since I didn't create a war inside by attacking/criticizing myself, there was no need to create a war outside, disguised as what many of us call "defense".

I could have blamed myself with an inner thought like, "What a stupid thing to say; now you've offended these people."

Now I wonder if perhaps attacking *oneself* is the first act of war.

That is what I did with the woman riding her bike past me on the sidewalk, and with the owner of the restaurant that had the loudly banging restroom door. First I blamed me, then in order to "fight back" and defend myself, I internally blamed them and externalized a war situation originally created inside myself by myself.

I've seen it again and again. When I blame myself, I often if not always follow by blaming others. I become both attacker and defender. First I create the need to defend by attacking myself. Then I complete the war-circuit by attacking and blaming outside.

Note: A couple of months prior to publication of this book, I discovered a different view of "defense". If someone swings his fist to hit me, "defense" is me putting my arm up to block his punch.

Before, I thought if he punched me and I punched him back, he initiated the offensive aggression and I was only defending myself.

Now I've realized that if I "punch him back" in the type of situation I described above with the girl's boyfriend, I am putting out (initiating) the same type of aggression he did. By striking back, I put myself in the same unconscious state of mind as he was in when he struck me. With this discovery I realized the difference between defense and counteraggression, which is also referred to as retribution.

The Moocher Shortcut

Is the word *moocher* ever useful?

Here are some words that convey a truer picture, much fuller than can be carried by the shortcut of calling a person a moocher.

> She borrowed money, promised to return it later, then asked for more before she had given back the money she first borrowed.

In my view, this description carries a very different feel than the socially-charged words *she is a moocher*.

But how could it be beneficial to use so many more words rather than just using what I am calling the moocher shortcut?

I have a friend I will call Jane. The first time I lent money to Jane, she returned about half of the $500 over a nine-month period. Then before she paid back the other half, she asked to borrow $600 for a medical emergency. She paid that back the next day as promised. Then again before she paid back the other half she asked for an additional $50, promising to pay it back soon. Years later she still owes me $300.

What's the difference between that lengthy description and just coming out and saying that *Jane is a moocher*?

Even if we restrict the topic to money, I see the wordy version as giving a much fuller picture by describing the facts rather than using a derogatory single-word label.

Now let's widen the view. Jane and I were good buddies for years at the office where we worked. We were also frequent lunch partners and social friends outside of work. Our years-long friendship was filled with positive experiences we shared and enjoyed.

To say *Jane is a moocher* is as narrow and limiting as telling a child seeing a flower for the first time *That is a flower*.

That colorful, complex living being we see in the distance is not the word "flower". That beautiful and complex being is not these six symbols formed from ink: F-L-O-W-E-R. It is so much more than the symbolic tag supplied by the six ink squiggles of that word! Seeing the truth of this begins by getting close to it, smelling it, touching it, experiencing it.

When my kids were growing up, I was the worst offender. I rarely if ever encouraged them to walk up to the thing I named so that we could actually experience it. I was obsessed with naming everything when I was with my kids. *That's a dog. That is a street. That is a skunk. That's a swing set. That's a bridge.* When I was with my children, my name-jabbering never stopped. I thought viewing the world through word filters was the only way. It turns out I was teaching them to pile layer upon layer of symbols which ended up burying the connectedness to source they were born with. I thought putting names and labels to things was the most important skill to teach.

Now I have a different view of what's important.

There is a better way than saying to a child, as I did so many times, *That is a flower*. Now if I were with a young child who was first learning about the world, instead of immediately pointing and naming it, we would first physically walk right up to the flower and look closely as we smelled it, touched it, and experienced the Being of it. Then I would say: "We use the word *flower* when we want to tell other people about this."

In this way, we invite the child to explore and discover by going directly to life itself. What I did was ingrain my children with the idea that they must always wear their word-tool glasses so they can view life properly, through conceptual groupings only.

More and more I'm finally realizing the importance of acknowledging the difference between a symbolic system of language tools and real things in the world – the difference between symbols and the reality they were created to represent.

The six letters that form the word *flower* are just squiggles that form a label, a shortcut we use to quickly reference rather than actually experience. It doesn't tell the whole story or even most of a story. It carries only a miniscule part.

The word *moocher* is even worse. It not only doesn't come close to telling the story. It also misrepresents the value of the relationship between me and Jane. It pulls out one narrow aspect – borrowing money and not yet paying it back. It ignores the countless other aspects involved in this relationship between two complex Beings.

That is why it has become important to me to:

> *Use words in such a way as to highlight the Connectivity*
> *from which they come rather than the separations*
> *to which they lead.*

When I say *Jane is a moocher* I've let words be boss and I've shut out my awareness of a wider picture: reality. I've taken the whole of a human being and turned her into a tag because I took refuge in letting a shortcut be a truth-teller rather than making an effort to be fully aware of the whole of what is real.

By using the shortcut of the word *moocher*, as if it were the whole reality rather than the distortion of a human being that it is, I've detached words from living and turned their potential usefulness into destructive judgment.

More-Than and Have-To

I thought a constant drive for more brought more satisfaction to life.
I thought feeding that internal push to make more happen was the
way to happiness. I felt a little boost each time I "made something
happen." But the boost never lasted long.

Eventually I began to see the damage I was inflicting on myself.
Getting more took precedence over everything. It was more
important than my body, more important than any object I touched,
more important than people. Anything that didn't add to getting
more stuff and success, as the world defined it, was just in my way,
and I treated it brusquely because nothing in life was as worthy as
progress and profit.

At some point, I finally allowed myself to question these priorities
just a little. First I became aware of the nearly constant tension I
was holding in my face, neck, and many other parts of my body.
I began to notice my dismissive and almost rough brusqueness
toward things and people driven by my seeing them as pesky *have-
tos* that got in the way of the task at hand.

I began to notice that the *more-thans* spawned the *have-tos*. I had
to do things in order to make more things happen and get more
things. This was all food for my efficiency monster.

Throughout all of this driving tension I thought I was happy.
"Happy? Of course I'm happy, why shouldn't I be? I have a lot of
stuff, and I'm working to get more."

I told myself that I should be happy, but I didn't feel it. The
happiness was like the word-tools I worshiped – it was synthetic,

artificial, highly limited, frozen, and symbolic only. It was a happiness made up of images.

Life was made of knowing more than, having more than, earning more than, and feeling more special than. And it wasn't just more than others had. It was more than I had before. I thought happiness was about the continual push for more than before. Isn't that what our revered idea of progress is all about?

I subconsciously put *more-than* above the simple enjoyment of here and now in this moment. My focus was on measuring. Anything intended as fun or joyful had to be measured while it was happening in order to justify it, in order to make it a meaningful contributor to the ultimate "more".

I convinced myself that reaching for more was worth all the inner constriction. I viewed people who didn't compulsively reach for more as lazy and as "living off of my taxes". I believed that continual pushing for more was what supported life.

I finally discovered continual pushing was not supporting life – it was constricting it, it was choking it to death. Anything that couldn't be measured, proven, or logically demonstrated was excluded. And I embraced this exclusion. Because potentialities – what I don't know that I don't know – are not easily measured, proven, or demonstrated.

Life for me had become one *have-to* after another dictated by the drive for *more-than*.

I had to constantly achieve more at work. I had to constantly be better with personal relationships. I had to constantly be healthier, stronger, smarter, nicer, etc. I had to constantly have a cleaner, bigger, better house, car, office, etc.

I had equated being happy with constant *more-thans*, which only led to feeling that life was made up of no more than one damn *have-to* after another.

Happily I came to see that really living goes far beyond *more-thans* and *have-tos*. There is so much of life that doesn't involve measuring, proving, comparing, or pushing for more. I discovered that there could be simple enjoyment of what is – without any gain, without any progress – just Being, only Being.

Goals Are for Losers

Dilbert cartoonist Scott Adams wrote, "Goals are for losers."[8] This really surprised me when I first read it in his book *How to Fail at Almost Everything and Still Win Big: Kind of the Story of My Life*. Especially since at that time my job included helping office employees create goals.

How could this statement make any sense? Scott Adams explained that goals create an imaginary future endpoint that puts a person into a state of failure until it is complete. To illustrate, I might say to myself: "I will be successful upon the day of completion, six months from now. And then another goal-seeking period will start where I'm less-than and falling short every day until the end of that goal." On top of that, the continuous measurement takes attention away from the energy available for doing the work well.

As an alternative, Scott Adams suggests creating an ongoing system of actions rather than putting primary focus on an endpoint. This keeps the energy flow positive without the frequent criticism that comes with falling short. So going to the gym regularly works better than aiming to lose 100 pounds by June 30. Visiting the gym regularly puts attention on the activities themselves rather than a preconceived score I have to meet at some future time.

I've found most goals work better when I set up a system of action, rather than putting primary focus on an endpoint where I'm essentially failing until I reach that end. I have often tried to use a goal for an activity I've never done before. Setting goals for complex unstructured activities that are done infrequently easily create an image "failure" that is disconnected from reality. No goal at all would be better than misusing a preconception. What we often call a goal is really a misuse of word-tools.

---

[8] Scott Adams, *How to Fail at Almost Everything and Still Win Big: Kind of the Story of My Life,* page 3 (New York: Portfolio/Penguin, 2013).

If you've done the same rote task thousands of times, then sure, setting standards and criteria in the form of goals can be constructive and even fun. The key point is to keep the energy positive and avoid using goals as a form of disapproval or punishment. Using goals as a way to measure failure doesn't do anyone any good.

While writing, I sometimes have an urge to evaluate progress by comparing to some outside standards of writing or by looking toward some completion type of endpoint. When I allow these thoughts I feel a little less good; I feel doubt, less energy, and dampened enthusiasm. Too much focus on standards or on endpoints takes attention off my doing the activity. It's just another example of being lost in concepts.

When I shift attention away from evaluation and toward the writing itself, I almost always enjoy it and I feel pulled forward naturally. With the positive energy of attention on the writing itself, I feel excitement for what I am doing.

I've heard that in track and field sports, if a runner uses energy to look behind to see where other runners are in comparison, he/she almost always loses ground and then loses the race. When I focus on winning rather than on my involvement in the action itself, I lose.

Putting prime focus on an end result, or comparing to standards of judgment, slows me down. Energy is wasted looking toward some imagined future. Before this book, when I still believed in punishment and discipline, I thought it was beneficial to latch on to a goal as if completion were crucial. Now I view it as disabling. Connection to the now is my point of control, the only point from which I can take action.

Open positive energy flow – not the constricted feeling of not-enough, not-enough, not-enough – is what leads to enjoying whatever I'm doing right now. And although I may occasionally focus on the next step, my work is best when it's the nearest next step.

When I plan too far ahead in time, I find that things have changed by the time I get there. My preconceived endpoint no longer fits the situation. It becomes a compulsion for me to follow through on what I decided, as if it were a post in cement. When I latch onto a decision and stick with it as an absolute *because I decided to do it*, it contributes less to life than if I had been flexible enough to change course when circumstances changed.

The reason it doesn't work is that reality is always changing like the constant movement of a stream. But our words freeze the movement of life as they form inflexible buckets like snapshots of reality. The this-not-that nature of word-tools makes them rigid. It's something I find very easy to forget as I manipulate words to create goals. That's why I remind myself not to take word-tools too seriously, and that goals are one type of word-tool product.

This doesn't mean there is no benefit in occasionally thinking forward to an end vision based on standards/criteria. My experience simply tells me that I do far too much of this type of tension producing monitoring. There is more life when I replace planning and assessment with simply focusing on what I'm doing in the now. It brings more enjoyment throughout the process and better quality with far less pressure.

Note: For more on goals, jump ahead to the section A Goal Without Consequence in Part 2: Connectivity.

Categorizing Stops the Flow

When material for writing pops into my head, I often feel a tug to categorize before it's written. My boss-mind wants to name it now; it wants to create comfort for itself by creating a bucket to immediately put the writing in.

But I know from experience that things flow better when I type the whole section first. Then I can read it and let the title flow naturally out of the whole of the piece.

Worse than that, sometimes while writing, I have the urge to evaluate a word, a sentence, or the ordering of thoughts – good/bad, right/wrong, etc. Evaluating is another form of categorizing. I know darn well not to do this while I'm drafting, yet my mind tugs me toward it.

Categorizing and evaluating stop the flow of what's happening. Even though I'm using word-tools as I write, using them to categorize the flow of writing stifles the motion of the writing itself. The this-not-that limiting nature of putting something in a word bucket closes the door on the process.

It does this in daily interactions with people too. My mind wants to go directly into category-matching as I look for things we agree on, where our histories may be similar, and if we know the same people, etc. I'm like a robot programmed to match things – in this case it's matching my word-dominated existence with the word-dominated existence of the other person.

Most of us have been trained to use this matching exercise as the basis of our communications. Rather than really being with each other, we are actually just slotting ourselves into familiar categories as one conditioned surface self checks out the conditioning of another.

But there are other options for us to discover. If I breathe and quiet my mind when I speak to a person I often become open enough for something more than matching. If I also then remind myself about my matching habits, I can continue the interaction with an awareness that is wider than my robot-like surface self.

If I forget these reminders, then instead of being open to new discoveries, I easily get swept into a machine-like process of closed, frozen, word-tool correlation. The flow is stopped because recognition of the whole reality of life is stopped. Life is dismissed as all my mental attention is filtered through my word structures.

My mind seems comforted as it overlays various categories onto a person I'm talking to or onto other people or aspects of life. It as if my mind takes satisfaction in "knowing" because it puts words on life. But this kind of "knowing" amounts to nothing because I've forgotten the limitations of the word-tools I'm using. I forget that I'm engaged in a matching process using symbols that freeze the movement of life and narrow it to a this-not-that bucket, symbols that merely provide what amounts to name tags.

"Oh, you know Sam too! From the same school that I went to! Yeah, he's a nice guy but sometimes he overreacts." I may feel excited by this matching and categorizing, but it actually carries a deep-down discomfort because the jump to match and place judgment labels detaches me from experiencing the interaction. It stops the flow of being open and curious about the person I'm looking at and talking to right here right now. In this example, we've both gotten lost in a frozen world of symbols assigned to a person called Sam who is not even present as we talk.

I remind myself that finding things in common is fine. But when it is a dominant focus, it overshadows the complexity and movement of life. I miss what I may have gained if I had not been immersed in preconceived categories.

This anxious stress to label partly comes out of my need to relate to the world out of a place of superiority. *Ahh, now I know what it is – it's a flower or a dog or a moocher or a liar. That's me, I'm the one who knows.*

And as I jump to immediately put words on everything, I miss the rich, unique detail of what I could experience in a state of neutral openness. I experience only a cluster of generalizations. Instead of experiencing a whole human being as a whole human being, I've only dropped him or her into my preformed judgment/comparison buckets. I'm like a little kid putting the red beads in this bucket and the yellow ones in that bucket. And these buckets are closed and inflexibly motionless.

And this closed stopping of motion also happens when I categorize and evaluate during the flow of writing or during the flow of speaking with someone. The process, movement, and aliveness is stifled, limited, and sometimes stopped by the nature of how categorizing works.

Happily, if I notice when my mind jumps to stopping life through words, I can take a conscious breath and relax my tight face muscles. Sometimes this quiets the urge to place myself above, through labeling, judging, and thinking I own the truth because I named it. Once I've seen and dropped my superiority, I can return to my writing or to the conversation and allow it to flow more naturally.

Stopping movement is in the nature of word-tools. It's something every word does. It pulls a snapshot from the rapidly moving reality of life. It stops the movement, and snatches only a sliver.

This reminds me of how much I like photos of people who don't know they are being photographed as opposed to photos of people posing. I like to see the spontaneity of people being just as they are. It's as if some of the movement of life is captured when they are not posing. When people pose, life has been frozen/stopped two times – once by the process of taking a photo; and a second time by the pose which stops/stifles the flow of the person's real being.

In so many ways, we miss so much of life when we freeze the movement of it. I miss out when I evaluate my writing while it is flowing just as I miss out when my interactions with people are dominated by category matching and judgments.

Categorizing and evaluating kills the flow of living whether I'm doing the work of writing, or interacting with a spouse, child, coworker, or friend. It artificializes life, and like a posed photo, it stops the moving, growing, creative flow of life and closes off the curious sense of wonder I feel when I quiet my categorization.

Creating My Reality through Categories I Choose

We choose what we group together into a category depending on what we want to achieve. In this book, thinking is grouped together with feeling/emotion. I did this to highlight a difference I found in my own experience. In this case the difference is thinking/feeling (including emotion) vs Being.

I've seen that if I label my friend as "closed to discovering new things" and "afraid of the world", I react to him based on that labeling. Instead, I could carry something less definite, and less arrogantly judgmental, such as: I really like being around him, and sometimes I feel a little less connected than other times.

By shifting my labeling, which is to say my thinking, I experience different emotions. When I'm more negative and definite, interactions with people feel different than when I'm more positive and open. In this book, thinking/emotion are put together to emphasize that Being is different from both.

My emotions change when I shift my thinking. Thoughts and emotions are closely intertwined. When I go to a business meeting with a "bad manager" thought, I feel dismissive and ready to criticize. When I approach that same meeting with the thoughts "he does a great job leading meetings with his employees", I feel relaxed and open to working with him.

A friend recently gave an example of how people feel different emotions about the same thing. One person feels very good about a rice cooker because his grandmother cooked family meals with it; warm feelings of affection come up when he remembers this. But another person, who knew victims of the April 2013 Boston Marathon bombing, which was set-off by a rice cooker, may feel very differently when she thinks about rice cookers.

What's the difference? The thoughts and experiences that led to the emotions.

Once I began to sense Being, which arose for me after I became more aware of the limitations of word-tools, the connection between thinking and feelings/emotions became clearer. The importance of my long-used distinction between thinking and emotion lessened as I experienced this new sense of Being as something much more fundamental.

I sense Being as much deeper and much less specific than emotion. And Being arises when my thinking is quieted, not going round and round as it usually does. Once I realized this sense of Being, it became something I could choose to point myself toward.

So I've chosen to create a category I call *thinking/feeling* in order to highlight the difference I experience with Being. Compared to Being, thinking goes together with the arena of feeling and emotion.

When I'm in a mountain meadow and see a variety of different-colored things near to the ground, if I also notice that they are different from the really tall brown stalks with green at the top, I can give the first things the name *flower* and the second the name *tree*. I selected where I pointed my attention and the categories of *flower* and *tree* had an impact on me.

If I choose to focus on geography instead of plants, I'm more likely to pull the following categories out of my experience: *meadow*, *stream*, *pond*, and *mountain*. Noticing that I choose to focus on geography rather than plants helps me become aware that I select what I choose to put my attention on.

This process of creating categories based on where I place my attention works the same with more abstract concepts which are farther away from the things we can see and touch.

I'm thinking here of the many negative concepts that have plagued my mind for so long: *problems, bad feelings, stupid people, rude people, incompetent people,* etc. I can form other more abstract groupings that include these negatives by saying "that's reality, that's the way the world is." Another example of this type of abstract category is what has been called Murphy's Law, which says, if anything can go wrong, it will.

By building wrongness into everything, Murphy's Law fulfills its own expectations. Since it selects *wrong* but not *right* as the basis of attention, it pre-selects a world view just as my flaw finding does. In the same way I've focused on flaws, I can focus on anything that may go wrong and I will find I've chosen a circle that is a self-fulfilling prophesy. Because I've set my mind to notice things that go wrong, it appears they do. Just as I create my own reality with flaw finding, I can do it with things that go wrong.

When I looked for negatives, I almost always found them. That is why I spent most of my life troubled and dissatisfied. Since changing the categories I hold and use, life has grown more expansive and enjoyable. And through that change I've seen even more clearly that what I think leads to what I feel.

Once formed and embraced, the categories I choose take on importance. My mind is drenched with the sense that these negatives are real. I express them in formulations that help hide what is happening such as "the nature of life" or "the nature of my life." The mind-set I choose becomes what life is, and I don't even realize these thoughts are causing me to feel troubled, dissatisfied, and incredibly stressed.

Without awareness of the limited role of word-tools, and how I had been misusing them, I gravitated toward negative categories. These categories, which could be called *attitudes* or *world views*, became as real as rocks, trees, cars, and houses. I viewed them as objectively real, true for all people, part of the nature of life. And as I watched more closely I began to feel the tension of resistance that goes with these negative views rising up to the surface where I could feel the negative effects more often.

Much of what reduced this tension of resistance was seeing and repeatedly reminding myself of several concepts: the limitations of word-tools, the vast arena of what I don't know that I don't know, and the fact that I choose where to point my attention.

These three – the limitations, the vast arena of not knowing, and my choosing what I point my attention toward – led to discovering that I choose the categories I use; reality doesn't choose them for me.

When I misuse word-tools, I forget my role in choosing. When I misuse and forget, it seems my attention was determined by objective facts. I forget that pointing attention to a negative category brought it into my mind and allowed it to be validated, authorized, certified, and even blessed through my use of it. I took it in and I colored life with it.

When I wake up with a grimace supported by the unquestioned thought, *Argh! Another day to struggle through!*, I play the role of creator by selecting those particular eyeglasses through which to view the world.

Happily I now know how to gently put it in its full context by saying to the negative thought: "Hi, nice to see you again. I know you like to wander through my mind in the morning, and I also know that you don't carry the truth about me or my life in the world."

Then as I'm just about to get out of bed, I can look for anything positive in my body or in the room. I can for example remind myself how good it is to breathe and feel the movement of my body. I can notice how the light coming into my room helps bring out the color of the walls.

I create my reality in these ways. Yes my word-tools are limited, but if I'm aware of their limits, I can use them as powerful aids as I practice pointing my attention to change my life experience.

Little Me, Superior Me

As I walked home from coffee, I saw a hamburger place where, years ago, I often got a toasted tuna sandwich for lunch. It was near my former workplace, and I had not been there for about three years.

I went in and bought a tuna sandwich. It was nice to talk to some of the same employees who were still there. As I said goodbye to them and continued walking home, the feeling of "little me" which was much more common three years ago came back. It seemed so clear now that this "little me" had been a position I often took on back then, now less often.

It's like choosing to play a role. Identifying with "little me" has the sense of putting on a costume in order to play a particular character in a play. And when I believed I *was* "little me", rather than viewing it as just playing a role, I felt globally bad in a deeply dark way. Now as I walked, it was as if that feeling was mostly gone, on the outskirts of my memories.

This is what it feels like to identify myself with a specific characteristic or role or position. It's like putting the shackles of word-tool limitations on myself, being trapped in a this-not-that bucket of "small".

As I continued walking, remembering these feelings and acknowledging that they still arise, I realized that when I feel superior, it's the same pattern as when I feel "little me".

Me as superior, usually in some intellectual or moral way, is also me cloaking myself in the robes of a role for a play, adopting a position, taking on a characterization that compensates for "little me" by forcing others (mentally) into the "little me" position. If I make them even more little than me, then I feel bigger and better.

My superiority functions to compensate for a need to boost myself up: *I am right. I'm strong. I work hard and put in extra effort. I'm smart. I've earned my way. I am good.*

However, making others little in order to feel bigger was never conscious – I had been unaware of it. I simply believed, usually with intense conviction, that I was right and the other was wrong. It wasn't conscious and it wasn't intentional to squash the other person into being "even more little than me".

As I write this now, I see that I use these boosts when I feel or fear that I am the opposite: wrong, weak, lazy, stupid, undeserving, and not good. Here again is the devil of comparison trying to compensate for my label-engulfed, name-calling insecurities by conjuring up fantasies about superiority.

The truth is that this compensation is both unnecessary and unfulfillable. When I'm in touch with Source, when I feel deep gratitude for the amazing functioning of my body, for nature, for people – then my needs to compensate, feel superior, and compare, all dissolve back into the thin air of illusion. When I'm in touch with gratitude and Connectivity, "little me" and all its partners become clearly unreal.

Even though the "little me" and the "superior me" still arise, it is refreshing to be able to watch them and feel free to stop embracing them. It feels good to disinherit these roles, not because I will be better than I was before or better than others (although I occasionally still fall into this) but because of the sheer enjoyment of feeling the free space of standing back and watching. This is a much better feeling than the constriction of being swallowed up in believing that I *am* it.

Miss-Taking a Word for Reality

When a child plays with your cat then is exposed to two cats next door, that child has the experience base to form the concept *cat*. But it requires that the child has also experienced other kinds of things, perhaps dogs, cookies, tables, chairs, etc. The comparison to other groupings or things is needed.

At some point the child mentally puts together your cat with the neighbor's two cats and creates a grouping called *cat*. Then when the child meets a cat he/she has never seen before, he/she will view it as part of the grouping, and will point an`d say *cat*.

The process of learning language is one of forming groupings (concepts) and giving each grouping a name (word).

Difference and sameness are intertwined in order to make the groups. We see a few cats, each one different from the other. We view the differences in the cats as less important than the sameness. We form the grouping *cats* by keeping the sameness and disregarding the differences.

Then we see a few dogs, each also different. And we view the differences in the dogs as less important than the sameness. Again, we form the grouping *dogs* by keeping the sameness and disregarding the differences.

The uniqueness of each cat and of each dog is lost when we use the word *cat* and the word *dog*. The difference that becomes important is the difference in groupings: cats-not-dogs becomes the important difference.

In reality every cat is different from every other cat. Same with every dog. But our word-tool system works by setting aside these unique differences. Word-tools favor the sameness of a group while disregarding the uniqueness of individuals in those groups.

Those four-legged furry things (*cats*) are more like each other than these other four-legged furry things (*dogs*). And cats and dogs are more like each other than these other four-legged things (*tables*).

If throwing tables into the mix felt like a bit of a jolt, it may be because we start seeing the world through our groupings. We were considering alive things, and then suddenly realized there are also four-legged things that are not alive.

Through this process of creating groupings, we give up unique reality in trade for making the mental objects we call *concepts*. The word-tools that result give us shortcuts for communicating.

The unique reality we give up includes all the differences across the cats that we ignore when we put them in the same group and use the one word *cat*.

The object is the one mental "it", which is the concept, carried by the one symbol, the word *cat*.

And as a this-not-that grouping, each word emphasizes the "not". The "this" of the sameness of *cats* nots-out (eliminates) all the "that": *dogs, frogs, fences, grass, flowers, cars, computers*, etc. The emphasis is on exclusion. This may be helpful in creating our word-tool shortcuts. But it's hurtful if we aren't aware of the extent of what we exclude when we create these shortcuts.

What does this process, the nature of the word-tools themselves, do to our viewpoints about people?

Here are a couple of examples from the TV/movie realm.

I recently saw an episode from a TV series *Touched by an Angel*. In it, an adult male travelled home to be with his family at Christmas. His mother, sister, and father were delighted to see him, and it was obvious there was a great deal of caring and love between them. The father especially showed a lot of interest, affection, and happiness while with his son. A couple of days later the son told his family he had AIDS and was going to die soon.

The father was shocked to discover his son was gay, and he no longer wanted anything to do with his son. As soon as the father used the mental grouping *gay*, everything about his son, all the uniqueness, was suddenly nonexistent in the father's mind. The one word wiped out a lifetime of experiences.

The word *gay* forms a grouping based only on sexual preference. It ignores all the other differences, in order to create this shortcut for communication. Just like with *cats* and *dogs*, now the difference in the grouping pulls our attention. The reality of the uniqueness of this human being was now made negligible to the father as his attention was drawn to the single aspect of sexual preference. Word-tools carry only one thin slice of reality.

This father nearly destroyed his relationship with his son by refusing to talk to him as he lay dying in a hospice during the last days of his life. All because one symbolic object of ink/sound-waves, the word *gay*, was held to be more important than a lifetime of experience and caring with his own child.

Minutes before the son died the father went to see the son and apologized. He finally saw his mistake in priorities, his error of putting the this-not-that aspect of sexual preference over life itself. He realized that he did not want to let the one concept/word grouping *gay* wipe out a lifetime of love.[9]

When I defend my use of negative judgments, my surface self/ego says that the word *gay* is actually neutral and doesn't have to be used the way this father did. And this of course is true. The way we use our word-tools is a choice.

But it simply isn't the way most of us use words in today's world.

Along the same lines, in a movie called *Jenny's Wedding*, a daughter tells her parents that she's gay and wants to marry her partner. Again this single characteristic of sexual orientation overshadows life itself as illustrated by the mother saying, "She's a completely different person." One day she's a beloved daughter; the next day because of one word, she's "a completely different person".[10]

My experience with my own mind is that I mistake my word-tools for the reality itself.

I forget about the fullness of reality as I favor the this-not-that convenience of my words. I forget that before we had these shortcuts, if I wanted to show something to my friends, I would have taken them to the unique place, animal, or whatever, and pointed to it so these friends could experience for themselves the uniqueness of what I wanted them to see.

---

[9] *Touched by an Angel,* television series episode "The Violin Lesson", directed by Peter H. Hunt (New York: CBS Productions, 22 December 1996).

[10] *Jenny's Wedding*, directed by Mary Agnes Donoghue (Philadelphia, PA: PalmStar Media, 2015) DVD.

It's so easy to say to my child "that's a flower" as I forget that the word is only a symbol, only a label we use as a shortcut. Gradually I'm shifting toward saying "we use the word *flower* when we talk to someone about this kind of thing."

I continue to practice being more aware of my tendency to mistake the word symbol for the reality.

I Have a Right! – Follow the Rules!

Driving home, I was waiting at a light to turn left. When the green left-turn arrow appeared, some pedestrians started crossing the street without their signal to walk. Guess what my first thoughts were? *You don't have a right to cross now! I have the right-of-way! It's my turn to go and you're slowing me down! I need to get home and get things done!*

Then I wondered: what are rights and rules for? What do they depend on?

The answer from my mind was: they are to make sure people don't take advantage of each other, to ensure every person gets what he/she deserves.

I felt the me-vs-them enemy mentality rise up inside. I sensed the underlying idea that "I am separate from others" (as if in a vacuum). Though I'm shifting away from these views, my mind continues to hold them and to resist people and situations by hiding behind rights and rules. My mind says, *These people aren't behaving responsibly; they should honor my rights and follow the rules.*

Yes, following the traffic rules makes things flow smoothly. But what's the ultimate value of flowing smoothly? People. Growing, feeling good, and doing things that contribute to life. When I remind myself of this ultimate value, I notice I've made word-tools, expressed in the form of rights and rules, more important than the living they were meant to enhance.

We create rules to make life better for all of us, not to use as clubs for beating people up. They are not for judging, blaming, and punishing. Yet, I use them this way. Rules are not meant to create negative energy, yet rule-dominated people use them for that.

When I think of all of us who criticize and judge people for not following rules, and of all the negativity this generates, I realize how much energy we all waste. We could instead use that energy to point attention toward gratitude. There is so much in life to enjoy: color, shapes, buildings, plants, animals; and if I shift away from using rights and rules to blame, I can enjoy those pedestrians as fellow human beings walking across the street.

So I realized that I was blaming these people and justifying it by hiding behind the ideas that people should follow rules and uphold rights. With gentleness, I told myself, *That's okay, now you are aware and awake again to the value of people.* As I waited for the people to finish crossing the street, I shifted my attention to colors of spring flowers and to the clear air I was breathing, the same air I shared with these pedestrians whose right to Be was greater than any rules we may create.

Here's a different example illustrating the function of rules. When I was a director/principal for a private school, a first-grade teacher came to me with a dilemma. She had a student who occasionally misbehaved, and she had sent notes home to his parents a few times.

But the last time she sent a note, the parents punished the boy by putting him in the backyard and making him fill a five gallon bucket with rocks. Then the boy was forced to carry the bucket to the other end of the yard and dump out the rocks. Guess what came next?

The boy was then required to put those same rocks back in the bucket, carry it back to the starting point, and empty it again. Then he had to fill it again, and carry it to the other side of the yard again. This repetition continued.

I didn't immediately know what we should do so I said to the teacher, "Let's think through the purpose of the rule for sending notes home to parents."

I considered the situation and came up with this statement:

> By sending notes home, we are trying to engage parents as members of our education team. We hope they will help us encourage the child in understanding the value and enjoyment of learning. We work hard to connect education to the child's own life, to show that he/she can have fun with learning and gain from it.

Would sending a note home to these parents at this time accomplish this? Probably not.

Would the rule function as intended? How would punishing the child as the parents did encourage him to learn? In this case, following our "send a note home" rule would go against the reason for creating the rule.

This experience, which happened about fifteen years ago, has stayed with me ever since. This is another "marker" for me. Repeatedly I was reminded that the reason we create any kind of rule or procedure is to contribute to people's well-being, not to make tools we can use to punish. And even though the rule may work in most cases, there will be times when breaking a rule fits its purpose even better than following it.

Following a rule can be counter to what underlies the rule. It can go against a deeper meaning.

In this school situation I saw with new clarity that rules are not absolutes and that they are limited to specific purposes.

The experience helped me see that structures formed by words are limited. Words are only tools, useful for indicating, unless that indicating actually goes against the very reason for creating any tool: to enhance life.

So just as my "right" to turn first before the pedestrians crossed was not an absolute, the school rule that teachers send notes home was not cast in stone. Considering the full reality fits any rule better because it fits life better.

As I catch myself using rights and rules to criticize and judge people, I wonder whether these concepts are ever used constructively rather than to just punish others for "inconveniencing" us. I feel superiority creep in when I use them, and it appears that others do too.

If people were robots, programmed to do exactly what rules dictate, life would not have the vibrancy I see all around. When I'm lost in concepts, that's just how I feel – like a deadened robot following a bunch of programmed rules.

But when I'm not trapped inside my thoughts, and believing word-tools as the carriers of truth, I appreciate our ability to put life above rules and I am grateful for the energetic liveliness that comes out of that, even when I don't get to go first as the rules say I should.

Earners with Entitlement Attitudes

When I interviewed candidates for employment, I avoided those who had an "entitlement attitude." To me at that time, an entitlement attitude was summed up by "the world owes me a living", and it belonged to lazy people who didn't want to work. I associated it with poor people who were on welfare. In my mind, entitlement was synonymous with acceptance of government assistance.

Separateness was deeply engrained in me then. I saw each of us as totally responsible for himself or herself. I viewed people like me who had earned what we had as rightful owners. Whereas those accepting government handouts were using a system where tax money was taken from these rightful owners through threat of imprisonment.

Doesn't it make sense? Don't the people who are forced to pay taxes take care of those who don't work for a living?

Being immersed in my world of word-tools and the feeling of separation that comes out of this-not-that functioning, it was natural for me to view these "kinds of people" as moochers/beggars and to see them as enemies of earners like me.

What I had missed, or ignored, is that I felt entitled. At least as much as anyone carrying a "world owes me a living" attitude. I had thought entitlement referred only to those who expected others to care for them financially or in a material sense. But once I was able to look within myself deeply enough, I was surprised to find that I expected others to care for me egoically.

I was a business manager and regional supervisor when I interviewed candidates, and boy did I think I was special. I thought I had earned all the money I was making and all the status that went with an authoritative, boss-like position. Even though I was the kinder, gentler type of supervisor, I still felt the superiority of being a management-level businessperson. I depended on carrying this image of myself, holding myself high above others.

And although I didn't carry the words "the world owes me a living" as a smart, business-manager type, I moved through the world as if I were entitled to more importance than others. I carried the words "the world owes me the respect and privilege of a higher status".

Since then my views have changed. Now, "seeing myself as better because I achieve and earn" is just another form of entitlement.

I remember feeling that my time was so much more valuable. *I shouldn't have to wait like all the others! How dare you slow my travel time down! I am important! I am entitled to better treatment!* The world owed me more because I had earned more.

How's that different from the moocher who feels the world owes him more, in the material sense, because he or she has suffered more? Have not the moochers come to deserve material resources from the world just as I have come to deserve ego-coddling? Why should any of us be above others in these ways?

I'm not saying that every person should receive the same amount of material payment from the material world. Effort, wisdom, and so many other factors are involved in any quality a person brings to being in the world.

But there are different types of efforts and earning. And there are different results than just material ones. I have met street people who looked me in the eyes, shared their wisdom, and listened more fully than many businesspeople I've met.

How will we, and how will I, learn to stop separating ourselves from others through using labels such as *earner* and *entitlement attitude*?

Becoming aware of the limitations of word-tools has helped. And this means realizing that the "10 percent visible part of the iceberg" that word-tools are able to symbolize conveys very little about what any human being is. A single characteristic having to do with material resources or money doesn't come close to carrying the reality of the whole of a person.

Misuse of word-tools narrows our ability to live. By blindly forcing experiences through the narrow filters of symbolic representations, rather than allowing them to be filled-up by the vast Connectivity that makes up reality, we constrict our Being, our interactions, our love, and our gratitude. So often I find my words stifling the flow and detracting from the enjoyment of experiences that are best savored in silence.

When I put attention on nonverbal connections with people, looking straight into their eyes, and at times touching their faces, it opens me to the vast web of interconnectedness that I can't see when I am lost in concepts. It opens up a vibrancy and fullness of living I had not known before. And my belief in the distinction *earner* vs *non-earner*, along with the meaning of the word *entitlement*, diminishes.

As long as we continue to live, we all breathe, drink, eat, and benefit from the same earth, sun, and air – we share so much of this vast interconnected reality. And I find that categories such as *earner* and *entitlement* rarely contribute to this shared reality.

Conceptual Force

For years I've felt tension toward a cluster of concepts that are generally accepted as "good". That cluster includes: goal, outcome, result, structure, discipline, etc.

Defending these as "good", my word-dominated mind asks: *Don't these push us in directions we want to go? Don't they serve as ways to pull people to finish what they want to do? Don't they inspire continued effort when hardships occur?*

But the whole-me asks: *Why is a pull necessary? Why am I resisting what I'm doing now such that a "pull" or "kick in the butt" seems needed? Why am I not enjoying my task enough to be drawn to finish it naturally? Why do I need the crutch of an artificial symbol, such as the word "should", which I so often misuse?*

My word-tooled mind counters by asking: *Isn't disciplined structure a helpful way to progress step-by-step? Aren't preconceived goals valuable in nudging or reminding me to make progress?*

As I write this I'm aware of how crazy it may sound for me to question these widely valued concepts. How can any progress happen without these types of pushes and endpoints? But my experience tells me I make more progress and do better quality work without them in my field of attention. So even if "it doesn't make sense" to my word-dominated mind in this word-dominated world, my experience gives evidence to the contrary.

Previously I excluded any possibility of the nonconceptual in my life. I was completely dominated by word-tools. But as I became just slightly aware of the nonconceptual, I began to sense a kind of word-tool force against myself. It's the kind of force that traps me in a commitment. It's as if I use it to put a *have-to* around my neck and the shackles of a threat of failure around my wrists and ankles. *You will lose if you don't lock yourself up in goals, absolute outcomes, discipline, and structure.* And lurking in the shadows of the background is a soft voice, or a loud one, that says, *Just like everybody else does.*

When I was almost completely trapped in the conceptual realm, progress without discipline seemed impossible. As I denied the whole of Source and believed that truth came only through word-tools, the very idea of doing something without being opposed, pressured, or punished was unimaginable. In my word-based world, it was either this or it's that. There was nothing else. The constant feeling of life as opposition appeared to be a reality.

Immersed in the this-not-that nature of word-tools, I was lost in a kind of word-based force that I used against myself and others.

I wonder if there is any constructive use for the concepts of goal, outcome, result, structure, discipline, etc. I wonder if we are trying to use a tool for something it is not suited for.

It's tricky because our word-tools are excellent at masquerading as what they aren't. The reason we don't see through their masquerade is we've forgotten where they come from. We've forgotten that their original source is life experience, a source that flows naturally as it grows without force. We're immersed so deeply in our word world that we can't see the natural flow that is both within us and all around us.

As I began to see the closed, frozen nature of word-tools, I began to see that I don't need this type of external, synthetic push/pull to be creative. In fact, it slows or stops creative flow. Once I opened up to sense the nonconceptual, I was able to experience the *growing* of life as better than the *forcing* of life. I saw that the "progress" of growth doesn't come from the force of an external symbol-tool that creates the tension of resistance.

And now when I sense this resistance creeping in, I remind myself of the peaceful, playful enjoyment that comes out of putting attention on the task I'm doing right now. And then the specifics of the outcome of the task begin to fade away because the enjoyment overshadows the endpoint.

Do I still use "goal" tools? Yes, but not often. In a way they are always out there, functioning as a general direction of where I'm going. But, when I notice their tug, I use the tension as a signal that my attention is in the wrong place. In my view, goals are used far too often as clubs both within and between people, e.g., bosses and employees, and parents and children.

When I'm lost in the world of getting things done as primary, I feel resistance and find myself gritting my teeth as I push toward reaching a goal. I notice that I'm stuck between rebellion and compliance, with an unacknowledged stress hiding deep within.

When my focus is on the goal-tools of outcome, result, structure, and discipline, I find a tension akin to the this-not-that exclusionary nature of word-tools. With goals, it's me and life that's excluded; with word-tools, it's everything that doesn't fit into the word bucket. Me and life getting pushed out of the way in order to make progress toward a goal is very much like everything getting pushed away in order to form this very clear definite symbol we use as a word. Recall that the concept *dog*, excludes everything that is not dog.

Once I became more aware of the tension arising in those of us who take goals seriously, I began to see goal-oriented outcome and focused discipline as a kind of conceptual cage.

Why do we need to put ourselves in cages? Why not find ways to reduce resistance without setting up artificial force-agents made up of word-tools? Once I broke out of many of my own word-tool cages, I was able to experience "doing" as fueled by enjoyment rather than pressured by constraint.

That is why I refer to goal concepts as one kind of conceptual force.

By opening up to Source I discovered that there is no need for force. I've found a way to move forward that is comfortably easeful and enjoyable. In contrast to the firm lines set in front of me by the language of goals, structure, and discipline, the flow of moving in consonance with what's inside me and with everything around me fosters enjoyment rather than tension. The "happening" of getting things done seems to come out of the whole of me moving Arm-in-Arm with the whole of Source.

When I fall back into using conceptual force, which I still often do, I see that I've misused word-tools. I've tried to *make* something happen, using me as the main pressure point. And whenever I do this, I find the outcome I had put on a pedestal is low quality, the result of letting my work be dictated by a timeframe that didn't fit reality. I see it in a lack of fullness, a lack of Connectivity, and a lack of enjoyment.

But I was unaware of conceptual force when I believed word-tools were the only way to know and do. I could see it only after I tasted, touched, sensed Source.

What I am calling Source is a kind of nonconceptual life energy I had missed when I was lost in concepts. In the past, I often reinterpreted and denied any experience with Source as foolish and not real. I was in the habit of forcing Source experience through the narrow constriction of conceptual word-tools. Even though it presents a challenge every day, I've found new enjoyment in discovering the difference between Source-based growth and a conceptually-narrowed push for completion.

I couldn't have written this section until this morning, when it came to me. The writing just poured out without plan, goal, structure, vision, or discipline. As I read through it after finishing the first draft, my conceptual mind asked, *How can the writing of this section not be a product of thought?* My answer is that I experienced no sign of deliberation. No long careful consideration, no discussion or analysis. Almost no intention at all. Instead, it just happened.

I had never put the two words *conceptual* and *force* together until it flowed from my hand about thirty minutes after I began writing this section.

I've pulled away just enough conceptual layering to allow me to give Source a chance at times. That is, to hear and answer this mode of Being when I've been open enough to expose and remove some of the layers of word-tooled conditioning. When we are ready to meet up – Source and I – I'm now often able to accept the invitation.

When I do accept, we flow Arm-in-Arm as we create. Not out of commitment to goals, outcomes, results, structure, or discipline; but out of the joy of Being.

Facing Reality

As I approach a new situation or talk with someone, I interpret what's happening based on past conclusions and associations. I sometimes call these preconceptions. They are ideas already in my head. You could say they are the lenses through which I view things.

When I use these lenses I don't look at a situation or person with new eyes to see what might be there. It all gets filtered through the past conclusions and associations, through my frozen surface self with its judgment structures.

I saw a TV show with three people stuck in a bank vault after a bomb demolished the building. One person said it would be impossible to get out. Another person said, "We don't know what will happen, but I believe everything will be all right." A third person, who was stressed and sobbing said, "No, I prefer to face reality – we're going to die!"[11]

Moving to a different example, I have a friend who has been stuck with the following thoughts for years:

- I am single and approaching the age of forty.

- I will always be single and will never have the husband and child I want so much.

- I love a man who is with another woman. I'll never be with him and he doesn't love me. [My friend carries these thoughts despite the fact that this man says he is not happy with the other woman, quickly responds to emails or messages whenever she sends them, and expresses affection for her.]

---

[11] *Touched by an Angel*, television series episode "The Big Bang", directed by Chuck Bowman (New York: CBS Productions, 25 November 1995).

My friend sees her always/never statements as "facing reality" in the same way as the woman in the TV show.

Only one of my friend's statements is true: "I am single and approaching the age of forty." This fits what is real. Her two other statements are just guesses about the future, worst-picture conclusions coming out of her frozen surface self and its judgment structures.

Her first statement uses words as the tools they are suited for, as a simple description. Her second and third statements are a misuse of word-tools. They don't describe what is real but they are expressed as if they do, as if they have the same status of certainty as the first. Neither the second nor third statements are about reality – both are imagined worst-picture fears.

The stressed, sobbing person in the TV show did the same thing when she said "No, I prefer to face reality – we're going to die!"

So many of us have been conditioned to refer to worst-case fears about the future as "facing reality".

Why do we do this? Why do we become blind to the difference between simple statements that describe reality, and fear-based, abstract guesses about a future that is not real?

For me, it comes from misusing word-tools so much that I "can't see the forest *or* the trees". I'm lost in layers upon layers of using concepts to judge, evaluate, compare. A judgment such as *she is bad* has the same status as the description *she is wearing a red shirt*. Thinking *he's incompetent* is no different from thinking *he lives in the apartment next door to mine*. When my mind chatters that *John is a better person than Bill*, it's easy for me to view it as having the same factual status as *John is six feet tall and Bill is shorter at only five-foot-five.*

If anyone challenges me by saying that *bad, incompetent,* and *better* are not the same as perceptual observations, I can talk for hours about all the evidence that proves she is bad, he is incompetent, and he is a better person. By the time I've described all the perceptual evidence that supports my claims of *bad, incompetent,* and *better,* they seem as real as *red shirt, apartment next door,* and *six feet tall.*

I've noticed that when I judge, I become blind to my misuse of word-tools in the same way as my friend, and as the people on the TV show. Lost in the this-not-that definite nature of word-tools and in my conditioning to misuse them, I easily mix-up what is real with what is not and view them as one in the same.

Happily, I've found some clues that shine light on my judgment-based, worst-picture viewpoints which are more about me misusing words than "facing reality".

Rather than facing the reality that the worst will happen, I face the reality that words are limited tools and that they are extracted from reality as only symbolic indicators. This has helped with becoming aware that "I don't know what I don't know". It turns out that facing the reality of *not knowing* is much more realistic than my fear-ridden worst-picture guesses about what might happen.

Carrying with me "I don't know what I don't know" gives me a new set of lenses that allow a wider view. It opens me to potentials and shines light on fields that are currently outside the conditioned associations and preconceived conclusions I habitually jump to. I shift from "whatever comes through my thoughts is real" to "there is so much I don't know".

I want to add here that I've adopted the habit of saying, with a smile of playful affection, *I don't know nothin'*. I say this in answer to my own thoughts, and I say it out loud when I talk with people. I say it in a lighthearted, nonderogatory way and with friendliness toward myself.

But when I'm enveloped in fear-ridden worst-picture guesses, there seems to be no such thing as "what I don't know". There are no other potentialities – only this reality I'm so certain I need to face. I function as if I know everything.

When I exclude potentialities, it's as if I'm acting like *I am* a word-tool. I exclude everything except what fits the category I stand for. I also blot out the uniqueness in everything I use a word for. The grouping process that creates a concept is intended to narrow my focus by excluding the detail of every unique tree, every unique dog, and every unique person.

A word not only smooths over the richness of unique details, it also does not convey the Connectivity that is real all around us. I find it easy to forget that every word makes it appear that things are more separate than they are interconnected. Yet the interconnections are actually countless.

What a word fails to convey about reality is vast. Its function as a this-not-that, narrow pointer is exactly what makes it so convenient as a shortcut for trying to tell someone about something.

When I remind myself that every person breathes the same air, walks on the same earth, and drinks the same water, I am using words to point to the complexity that they can't convey. When I add awareness of the rich unique details that words exclude, my misuse of them becomes more apparent.

Words don't work correctly when we use them as if they are not limited. When I forget that "I don't know what I don't know", and when I forget that word-tools don't and can't carry uniqueness and Connectivity, then I stifle my ability to see the difference between what's real and what's not real. And that makes it easy for me to miss that when I believe I'm only facing reality, I am actually only feeding my egoic sense of superiority.

How often do you hear yourself or others use the words "facing reality" for fear-ridden worst-picture conclusions that seem real but aren't?

How often does "facing reality" deny the potential of what we don't know? How often do we mistakenly equate the unreal with the real because we've been conditioned to use words for more than what they are capable of, without the awareness that they are only tools designed to function as general indicators?

I find that the false surety I feel with word-tools gives more credence to imagining "the future" than to the area of the unknown. But which is more aligned with reality? That I can predict the future with surety? Or that there is more that is unknown to me than is known, and that I don't even know what that is?

One thing I know is this: I feed and strengthen my superiority, my ego, my surface self, when I misuse words to cling onto a certainty that isn't real. Then I feel a sense of righteousness when I say I am simply facing reality. But when I allow the realization that "I don't know what I don't know", I am more grounded and playfully peaceful.

Note: For more detail, see the sections "The Value of What I Don't Know" and "Uniqueness and Connectivity" in Part 2 and Part 3 respectively.

Synthetic Essentials (Words/Concepts)

I was at home doing morning exercise sometime around the year 2012. I happened to look over at a nearby bookcase and noticed an old book: *The Idea of the Holy* by Rudolf Otto. It had been part of a philosophy of religion course I took when I attended university in the 1970s.

I felt curious, and for no apparent reason, pulled it out and opened to page two, where I had written at the bottom of the page this sentence:

> *Rational attributes are synthetic essentials; they are predicate to a subject which they qualify and which cannot be comprehended in them.*

I really had no idea what this sentence meant, even though I had written it as an attempt to summarize the confusion I felt about what I had been reading on page two. Have you ever read something with the frustrated response "I have no idea what this means"? That's what this page was for me.

I didn't really know as a student in the 1970s what the words in that sentence meant: rational, attributes, synthetic, essentials, and predicate. Even now, I'm not sure what they mean.

But rediscovering it in 2012, I was fascinated with this sentence. It made me think of a course on definitions I had taken in the year 2000. That course was the first time I sensed that words have a source, that we look out at the world and then mentally do something with what we see in order to create a concept and then a word to stand for it.

The sentence connected to that course in some way. I looked up the words – rational, attributes, synthetic, essentials, and predicate – to see if I could more fully understand the sentence in light of my experience with the definitions course.

The course's homework was to draw out definitions from our own life experiences and we wrote many pages for each of ten different words. This work of pulling definitions out of real life taught me that before words, there was life.

I ended up using this "before words, there was life" lesson repeatedly in situations at work. I saw that managers thought they knew the jobs of their staff. But the people who actually did the work each day usually knew the jobs better. We could say that "before there were managers, there were just people doing the work."

Just as words came out of experiences of living, managers came out of experiences of working. Words didn't come first and neither did managers. (Funny, now that I think of it, I was a manager for most of my professional career.)

So after seeing the applicability of the definitions course at work, the sentence on synthetic essentials seemed more meaningful. I now saw the word *subject* in the sentence as a starting point, something that came first; I saw it as a base.

Noticing managers who thought they knew better but didn't, helped me see this misperception working in myself as a manager. I saw that in most cases, to be closer to the base is to know more.

Even if the manager had done that exact job in the past, things change. I began to see that when a base is filtered through layers of time and business and customer changes, the manager's previous firsthand experience is often soon outdated by change. When I'm farther away from it, in time or layers of business structure, I tend to mistakenly think I know more than I do. Those closest to the base almost always know most about that base.

These cognitive connections, between the sentence, the definitions course, and the work experiences, left me with strong promptings to explore the highly limited nature of our word-tools.

Now, I use *synthetic essentials* to refer to any word or combination of words created by human beings. And I use synthetic essentials as a synonym for the term "word-tools" used dominantly throughout the book.

Here are more synonyms as listed in the introductory section, "Terminology":

> word ⇔ word-tool ⇔ concept ⇔ category ⇔ synthetic essential ⇔ language ⇔ symbol ⇔ label ⇔ name ⇔ snapshot ⇔ this-not-that-tool ⇔ cognitive ⇔ in-the-head ⇔ symbol system

In this book, all of these terms refer to the same general arena of meaning and I use the term *synthetic essentials* interchangeably with any of them. Despite subtle differences, I view them as the same in comparison with the base of reality.

This arena of meaning includes all language, as well as anything formed from language, such as reason, logic, methods, rules, etc. And I admit this entire book is made up of synthetic essentials (word-tools); I am using word-tools to point to the nature of word-tools as I view them.

Words/concepts are synthetic because we human beings created them; they are not found in the reality of natural things. Before words, there were organisms and natural things of all sorts interacting: rocks, plants, animals, water, sun, etc. Life, nature, and even human beings, existed without words.

And although words seem to be indispensable parts of our current realities, they are still artificial symbols we created to represent a base, the origin of it all, the source that is reality. This is what is referred to by *a subject which they qualify and which cannot be comprehended in them.*

I use the word *synthetic* to mean derivative, extracted and made-up from the base that is reality. And as I remind myself that a symbol is not the thing itself, I also remember that reality can function without words. The words merely represent the things that functioned before they existed. The words are tools for thinking and communicating.

For those of you who want more on the sentence about synthetic essentials, read on for more details and repetition. But even though I find value in often rereading what follows, if you don't want more of this technical stuff, I encourage you to skip to another section.

We use words, or *rational attributes*, to name and describe things; but words are not the actual things.

Words are symbols we create to represent those things which are *subjects*.

Words like *big, small, white, brown, fast, slow* – these adjectives and adverbs are called modifiers, at least in my grammar school English classes. They may also be called *attributes*.

We use attributes to describe things we observe: That dog is *big*; that other dog is *small*. That is a *green* tree; that is a *yellow* flower.

"To predicate" is to give extra information about a subject or being. The extra information is secondary to the subject or being. Modifiers/attributes are examples of predicates.

Here's the sentence once again: *Rational attributes are synthetic essentials; they are predicate to a subject which they qualify and which cannot be comprehended in them.*

These words in particular stayed with me: *which cannot be comprehended in them*. This means that we can't know the base when we are far away from it. Adjectives, adverbs, modifiers, attributes, predicates – like the manager separated from the base by all the change that happened since – are all layers away from the base of the *subject*, away from the *what is* of reality.

At the same time, these far-from-the-base symbols I call word-tools give us handy shortcuts for communicating. Without them, if we saw something and wanted a friend to know about it, we would need to physically take her or him directly to the location and point to what we saw. For example, a dog, flower, stream, or car. With words, instead of traveling and pointing, we can just move our mouths and make sounds that symbolize but don't carry the fullness of what we saw.

I've found it worth remembering that words, as the shortcuts they are, can't replace taking the person to see and fully experience a thing first hand. The full firsthand experience is something more than words can describe.

Isn't there more to what you love – a person, a pet, or anything else – than any of us can describe in words? Isn't there more to you than what people see and describe as you? And notice that what they see as you is usually expressed in labels, judgments, evaluations, opinions, etc., that is, *attributes* in the form of evaluation.

Perhaps the something that is more than words can describe is *holy* or *sacred*. Not in the way so many of us were raised to view these words, with stories made up of synthetic essentials. But in a way *that cannot be comprehended in them*.

My experience with the synthetic essentials sentence helped me realize that words are second to the Being of the thing itself. Words can tell a little about the thing; they can indicate but can't give us enough to really know it. The Being of the thing itself comes before and is primary to any word symbols we create as shortcuts to describe it.

I've heard the example of someone doing a PhD on honey without ever having tasted honey. Of course they would have many facts about the physical properties of honey. They may know all the science but without the experience of actually tasting honey they remain far from the base of firsthand experience; they remain detached from the reality of the life of honey they thought they knew so well.

Ten ago I believed I knew the objective facts about fundamental reality, and I was closed to the "taste of honey" because that was just the stuff of simple living. Who needs to taste honey when you're expert enough in the conceptual realm to write a PhD dissertation on honey? I would have dismissed this book you are reading as ridiculous because I believed that reality could be viewed only through conceptual filters, only through synthetic essentials. I was lost in concepts.

I've come to see that the base, the subject, the whole, the inner qualities and interconnected nature of things and organisms, *cannot be comprehended* through word-tools alone. Words are only symbols; they are synthetic tools we created from experience with a reality that existed *without words and before they came to be*. Before words, reality was at the forefront. But that was a time when the symbols weren't seen as more important than the life from which they came.

If you choose to read through most of this book, you'll find many examples of how limiting word-tools are. What if there could be ways to communicate that were not as limiting as words? What if we could discover different tools that carry more of the reality we want to share with each other? What if we're so completely immersed in word-tools that we are missing the value of *subjects* we never imagined possible?

Wow! I Don't Believe in Right/Wrong Good/Bad Anymore!

After shifting my attention away from negatives for a couple of years, I was walking into a coffee shop one day when this exclamation suddenly popped-in: *Wow! I don't believe in right/ wrong, good/bad anymore!*

This really shocked me! The feeling of astonishment continued as I exclaimed, *I can't believe it! Me, the objective, principled, logical, reality-based thinker! How can I not believe in right/wrong?!*

Yet, despite my surprise, I didn't immediately throw it out as totally crazy nonsense. Instead, this pop-in stayed with me through weeks and months of wondering.

I remember asking myself, *Then how do you view mass murder, Hitler, or people who out of blind anger viciously beat someone as we see in the movies?*

Years before this book when I studied objective philosophy I held the view that evil must be destroyed or else it will keep destroying. When the World Trade Center in New York City was blown up I was filled with righteous tension. I believed, *The evil must be destroyed!*

At the same time whenever I felt such righteous tension, along with the superiority of judgmental fervor that accompanied it, my body and mind felt intensely bad about the world and about myself. But to me then, feeling bad was worth it; the tension, stress, and fear of righteous hatred, didn't matter – I had to do the right thing.

So how did I justify embracing the "kill bad guys" belief with such certainty?

I used word-tools to label them *bad* and *not like me*. I called them *evil destroyers*, and therefore considered them *not worthy of life* and as *less than human*. I did what Hitler did to the Jews, what American slave owners did to African Americans, and what those who destroyed the World Trade Center did to the United States. When we define our enemies as *nonpeople*, we feel justified in doing to them whatever we define as right.

Now I see that *I was* my destroyers. My reaction to destruction of the World Trade Center carried the same energy as those who destroyed it, the same energy as Hitler and the same superiority-based energy as abusive slave owners throughout history. I was using word-tools to narrowly limit my view of human beings just as the destroyers and enslavers did. I was my destroyers because we all placed our labels, evaluations, word-tools above life.

And this creates a back and forth that has occurred throughout history: *bad* guys attack us; so we attack them; then they attack us because we attacked them; then we attack again, etc. Through all this, everyone is tense, fearful, and filled with hatred as they use word-tools to redefine each other as *bad* and *not like me*.

We maintain and embrace a we-not-them viewpoint by putting our this-not-that word-tools above life.

This finally presented to me as a simple choice: let go of *evil*, *bad*, and *not like me*, along with its associated violence; or continue the tension of thinking I should judge and then counter their *evil* actions with my *good* actions. Either feel good by letting go of the never ending negative energy, or continue to feel bad by holding onto it as I ignore the ongoing tension.

Over the months that followed, my shock, surprise, and confusion began to shift and what started as a pop-in became the strength of a realization that was accompanied by a feeling of gratitude. As I applied it each day, I continued to realize more clearly the damage I did whenever I made words more important than life itself.

Then I wondered: *How do we improve the world situation without embracing the idea that we must destroy the destroyers? Don't we have to fight the bad guys? Shouldn't we execute murderers? How else will justice be done?* My answer at the time was: I don't know.

But I do know that the "kill the killers" viewpoint hasn't worked for me, just as it hasn't seemed to work throughout human history. My guess is that the feel-bad tension it caused in me is also experienced by killers who seem eager to start a fight and fighters for "righteousness" who believe they will establish justice by killing as retribution.

While I'm in the "killing-energy" state, I am too tense to see that approving of that energy creates more of it. I don't see that embracing it by appealing to justice uses circles of words that disconnect my energy from life. The evil I tell myself I'm trying to rid the world of actually grows and becomes stronger because my reaction carries the same seed as the evil I claim I'm fighting.

Defining human beings as *bad* or *evil* is misuse of word-tools. It is a form of unconsciousness that assumes there is no reality outside of what we can put into words. What we fight only gets stronger because we start from the unwarranted base of believing that negative judgment, blame, and punishment are valid. Our unconscious embrace of judgment arises from, or at least is made possible by, mistakenly using concepts such as *bad* and *good* for something these word-tools are totally unsuited for.

I've seen it inside myself, during the destruction of the World Trade Center and anytime I lose my temper with another person. I've watched tension-filled fears create a fight for "right" that's like a corrosive element inside me and people around me.

As I sensed that my righteous moral justice carried the same energy as that of the killers throughout history, I wondered, *Are we all lost in the same confusion?*

It's obvious that feeling killer energy does not equal the action of killing. I may feel the energy of a killer while I'm yelling at my sister in anger. And though I may hurt her emotionally with my raging, I certainly have not ended her life in the way a killer ends a life.

Yet if I look inside myself when I experience killer energy, I feel the destructiveness firsthand. The evidence is inside me, if only I will look. I think of looking at this evidence inside me as a form of self-science which I have learned to take even more seriously than the body of science outside me.

I also remind myself that the body of science outside me has recently shown that everything and everybody emits energy. Energy is emitted from one body and it flows out and impacts others. Bad energy from me floats out and affects what's around me. Although scientists have proven this, it is easy to dismiss it as hocus pocus, especially if I hold to the beliefs that I am separate as if in a vacuum and righteously superior as if I own the truth.

So again I ask, if I continue to embrace the judgment mentality of right/wrong good/bad, am I not embracing the same process and emitting the same energy as Hitler when he declared the Jews to be bad and worthy of destruction?

What I know is that I no longer see the point of continuing the tension these judgments bring. For me it goes against life energy and against a feeling of gratitude for life itself.

I see the destruction of right/wrong good/bad inside me, and I see it outside. As I release myself from the hold of this energy of righteous superiority, I find peace inside. Now, after experiencing Connectivity with people and with Source, I see the potential for peace outside me as well.

I was glad to experience two more pop-ins within the months that followed: "Selectivity" which means taking action with a nonjudgmental, emotionally neutral energy; and "A New Kind of Right". See these sections in Parts 2 and 3 respectively.

We Choose Our Authorities

Years before writing this book, I hired a life coach to help me become aware of issues that were holding me back, issues I may not have been seeing. At one point in our work, I resisted her tools and techniques to such an extent that I yelled at her in a rage. It was a state of anger I occasionally experience where my fury is so intense that I can't remember much of what I say. I was so totally unconscious that I remembered nothing of what I yelled. I only remembered what she said, the things that fueled my anger.

I had viewed my anger as justified. I thought I was angry about what I saw as mindless repetition in some of the coaching techniques she had been using. Perhaps these techniques didn't fit my way of approaching life. On the other hand, I believe there is truth in the statement "I am never upset for the reason I think".[12] So what had really upset me?

As I continued to feel the rage, I realized I had unconsciously labeled her. In the background of my mind I had pinned her with the label *authority*, and as such "she had certain responsibilities".

I had trapped her (and me) inside a word-tool bucket, a limiting container that holds a very narrow cluster of ideas. Once I put that label on her, my view was fixed. I saw her as someone in a position of power, a professional, an expert, and a superior. Deep in my mind, she was someone who tells me what I should do and someone I should listen to.

It is understandable that I would view her that way. We tend to view our doctors, lawyers, and accountants as people whose advice we should follow.

---

[12] Helen Schucman and William N. Thetford (scribed and edited by), *A Course in Miracles: Text, Workbook for Students, Manual for Teachers,* Workbook for Students Lesson 5, page 6 (Omaha: Course in Miracles Society, 2012).

Not only was this label buried deep in my mind, but I was behaving as though I was unconscious of the nature of word-tools, even though my work consists of studying and writing about them.

So as I continue to feel the anger I remind myself that the label *authority* is a limited, freeze-framed tool. It is extracted from the swirling movement of many of us who use experts for help in a certain area of life. The word *authority* is only a shortcut. It carries only a tiny sliver of meaning that, as it turns out, is something I created.

Digging a little deeper into creating an image of "someone I should listen to and follow", I noticed that it positions her above and me below. And this image generates a pressure to "do as she says", even if I don't connect with it. The label *authority* sets up an identity of me as viewed through an above/below comparison.

What I had missed are these two perspectives:

- I was paying her (I had hired her), and in that sense I could be viewed as the boss in this relationship.
- Any "authority/expert" is chosen by the person who applies the label.

I realized that I'd used the frozen, inflexible, closed container of a word-tool to create an above/below role which then became a reality in my mind.

But if I created the above/below image, am I not "above" because I am the author of that creation? It may appear I am below. But how can this be since I created the image and then chose to fit myself to it by playing the role of being below? By creating the image in the first place am I not actually above it?

I realize now that am above it, but only if I am able to be aware that I created it. If I'm not aware I created it, then the image becomes the boss of me by virtue of my lack of awareness. My lack of awareness keeps me in the below position.

If I'm aware I use word-tools to create images that become realities in my mind, it's as if I hold the key. But if I'm not aware, it's as if I locked myself in a jail cell and threw the key out the window. Of course I can always unbury the awareness that's waiting there deep inside me. Because in a sense the key is hooked to a string and I can pull it back and use it to free myself anytime I choose.

I know this deep down, but word-tools don't hold this kind of knowing. Their this-not-that limitations don't allow it.

I view *authority* as one of those word-tools that is misused most of the time. Every human being can be seen as an authority in some area; if not in the outer world, each is the prime authority of his or her own life experience.

I realized that anyone who I've viewed as an authority in my life – doctor, lawyer, teacher, religious leader, therapist, boss, etc. – is someone I gave that label to. And since I am always the prime authority of my life experience I'm never ultimately in a "below" position. Even if someone who hired me is called *boss*, I still have a choice to stay or leave. And if it doesn't seem I have an option to leave, I choose how I describe the relationship in my own mind. Changing my views about it can make working for even a harsh boss much better because I reduce the resistance that makes me so tense inside; I can let go of trapping me and my boss in the word-tool box *harsh*.

I had trapped my coach and myself in the narrow confines of a label. I had reacted to unhappy feelings of obligation, being controlled by another, being shackled and locked-up by an authority I "should and must" obey. But since I chose to work with this person, I am the one who put all these feelings into play.

All these thoughts/feelings sprung from the label *authority* which led my mind to enclose us in a specific and limiting framework. I chose this person, assigned her the role of controller, and then damned her for the status only I could give her.

I was lost in the label I chose as if it fully represented the whole reality of our relationship. But a word-tool label cannot hold all that's involved in the interactions between two people.

In the same way that the word *flower* doesn't carry the experience of smelling and touching a real flower, *authority* doesn't carry the vast array of swirling movement of the interactions involved between people of varying knowledge and experience.

As I remind myself that no one can be an authority over me unless I create an above/below image, I also realize that this experience taught me to simply avoid labels like *authority* and *expert*.

I find it beneficial to use longer descriptions so as not to mislead my mind. Instead of labelling someone an authority/expert, I say to myself, *I'm hiring someone who has studied a specific area because I want to see if I can benefit from their efforts and intensive focus in that area.* Then I remind myself that I own my decisions, that I can accept or reject all or part of what I hear, and that I chose and wanted to hear this person's viewpoints.

I find more value using more words because I'm less likely to mislead myself by using the shortcut of a single word, like *authority*, that can hold only a tiny sliver of what is real. My life flows much more smoothly when I:

> *Use words in such a way as to highlight the Connectivity from which they come rather than the separations to which they lead.*

Note: About a year after first drafting this section, the catalyst for my anger came to light. Back then when we worked together I thought I was angry at my coach because "she had not been with me" and I blamed the tools and techniques she had been using. I had felt pressured to adopt approaches that were too far from my stage of development and I felt she expected me to accept things I was not relating to.

But guess what happened? About a year later, it occurred to me that I myself often do exactly what I was accusing my coach of doing. I finally noticed that when I offer opinions or newfound beliefs to others, I frequently expect them to immediately accept what I'm saying. And I noticed that I am not "with the other person" because I've made promoting my position more important than understanding our interaction. When I'm in this promotion mode and expect others to see my opinion as truth, I am lost in concepts.

So it turns out that I was angry at my coach about what I was not ready to see in myself. I perceived in her something I didn't approve of in me. And without recognizing it at the time, my unacknowledged rejection of my own behavior caused the troubled state of resistance that was the real catalyst for the anger I directed toward her.

Part 2 Connectivity

A Brief Whisper of Connectivity

Just before my divorce, I lived apart from my wife for a couple of months. I was in California while she was home in Utah. I was looking for a job. My plan was to commute back and forth between California and Utah, as I had done another time during our marriage between Texas and Utah.

While searching for "the ideal job" in California, I had no social contact. I had set my mind to job hunting and philosophy studies, not allowing any other activities, even though I could have sought out some old friends who lived in California.

I felt more alone than at any other time in my life. I was isolated.

And I had one experience that stayed with me. I call this type of experience a *marker* because it's the kind of happening that comes back to my mind over and over again. A *marker* is something that seems to continue to tug at me as if it wants my attention.

Here's the *marker* experience that happened during this period of isolation.

I was going through the check stand at a hardware store, purchasing an item for the kitchen. As I gave the money to the checkout clerk, I looked up at him. My eyes met his for just a brief moment. I didn't dart my eyes away as I often do. I don't know why, but I was fully conscious of my eyes meeting his, for just that one moment. It felt like a genuine connection, as if our eyes had held each other.

During this time of loneliness, this eye contact felt like a comforting human touch.

As this experience repeatedly came to my mind, it occurred to me that it was a meaningful moment, the kind which I had not experienced for many years.

Without words, without intention, with only a brief instant of holding each other's glance, we became two connected human beings, not just people going through the motions of playing the roles of customer and checker. It was clear to me in that moment that each of us were of the same kind, with feelings and struggles that were in some way like each other's.

That was it. I never saw that man again. But that moment we shared seemed to be a precursor to the opening up to a sense of Connectivity that was coming next in my life. I'm glad I listened to this marker – I'm glad I gave it the space of my attention when it tugged.

Life as Process Not Frozen Snapshots

After breaking through some of the this-not-that bubbles I'd created by putting labels on things and people, I began to see life more as continuous processes rather than as distinct, separate, frozen buckets. Life became more like a movie than a snapshot, and I began to experience feelings as moving energies, rather than as the frozen, fixed tragedies I was so accustomed to.

I eat, I sleep, I wake up and exercise my body. I take a shower, put on clothes, and walk outside the house. If I try to stop the action by freezing one extracted part of the flow, I lose the sense of what my living is.

But this-not-that tools hold only one frozen spot of life's movement. I so often hold in mind an image or snapshot of a flower, a dog, or a person. Most of the time, I do this in the form of word-accompanied pictures: large and yellow with a light-green stem; fluffy fur, medium sized; tall and slender with brown hair.

These may seem detailed at first, but they miss so much of the interconnected movement that makes each one what it is. They miss the aliveness as they draw me into the gravity of feeling that "I know" because I've attached a few words.

Words used as evaluation do even more damage to conveying the full picture of the flow of life. When I use words like good/bad, right/wrong, lazy/hard-working, they "play" as if they carry a story worth telling. But these words carry only a miniscule sliver, only a narrow, surface aspect that appears "real" but are actually only freeze-frames of conceptualization that are then held in my thoughts/feelings.

My first glimpse of this is described in "Crazy Thoughts" where I saw how stories in my mind that seemed so important could shrink to meaningless distortions of the full reality of the moving whole.

Life, reality, Source. These are the "what is" wholes of Being. They existed prior to word-tools because they are what the word-tools come out of.

Words/concepts are frozen slivers of information pulled out of the movement of what is. They are merely shortcuts we create to indicate the general idea of what we're thinking in a certain situation.

While we busily use concepts and words to communicate and coordinate with each other, our sense of life/reality/Source moves right past. It continues to Be without stopping to create the symbolic freeze-frames we call words. Life itself, reality itself, has no need of synthetic symbols. Life and reality simply are; they Be without needing to be communicated in the form of word-tools.

To expand my awareness of reality as a continuous flow, I needed to step back from the freeze-framed symbols of words and see them for what they are. That's how I began to get a sense of the fullness of Being and to see, at least occasionally, the "what is" before it gets filtered through and diminished by our highly limited word-tools.

Vulnerability

Just after a divorce from my wife of sixteen years, I had an experience that touched me in a way I had not allowed for a very long time.

I was working as an upper-level manager in a company where I reported to the CEO. Because I had a master's degree in psychology and had studied philosophy, I viewed myself as a smart guy, an intellectual of sorts. I felt superior to most of the employees I encountered.

I myself never liked encountering a "know-it-all", even though I felt superior to so many people around me. Thankfully, there are experiences that can make little cracks in the hard shell of a superiority illusion.

The first year after our divorce was the most tenderizing and painful period of my life. I felt numb and emotionally lost most of the time. I often took walks around our building at work. I remember thinking, *Just keep putting one foot in front of the other. You can keep going – you just need to take one step right now, and then another.*

During this emotional time, I volunteered to be part of a development group at work consisting of employees from all levels of the company, not just managers. As I thought about going to the first meeting, I remember wanting to be there without the usual feelings of know-it-all superiority rising up inside.

I still don't understand why I wanted to do this, but I remember walking into the meeting with the idea of not allowing my superiority attitude to take over as I had with so many other interactions at work. I wondered what it would feel like to face the group as a regular person, just like them, rather than as someone above and looking down. Because of my divorce, I had just begun feeling connection to people who were feeling pain from a loss. And my new feelings of loss made me curious about how it might feel to be free of the need to constantly prove I was smarter and to let go of the superiority image that I had identified with.

As each participant spoke, I thought about the unique knowledge of each person and how their contribution was beneficial to the company. Doing this kept my mind busy on positives, instead of judging and demeaning these fellow employees. I didn't dominate the group as I had at times in the past. When I spoke, I thought of the valued uniqueness of each person I'd heard, and I was able to speak as one *of them* rather than as one *above them*.

As I walked away from the meeting, I was surprised, almost mystified, by my own feelings. I felt quietly good. I didn't know at first what to call this strange feeling. Then the word *vulnerable* popped into my mind. I thought, *Wow! I never knew that feeling vulnerable could feel good!* This seemed very new to me, something I had previously not allowed as possible because I had been so busy using superiority as a shield. For that brief moment, it was as though I had always been in constant battle and now discovered there was no need to be.

The feeling was soothing and gentle and pleasantly unusual, with a softness that carried none of the harsh edges I'd been used to. This meeting felt different from the inner tension I had generated in so many other meetings where I'd been a know-it-all. It was a brief moment of feeling genuine and at peace within myself and with the people in this office where we all worked.

Restroom Battles – Word-Tools vs Connectivity

I walked into the coffee shop restroom, toothpaste and toothbrush in hand, needing to use the urinal. My multitasking compulsion, part of what I call my efficiency monster, insists that I save time by brushing my teeth while I use the urinal. I started doing this long ago when a dental hygienist told me to brush slowly, using gentle circles at the gum line. Who has time for that? But since I have a free hand while are I'm at the urinal, I reasoned that I could take the extra time then for slow, gentle, circular brushing.

Anyway, this particular coffee shop restroom had one urinal and one stall, so more than one person could use the room at the same time. But most of the time, I had the room all to myself.

A man who seemed to be in his 80s was using the urinal when I entered. I felt agitated, thinking he was in my way and that I would lose time because I couldn't do my usual routine of brushing as I used the urinal. I felt this slow-moving older man was interfering with my need to always use my time efficiently.

Both my efficiency monster and next-next-next compulsions were thwarted by this situation. Since I must be efficient and since I'm always a step ahead and wanting to get to the next thing, this slowdown created agitation, frustration, and resistance toward this man and the existence of other people in general.

Crazy, huh? Especially since I get so much from people and would not want to live without them, even if that were possible.

Ten years ago, I resisted life almost continuously because it seemed as though people everywhere were "in my way". It was as if I were standing around, tapping my foot and staring, as I waited for people who slowed me down. I blamed them for getting in the way of efficiency. I resisted the living that happened throughout the day every day. This resistance made my body tighten up, something I was unaware of until I began to watch and question my thoughts.

People were like objects in my way, and this older man in the restroom was one of them. And since the grouping process that leads to concepts/words leaves out uniqueness, making this man into the generalized object of "something in my way" was easy to do, at least for me.

But somehow during this restroom visit, I was aware enough to notice the meaninglessness of all this complaining superiority inside me. I was able to step back and see it as another example of my crazy thoughts.

I reminded myself that thought/feelings are word-tool based, and as such they carry only miniscule amounts of information. I reminded myself that words are tools to help me communicate with people, not to turn people into objects so I can push them around. I remembered that words pull me into believing I am separate, as if in a vacuum, and then I reminded myself that Connectivity is real and separateness is symbolic. I realized again that people matter to me and that using these labels about the man, "older" and "slow moving," along with my belief that I must be efficient, had been typical ways of mine to use the tools of words and thoughts to push life away.

These reminders helped me highlight my impatience, see it as unreal, and realize that this agitated frustration was actually only a product of crazy thoughts in my head.

It's not that I pretended my initial negative responses didn't exist. I just decided to not give them any credit as truths; I chose not to take them seriously. And with a bit of gentleness toward myself and toward the negativity and frustration, I shifted the negatives to the side as inconsequential.

Then I realized how grateful I was to be living in a world with real people, rather than as me alone in a vacuum. I reflected on moments of Connectivity. And once I stripped away my initial negative labeling by recognizing my thoughts as an invalid function of word-tools, I actually felt genuine appreciation toward people around me including this man in the restroom.

Finally after these reminders, I focused on my breathing and quieted my mind of its noisy word-tool domination. I actually looked at the man standing at the urinal and saw his face. Once I'd set aside the word-symbol labeling, I was able to allow the uniqueness of this man to enter my consciousness and I immediately felt warmth and friendliness. It was as if the thoughts of being "interfered with" or "slowed down" dissolved into the sink as the man washed his hands. I said "Hi, how are you doing today?" He smiled and said, "I'm fine today." Then as he was leaving I said, "I hope you have an enjoyable day."

As I left the restroom there was no agitation or frustration, no resistance, no negative feeling. There was only warmth, caring, and kindness toward a human being I was glad to have met.

Connectivity makes a difference to me almost every day in ways like this. And it continues to amaze me that in just a few moments, my feelings can change from so much negativity to a warmly positive goodwill toward life.

Talking To My Dog in My Mind

My friends have a little dog they call Snoopy. I often take him out for walks on the trails across the street from his house. I love to watch the little bounce in Snoopy's steps as he runs ahead, then turns to look back at me. There is so much joy in his movements as he so busily engages with smelling all sorts of stuff at the sides of the trail.

The trails are surrounded by nature: trees, open space, birds, grassy fields, and occasionally other people walking – it's quiet and peaceful. In the near distance, there are mountains encircling the area. It's a perfect setting to feel relaxed and peaceful while walking and enjoying Snoopy's energy for living. At times I consciously look at the mountains, clouds, and other sights; and occasionally I even focus on my breathing.

But many times on these walks, I have caught myself feeling a bit tight, not relaxed. I began to wonder how I could feel tense in this peaceful, undemanding setting.

Then one day when Snoopy and I were quietly walking, something new happened: I noticed I was having a conversation with him in my mind. *Ahh, Snoopy, I forgot to give you water before we left. I wonder if you are thirsty. I wonder if you'd like to go to the off-leash park this afternoon, the one where there are usually lots of little dogs like you.*

I also noticed tension in my forehead, cheeks, and neck. At one point I noticed a connection between the talking in my mind and the tension. I stopped the words by consciously breathing and putting *full* attention on a tree, mountain, or cloud. This worked – I felt my face relax!

A few minutes later, or perhaps only a few seconds later, I started talking in my head to Snoopy again. During this hour long walk, I bet I caught myself talking to him about six times. But it was amazing how easy it was to turn off the thoughts, at least for a few seconds or minutes, and to feel relaxed and almost at peace.

Before this, I was not much aware of conversations in my mind. But on this day, I noticed very clearly the tension in my body and that it was there when I was talking to Snoopy in my head and gone when I put full attention on something else. There was so much in the surroundings that didn't require anything from me such as a tree or the clouds, and this contrast to the tension seemed to shine a light on my pattern of useless mind chatter.

Later I discovered that I have conversations in my mind a lot. I notice anticipating how a conversation may go as I drive to meet someone for a meal or appointment. Sometimes as I wash the dishes, I'm talking to myself in my mind about interactions with people earlier in the day. Usually I'm evaluating and revising those interactions, as if I could now change what happened in the past.

Recently I worried about a future interaction with my property manager who made an error of taking two rent payments from my bank account in January; I worried because I didn't want to lose my temper and blame him for an understandable mistake.

Do these conversations in my mind mean I am crazy? Am I the only one having these kinds of chats in the head? Or is it a common occurrence for other people too?

I feel the pull of the world to anticipate, plan, and to "know" *what might happen* in advance. And I can feel the churning of evaluation/judgment of myself and others about *what did happen or should have happened*. For me, talking in my head, whether to

Snoopy or to people, is dominated by evaluation/judgment of what might happen and what should have happened. Worries and doubts.

Noticing is the first step toward something better. What seems like a negative is actually a positive. It's like the positive of the gasoline indicator telling me my car is almost out of gas. Noticing is better than not noticing.

What matters most is not that I catch myself again and again and again having conversations with Snoopy, and with many others, in my mind. What matters is noticing the tension that accompanies these conversations in my head, and then sensing the peace that arises when the thoughts are quieted.

Noticing that I have talks with Snoopy in my head gave me something new to be aware of, a pattern I hadn't clearly noticed before, and a way to reduce inner stress by putting attention on something that demands nothing of me. The tree, mountain, or cloud, along with a conscious breath, releases me from the demands of my own mind chatter. And it frees me to enjoy *this moment of living*, such as the simple movements of walking the trails with the Being of this little dog I love who happens to be called Snoopy.

The Value of What I Don't Know

Suppose you could put everything you know, every thought and belief you've ever had, onto one small space, maybe a 3" x 3" square. Then consider that outside the square, spreading over one hundred feet in all directions, are things you don't yet know, and that you don't even know that you don't know.

I had never thought of such an idea until I heard it in Kevin Trudeau's audio series *Your Wish is Your Command*. He called the 3" x 3" square a "radar screen."[13] I also call it my "frozen reality" because of the nature of how words come to be: they are extracted from life experience by freezing a tiny sliver of the moving flow that is life; words pull a snapshot out of the whole of intertwined reality we could call Source.

So I began watching for examples, to see if "what I don't know that I don't know" could be real. Here's one of my first.

I was having lunch with a friend who is a golfer. We were sitting at a table next to a golf course eating sandwiches. It was a gray day, darkened by an overcast, cloudy sky. Suddenly a loud siren sounded, and golfers began to leave the fairways and putting greens. I know almost nothing about golf, so my friend explained what was happening. He said there are electric devices around the golf course that monitor electricity in the air, and when the electrical charge reaches a certain level, the siren sounds to warn golfers about the danger of lightning.

The existence of these electrical monitors had been outside my radar screen, not part of my frozen reality. Suddenly, I became aware of something "I didn't know that I didn't know" and I realized

---

[13] Kevin Trudeau, *Your Wish is Your Command,* audio read by the author, cd 6, track 5, 01:59 (New York: Global Information Network, 2009).

this arena of "not knowing" could be real. Just because I didn't know it beforehand, doesn't mean it's imaginary.

Then, as I remember it, my friend said he had not taken the sirens very seriously at first. But one afternoon when he was sitting in his backyard looking at a flag in a hole on one of the greens, he heard the siren sound. Soon afterward, lightning struck the flag. It shot high up into the air and broke in pieces, both flag and pole smoking and blackened from the lightning.

For my friend too, it seemed that the danger had at first been outside his radar screen. It had been only theoretical in nature, a belief carried only in the form of word-tools. But when he saw the lightning for himself the danger became very real. From then on he took it seriously.

As I continued to watch for "what I don't know that I don't know", I began to see a huge amount of value in embracing it. The sharpness that pervaded my mind when I felt superior to people because they thought differently than I did began to erode. I found so many examples from life where I did not "own the truth" as I had previously thought.

I began to realize that what was outside my radar screen was something I wanted to take seriously, even if I could never specify it ahead of time. As I integrated this idea with the limitations of word-tools, I began to view the content in my radar screen differently. I saw that what was inside my radar screen was only a product of word-tooled knowledge; it is frozen, doesn't move, and doesn't change. It's inflexible. My concepts/words are fixed buckets that hold only slivers of the reality they attempt to represent.

A friend of mine referred to "what you don't know" as the only space for growth. In addition to viewing it as a space for growth, I like thinking of it as a source of adventure and as an antidote for my superiority, my error of thinking that I own the truth. When I catch myself thinking I own the truth, I now add that I am stuck in my very small frozen reality, my 3" x 3" radar screen.

I recently heard someone refer to "becoming strong in not knowing". For me, it is logical to acknowledge the unknown and to become strong in it. How would I have learned anything at the start if I had been closed to what was outside my then-current knowledge? And when I know something for sure, have I not built a wall to keep away anything that doesn't fit this knowledge I am so certain about? That sounds more like becoming weak than strong – weak with the fear of not being right.

At the same time, "becoming strong in what I don't know" doesn't fit logic because I can't name it specifically, I can't put my finger on it in word-tool terms. So what does this mean? It means that the content of "what I don't know" can be embraced only in a noncognitive way, without specific words.

I like something I heard Eckhart Tolle say: "You can't really understand it conceptually but you can realize it experientially."[14] This fits my sense of honoring the noncognitive, acknowledging and paying tribute to what can't be expressed using word-tools.

But when I cling tight to my frozen reality as if it is The Truth, then I am closing out the moving reality that was its source. Holding tight to my radar screen is shutting out the vast arena of what I don't know, the arena I implicitly had to have "trusted" in order to come to know anything in the first place.

I honor what I don't know because I realize that everything comes out of it. Before words, there was life without words. And that life, which is unknown to me until I experience it, is of value to me.

---

[14] From a video I heard through the "Eckhart Tolle Now" subscription. I know I heard it because I wrote it word for word on a note. But I did not note the name of the specific video.

I Use Absolutes to Blame

As I stepped bit by bit out of a concepts-dominated existence,
I began to feel more satisfaction, happiness, and playfulness. I
gradually came to view living beings as more important than
achievement, accomplishment, productivity, rules, and guides, such
as morality. Isn't the purpose of all of these to allow living beings to
flourish and experience joy in life?

Yet I so easily forget that life can be enjoyed. As I drive to work, just
in time for a scheduled meeting, I notice an inner urgency and a
hint of tightness. One driver cuts in front of me then drives half the
speed limit. Another driver is stalled, with his car blocking the road.

I've discovered I have many choices about where to point my attention.

Based on my absolutist high standards, my first impulse is to
curse the driver who cut in front of me. I can label him as *short-sighted*.
Then I can complain about the driver with a stalled car. I
can believe my thought that he "must have been lazy, not taking
proper care of his vehicle". After all, I've never had a stalled car
that stopped traffic. I can add to this by thinking that people are
generally "rude and stupid". These types of blaming, labeling, and
tense constriction were my standard ways of functioning for years.

But if I widen my focus, other scenarios are possible. I can remind
myself that both the driver who cut me off and the one with a
stalled car are people with needs, feelings, and confusions like
mine. I can let go of the idea that being on time is a standard that
must be followed and that being late would be tragic. I can take
a breath and remind myself of my engrained flaw-finding habit
of negatively judging everything, including people who are likely
doing the best they can. I can remember that these people have
their own lives and their purpose is not to cater to mine.

With this widened view, I am able to realize that any of the absolutist standards I consider to be part of "objective reality" can't be truly objective if they always function to make me right and others wrong, or if they always make everyone wrong including me. When I am blamed for being late for work, I tend to pass it on by saying *I was late because he made me late*. That's how my absolutist blaming works.

While immersed in a blame-oriented world of absolutes, there are always cause-and-effect arguments and logic that prove why being late and blocking traffic *should* be blamed as "bad." *We must achieve, accomplish, and produce so that we have what we need to live! And if we don't follow rules supporting these needs, we will die!* My word-tooled mind loves to justify its blaming.

I embraced blaming and justified it by using absolutist word-tools, such as cause-and-effect, logic, responsibility, and morality.

When I was nearly 100 percent mentally committed to blaming in order to uphold absolutist high standards, I felt anxious, tense, constricted, and angry at the world. Given what is "right" and "true", I had to blame myself for being late and others for cutting in front of me and blocking the road. And I had to view blaming itself as "right" and "true".

But then I found another way. By acknowledging the limitations of how my mind uses concepts/word-tools, I was able to open up, calm down, reduce blaming/judging, and feel much better more often.

Noticing that I allowed word-tools to take precedence over the living they are intended to enhance, I was able to better see that judging and blaming is a form of positioning me above those I judge. And then I was able to see my strong leaning toward superiority more clearly. I was able to see blaming as a distortion, not as an objective, high-standards way of being.

As I watched more carefully how I used the high standards I considered as absolutes, I found I used them to beat people down, to criticize, to blame. I wonder now if any absolutist idea can be used for anything but some form of blaming.

By reminding myself that life comes first and that people are more important than timeframes and smooth traffic, I began to see through the this-not-that belief that we are separate beings who must battle each other for survival. And then I was able to get closer to actually feeling Connectivity with the world around me.

Next-Next-Next

Lately I've been turning the water off while I brush my teeth. I put the toothpaste on the brush, turn the water on to wet it, then turn the water off. This is new. Before this, my superior surface self had no problem wasting water, leaving it running from start to finish as I brushed. Now I'm just a bit more comfortable hearing silence in place of the constant sound of water running down the drain for no reason.

But can you guess what happens while the water is off? I feel the pull of an irresistible urge to reach my hand to turn the water back on before I'm ready to rinse. I catch myself and pull my hand back. Then about two seconds later, I reach again even though I'm still not ready. This happens repeatedly until I am actually ready to rinse. Sometimes I even go as far as turning it on then back off again because I'm not yet ready to rinse.

Walking to the bathroom, I begin unzipping my pants long before I get to the toilet. And when I'm standing at the toilet urinating, I have an impulse to push the flush lever down before I am finished. Again I pull my hand back, and again I reach repeatedly before I'm ready.

It's almost like whatever is coming next is wired into my cells. I'm constantly moving toward what I will do next.

As I walk out my back door, my thought is already on the road I will drive on. Then as I walk to my car, my mind is asking which coffee shop I'll go to today. Then as I drive, I'm planning what I'll do after my writing at the coffee shop. Always one step ahead. Isn't this regarded as "good" in our hurry-up, multitasking world?

Philosopher Alan Watts wrote:

> What is the use of planning to be able to eat next week unless I can really enjoy the meals when they come? If I am so busy planning how to eat next week that I cannot fully enjoy what I am eating now, I will be in the same predicament when next week's meals become "now".[15]

As I talk with a friend, I often think about the next thing I want to say instead of listening. As I make my bed, I can't wait to get it done and make breakfast. As I sit on the toilet cleaning myself, I rush through it brusquely, to finish as soon as possible so that I can shower and dress.

And guess what's on my mind while I shower and dress? Who knows? But one thing is sure, it's *not* on the experience of feeling the water, or the touch of my hands on my hair and skin as I wash, or how it feels to put on my clothes while I'm dressing. Wherever my mind is, it's some place other than where I am. You could say, wherever I am, I'm always somewhere else.

And when I'm always somewhere else, one step ahead in this case, I'm *in "the there"*, rather than *here*. Sometimes I use this cute reminder: if you cross out the *t* in *there*, what do you have? *Here* ☺

Tied to next-next-next is the idea that whatever I'm doing is only a "means to an end". That feeling of "gotta get through this so I can get to that" is so prevalent, it's as if I am living a life filled with "one damn means to an end after another" with no enjoyment of what I'm actually doing in the moment. Enjoyment is always ahead of me in the next step. And that next step never comes because before it does, it's replaced by the step that comes after.

---

[15] Alan Watts, *The Wisdom of Insecurity*, Chapter II: Pain and Time, page 35 (New York: Vintage Books, 1951).

So, next-next-next is a major source of dis-ease for me. It's something that never stops unless I take a breath and shift my attention. Once I began to watch for it, I discovered that every thought of "next" creates just a little bit of tension. That tension, usually in my facial muscles, has become an indicator of next-next-next. When I'm aware enough to sense the tension, my frantic next-ing can slow down enough to notice what's happening: next-next-next is running me forward toward a never-to-be reached end, far away from the living happening right here right now.

Whenever I sense the next moment to be more important than this one, whenever I feel that what I'm doing is only a means to an end, whenever I feel that tense drive to get this out of the way so I can get to some other thing – that's when I know I'm in the grips of next-next-next.

And each time I notice it, I discover so many pleasures of the moment I never knew existed. It's as if a world of satisfaction, never before within reach, suddenly opens up. I wonder if next-next-next is why so many of us connect to the song "(I Can't Get No) Satisfaction".[16]

Last week, I think I brushed my teeth twice without the impulse to turn the water on before I was ready. And if I'm not stuck in next-next-next, I have mental space to notice how good the brush feels on my gums. One time, it felt as if my gums were thanking me for giving them such full attention. Crazy, huh? But, it felt good – each moment of staying fully with my brushing was like a rare experience of living interactively with my gums. It was a first for me.

Cleaning myself after a bowel movement has become a chance to be gentle instead of brusque and harsh. To me it's amazing to turn a cleaning job, one that had habitually been only a

---

[16] Rolling Stones, "(I Can't Get No) Satisfaction", by Mick Jagger and Keith Richards, track 7 on *Out of Our Heads*, London Records, 1965.

distasteful means to an end, into a gentle, self-caring, and nurturing experience.

When I do things merely as a "means to an end" life feels phony, like I'm just going through the motions, like I'm doing things I don't want to do in order to get to things that I imagine I do want to do. When I get to those imagined things, my mind is in a state of busy, slightly frenzied franticness about the next imagined thing. While I'm doing what I said I wanted to do, I miss that moment I had looked forward to because when I get there my mind is on the next. It's as if I've formed a pathway or a rut in my nervous system that continually pulls my mind into next-next-next.

Happily, awareness is expanding, and I more often catch myself when I'm in next-next-next. As the unconsciousness decreases, enjoyment increases.

I don't know where I heard this, but lately I've enjoyed reminding myself that: "This moment is no less important than the next". And here's a more recent version I like even better: "Where I'm going is no more important than where I am right now."

Previously, enjoyment had been covered up by layers of false values: multitasking, the goodness of continuously planning one step ahead, and compulsive efficiency. These "values" lurk around as structural supports for my next-next-next, means to an end functioning.

As I catch myself in next-next-next more often, it seems as though the pathway or rut in my nervous system is gradually diminishing. I often feel each foot as I walk upstairs in my house. As I cut vegetables for dinner, I feel the serrated knife as it saws through the hard resistance of the carrot and red pepper, glides through the softness of a mushroom or avocado, and as it works through the resilient texture of cooked chicken breast.

When I catch myself hurrying to hang up clothes from the dryer, or to make the bed (something I don't like doing[17]), I can stop and remind myself that there is something more. I can notice the smell of the freshly cleaned fabric and the texture of the sheets as I pull them tight across the mattress.

So my dis-ease of next-next-next becomes a positive when I use it to shift attention to something that feels good "now". Reminding myself that "Where I'm going is no more important than where I am right now" becomes something I enjoy whenever I'm aware enough to place it in the forefront of my attention.[18]

---

[17] The words *I don't like doing* accomplish nothing – they only leave me with a bad feeling. When I judge making the bed as a *don't like* task, it blocks my awareness of aspects of making the bed that I could enjoy. My *I don't like this* thoughts go with the feeling of *this is only a means to an end, so let's get it done ASAP*. This all helps maintain the next-next-next resistance to the "now".

[18] There are many points of Connectivity woven throughout this section. When I feel the brush on my gums, the knife on the vegetables, the texture of the fabrics, and my hand as I clean myself, I am connecting my hand with: the toothbrush, the knife, the toilet paper, and my own skin. When I fully feel my feet as I walk up the stairs, I am immersing myself in a Connectivity that includes my feet, the floorboards, the foundation that keeps those boards solid, and the earth the house sits on.

Flow of Giving

As I felt less "me-vs-them" toward people, I discovered I could enjoy giving. It was a gradual and growing enjoyment that started with little things like bringing a bubble tea to work for a coworker, or a chocolate treat home to my roommate. Or at times I was able to give full attention to an acquaintance who wanted to talk.

This natural flow of "giving" now extends to saying "hello" to strangers wherever I go. And I experience it when I take the time to listen to a person on the street asking for money, even when I say no.

As this feeling of generosity grew, I would at times criticize myself – I would accuse myself of doing things so that people would like me, or so that I'd feel desirable or popular. Looking back, I see that having the feeling of being liked was part of what was happening. There was a little bit of surface self/ego in my giving to girls at work and my roommate. They were cute, engaging girls and I noticed feeling a boost to my self-image when I was with them at lunch or out on the street walking.

But that didn't account for all my motivation. Those self-image boosts were only a part of the whole picture. And they weren't the source of my deepest enjoyment.

I remember being surprised by something that seemed mysterious to me. It felt good to care, even if there was a dose of "me-so-nice, I-feel-liked" mixed in. Beyond feeling good, there was something more here than just the giving.

It's as if I had created an inner reality of benevolence that held generosity, affection, and love for people. I experienced many hours, and even whole days, when I felt these positive emotions flowing out toward whatever crossed my path.

Sometimes the giving flows the other direction, from others toward me. I remember being surprised one night when a person I wasn't even looking at smiled and said hi to me. I appreciated his friendliness, but again the simple act was not the deepest core of what I was beginning to sense.

I felt I had begun to allow a glow to rise up from deep inside me, one that had been buried for a long time. It was like a natural lightness, a shining from inside, like the sun, happy to spread its energy in all directions.

My mind is telling me how stupid this probably sounds to many of you. And I admit that I don't feel this "flow of giving and benevolence" all the time, perhaps not even a majority of the time. But to an edgy "mister know-it-all" like me who felt superior for so long, feeling this flow of giving seemed miraculous.

Previously, I hadn't been aware of the hooks of expectation that my giving had carried. Now I see it had been littered with feelings of obligation and/or expectation of getting something back. Usually in the past there was a hidden if not explicit tit-for-tat underlying my giving. I thought that was just how giving worked – I thought expecting something back was the reality of a situation of giving. Sometimes I still feel that.

But I've found that when I feel that hook, expecting to get something from people I give to, my natural inner energy of goodwill is stifled. It's as if I've leashed my energy to an outside surface phenomenon, instead of staying rooted with the natural flow within, and it constricts my inner aliveness. The benevolent joy isn't there when the hook is.

Do I expect something back for many of the things I do? Yes, absolutely. But these are mostly limited to business interactions; e.g., shopping at a store where it's clear that if I give them two dollars, they give me a jug of milk. This expectation of getting back, of tit-for-tat, applies to shopping, doing a specific job for a specific amount of pay, and many other trade-based activities.

But this other type of giving, an outflow of something inside me connecting to something outside, is like a kindness toward life that doesn't need a reason. With this giving I've begun to experience a new kind of delight in being alive, without the old hitches of tit-for-tat expectation. And this positive outflow of delight can accompany even the trade-based interactions, such as at the grocery store or gym, because there are people at those places I look at and speak to.

The delight of this no-hook giving feels like a catalyst for positive energy flow. It's like fuel that creates inside me the kind of world I like to see outside. It's fuel for an inner benevolence that's somehow intertwined with contributing to a benevolent world outside.

This flow of giving has uncovered a feeling of deep gratitude for people, including myself, and even for the natural energy forms of animals, plants, and rocks. It feels all-embracing. It's become a new kind of appreciation of life, one I am grateful for whenever I sense it.

In some strange way, it's the flow itself that makes the difference. Not needing anything back is somehow more connected with the flow of bringing more to me inside than to anyone or anything outside. And yet sensing the feeling reflected outside is part of what makes the flow feel so good.

It's a strange and wonderful circle, this generous, benevolent flow inside me that seems to reflect out onto the world. Without any reason, without me getting anything back, the "reality out there" feels like the one that's taken form "in here".

Disengaging Word-Tools to Engage with Life

I went to the coffee shop with a plan to write. A friendly couple, an older man and woman who I had talked to before, began to tell me about a funeral they just attended. They began to describe details about the ceremony and about the man who died.

I felt an internal drawing of a line of separation, sort of like a judgment. It was the slight edginess that comes out of my this-not-that buckets that word-tools provide. My mind asked: *Why should I take time to hear about a funeral? What would justify missing my writing time to listen to this?*

It was just a slight feeling of being restricted by my plan to write, of not wanting to cross the lines of the plan I'd created. I felt a whisper of hesitation about continuing to listen to this couple. Lurking in the background of my mind was the idea to reject this conversation, to resist it.

I heard my rigid voice go on to say, *Why use my time this way? I don't know the person who died, and I don't really care about funerals.*

But I remembered many talks I had enjoyed with these friends and that I'd felt affection toward them during previous visits. That's when my rigid voice backed away just a bit and I felt myself making eye contact and attending more fully to what they were saying.

As I began to really listen to their description of the funeral ceremony, a colorful image of the deceased started to take shape. I envisioned a man I would have liked talking to and spending time with. It felt as if I was getting to know this man through my friends' vivid descriptions of what happened at the funeral. It sounded like the kind of ceremony that was a celebration of life. Once I got over the slight effort to shift out of the enclosure of my plan, I was fully engaged in just relaxing, listening, and exchanging with these friends.

My clinging to the plan dissolved, as did the edginess about spending time on something I thought I wasn't interested in. I felt the disengagement of my word-tool thoughts about *my* plan and *my* writing time. It felt like the release of an artificial hold that I had almost allowed myself to be taken over by at first. As the conceptual edginess softened/faded, I was able to fully engage with myself and with these coffee shop friends. I allowed life to flow in a natural way without resistance.

It was enjoyable and even exciting to hear about this deceased man and his life. I felt an open, gracious, sharing – a flow of positive energies from me to them and from them to me. I felt the surprise of discovering that this was something I was interested in.

Once I let go of my pseudo-separateness, I was alive again, rather than locked up in the frozen word-tooled world of my surface self.

Afterward I thought, this *is* my work, it's just work in a different form from my writing. What does work consist of if not to connect and engage with "the we" of which I am?

Connectivity – What It Is and What It Is Not

We created words as tools for communication. I once saw an unusual dog that looked like a panda bear. If I want to tell a friend about this, I can use a lot of words to try to describe it: a medium-sized brown-and-white dog that looked like a panda bear. I can tell my friend that the owner who was walking the dog said it was a Mini Golden Doodle.

But my words are only a shorthand. A photo would provide much more, but even that would not give my friend the full reality of seeing and touching this animal in person. The words and the photo are symbolic, synthetic representations.

If I want to really convey the experiencing of this dog, I must take my friend to the dog so she can see, touch, smell, feel it for herself. My friend needs to actually Be there with the dog. This would be communication at its root, without the shortcuts of artificial symbols that can only indicate but never fully bring to life something I want my friend to know about. To really know something is in essence experiential not word based.

Life can *Be* without words.

Trees, animals, plants, earth – they *Be* without words.

Wind, sun, air, fire – relate to everybody and everything, all without words.

My body functions without words – my thyroid, pancreas, creation of blood in my bone marrow, organs such as heart and kidneys – all these do what they do without words, without books, without universities, without science.

Words are a tool, and I have unfairly tried to push them into being more than they can be. By judging and evaluating people and life situations, I've misused words as if they carry the whole picture of a particular person, event, or situation, as if they are absolutes worth criticizing for, blaming for, and even killing for. Throughout history, people have killed others because they had different ideas, that is, because they used different words. These killings occurred because, like me, people believed their word-tooled judgments to be truths that must be followed.

When I was unaware of the limits of word-tools, I used them to destroy and damage myself and life. But word-tools can of course be used in positive ways. They can help remind us of the reality of Connectivity. Isn't that what communication is, a way to bring us together by conveying our thoughts/feelings? When I communicate, I'm trying to share an image or idea that's in my mind. As long as I remain aware of their limitations, words contribute to this sharing and to realizing Connectivity.

But misusing cognitive tools – words, concepts, logic, reason, etc. – as I so often do, destroys Connectivity and the purpose they were meant to serve. I've used word-tools as if Connectivity didn't even exist. I've used them in ways that hurt people. I've used them to justify destructive, even cruel actions, toward people, other life forms, and the earth.

How often do the tools we initially create to contribute to life, end up destroying or harming it because we misuse them? When a killer kills because he was "just following orders", he was putting a limited, symbolic system of word-tools above life itself.

For me, Connectivity is my reminder of the interrelationships that word-tools don't adequately carry. It prompts me to expand my attention to include a perspective that is wider than this-not-that.

In this book, Connectivity means awareness of interrelationships. It means that they are real, everywhere, and inescapable.

- We all breathe the same air.

- I'm sitting on this chair, on the floor, in this room, in this building, on this part of the Earth, in this solar system, etc.

- When I talk with a person, what I say depends on what that person says, how they look, their facial expressions, and much more.

My actions continuously relate to what's around me. The environment I'm in affects me, my actions, thoughts, emotions, etc.

I am not suspended in mid-air with nothing under, over, or next to me. I do not exist in a vacuum. I am not separate. Whether I like it or not, I am an interconnected being.

When I forget this reality of Connectivity and get drawn in by the separation that words pull me toward, my energy flows against what is real. Without reminders, I find it difficult to be aware of the ever-present countless interconnections because our word-tools don't support that wider viewpoint. I find it easy to forget, and even deny Connectivity when I lose myself in word-tools.

My discovery of Connectivity arose through interactions with other people. When I began to allow myself to look beyond word-based preconceptions, I was surprised by the positive regard and affection I could feel toward someone who, only minutes before, I had judged as negative or undesirable.

I remember a regular coffee shop visitor who I'd seen many times over several years. I felt a generalized negativity because I could not tell if this person was a man or a woman. I remember hearing the person talk about a sex-change operation, and I thought "that explains my confusion". But I still felt the negativity.

Many months later, this person was sitting at the table right next to me. I finally said hi and we began talking. After a short time, I became interested in what the person was saying; I felt respect and affection, and thought I would enjoy talking again. I didn't find out if the person preferred to be defined as male or a female, and it didn't matter anymore. I just thought of her/him as a human being. It was as if the importance of knowing if the person was male or female dissolved. In the shadow of experiencing Connectivity with this person, the words that had before seemed so important became needless.

As a young boy, I loved dot-to-dot coloring books. I view Connectivity as a massive dot-to-dot flowing out endlessly in all directions. I like it because it has a never-ending supply of dots to connect with. This image helps draw my attention to the always present interrelationships of me to everything. I can draw lines from this chair to that floor to this room to this building, etc. It is like an ever-expanding web of connector lines that never stops.

In this book, Connectivity does *not* refer to surface interaction such as:

- It's who you know, not what you know.

- Tit-for-tat commercial trading, limited to two people who are only playing roles, for example a "clerk" exchanging with a "customer." (Although these types of interactions can include a real Being-to-Being connection that can take precedence over the clerk and customer functioning.)

- Status-based connections, including business networking driven by thoughts of "what can we get from each other?"

- Any form of connecting when the prime motivation is to gain from the "other" as opposed to simply enjoying.

Connectivity goes deeper. It is the view, outlook, or perspective of *me as-and-with we*. Its prime motivation is the simple joy of Being, which includes all of this reality, not just surface roles/functions we play. It does not seek to change what is, or to fill a gap or a lack or to satisfy a need for superiority or any other ego need. It simply acknowledges the reality of our interrelationships. Connectivity doesn't primarily need or want something from interrelationships – it merely enjoys them.

I was at the gym talking to a woman in the sauna. At first, our conversation felt pure, as if we were both spontaneously interacting as two human beings flowing with enjoyment. Then a thought arose in my mind, "I feel attracted to her". Suddenly a whole cluster of associations came to mind. They were about men and women, dating, and definitions about what relationships were made up of in this word-dominated world.

All of the sudden I felt veils, shields, separators coming between us and stifling the flow. The energy now seemed "fake". There was a clear feeling inside me of wanting something from this attractive woman, perhaps something romantic. And that stopped the human-to-human spontaneity of enjoying each other in the moment.

This change in flow was abrupt and blatantly obvious. My word-tooled associations shifted the whole interaction from pure enjoyment to a means-to-an-end wanting.

There is a difference between merely enjoying another person and wanting that person to fill a lack or a need. Lack is a self-created "hole" that makes me yearn to fill it. It is concept-based, not reality-based. It requires comparison, and only leads to suffering when I put my attention on it. Connectivity has no hooks of this type. It has no ties to lacking, longing, wanting to be with, or needing "love" of another to be happy.

Connectivity is sheer enjoyment of Being, and of all the Beings of people and surroundings, as we move through the interconnected reality of "what is". When I feel Connectivity, I experience affection and a sense of honoring all that is around me embedded in acknowledgement of the environment from which I grow.

Energy of a Killer

My poor wife. (Actually she is now my ex-wife.) She put up with so much unconscious behavior from me. When we were together, I would become viciously angry about things as silly as "the right way to load the dishwasher". I believed there were definite right and wrong ways to put the silverware in. Putting the tips of knives pointing down, not up, was the right way because then people wouldn't cut their hands when they reached into the dishwasher. Forks needed to point down for the same reason, but spoons could point up.

But she didn't always put the knife tips down. And when I cut my hand, I burst out at her with malicious, blaming anger for doing it wrong. Now that I had cut myself, I had proved that my way was right. "See what happens when you put knife-points up!" It was almost as if I had been waiting for the accidental cut so that I could show her how wrong she was.

Of course at that time, I was closed to the idea that the person putting their hand in the dishwasher could be watchful. I did not allow the possibility of taking responsibility for the movement of my own hand in order to avoid cutting myself. I was so lost in the this-not-that of the right way and the wrong way — I couldn't even imagine the possibility of being consciously careful when I reached into the dishwasher. Being lost in concepts had made me blind to life.

I operated under the conditioning that I had a right to live unconsciously, and to blame others for "bad" things that would happen. It was not my unconsciousness, it was the enemy "others" that were to blame.

Viewing the world as separate people, as if each was in their own vacuum-bubble existence, allowed me to justify being disconnected from my surroundings. This led to disowning the consequences of my failure to connect with people and circumstances. As a know-it-all in a vacuum, I had made myself blind to the details and vibrancy of everything around me (knife points being one of those vibrant details).

Later, I saw that the negative energy I had pushed out toward my wife damaged both me and our relationship. This year, I caught myself with that same energy as I yelled viciously at my sister. I was trying to get her to see my point of view, to see that I was right and she was wrong. Then something came to me.

In both situations, what I felt is the kind of energy that a killer has. Sure, yelling is not killing. The actions are different, but the energy seems the same. When I unconsciously push my anger onto people or situations, my actions may be different but the energy is essentially the same as a killer's.

Before becoming aware of the limitations of word-tools, and before acknowledging that I don't know what I don't know, I held tightly to the belief that I knew The Truth, but others did not. This was significant in my carrying negative energies like those of a killer – the unconsciousness paired with belief that I knew but others did not, that I was superior, that I owned The Truth.

Most killing throughout human history has been justified by an idea, an idea in the form of thoughts/emotions ultimately formed by word-tools.

When I am unconscious of the limits of word-tools and the vastness of what I don't know, isn't the energy of my belief that I know The Truth but others do not, the same as the killer's energy when he/she says: "I was just following orders" or "they deserved to die; the world is better without them"?

Some friends recently told me about a man who was writing an essay defending survival of the fittest as a fact about the nature of life. They asked me how I viewed the idea that each of us must strive to be strong so we can then use that strength to take resources from those who are weakest. Years ago, I agreed with these views as part of my enemy-mode ways of functioning. It seemed to me then that fighting others was woven into the nature of existence.

But now I don't see it that way. To justify abusing others by claiming survival of the fittest as "the way things are" is a form of being lost in concepts that is destructive to life rather than aligned with it. As I talked to these friends, I began to sense an argument boiling up inside me. I felt a fight response, an intense negative energy arising. It was as if the inside of me was yelling: "Those fear-based, enemy-mode survival of the fittest views are wrong! My views of Connectivity are right! That man is wrong and I'm right!"

Gladly I was conscious enough to immediately tell these friends about the intense negative energy I felt rising up inside me toward this man's essay. It was nice to then feel the negativity dissolve as we continued to talk. But whenever I fall back into clinging to the righteousness of holding my ideas as absolutely important, I unconsciously react with that intensely angry killer energy. And this is where words become my favorite weapons.

When I defend my views as right, I enter a process of fighting that seems to support the man's "survival of the fittest" ideas. Just as most killers throughout history, I'm in a fight mode that uses ideas as defense for a me-vs-them view of the world.

Actually none of this fighting is necessary. Instead it's a case of taking ideas too seriously and of being lost in a conceptual world that is detached from reality. Ideas and all word-tool products carry only a tiny amount of the reality they attempt to indicate. They are tips of icebergs that don't warrant that kind of righteousness. They are woefully unsuited as justifications for killing energy of any kind.

Word-tools do not take precedence over A Whole or over The Whole of life. When I get stuck in arguing for the rightness of my position, I've forgotten the highly limited nature of word-tools and misused them as posts in cement rather than posts in the sand. When I unconsciously use them as posts in cement, I give them the same false power that's been used to justify killing throughout human history.

Selectivity

As I move through the world of things and people, if I simply accept the first thing I bump into, and then the next, in a random fashion without judgment, I am like a leaf blowing anywhere the wind carries it.

Life is limited. If I don't judge this thing as good and that thing as bad, if I don't evaluate this person as more desirable to spend time with than that one, how will I get through my days? How can I manage my own life if I stop to help everyone I happen to encounter? How can I live if I hold the view that I should spend time with everyone?

If I feel allowance, affection, and even love, for every being in my world, wouldn't I use up my entire life helping anyone I run into? Shouldn't I judge them as worthy, or not worthy, before I take time to help?

Many people I pass on the street ask me for money. I give to some and not to others. My choice depends on many factors that I can't really put into words. I can try, but the words I use won't work because they do not hold the uniqueness of each situation. Since reality in each situation is unique, a flawless guideline about who to help or spend time with doesn't work.

My previous embrace of right/wrong and good/bad judgments made it easy. It was a cut-and-dried function of determining worth, deservedness, or goodness. I believed my black-and-white simplification of life and my word-tools made this narrow view easy to adopt due to their this-not-that functioning.

But now I am beginning to try out real life. I am beginning to Be in the world without the domination of symbolic rules and shoulds to guide my every action. Now I want to live *with* life, not just through symbolic representations of it.

Even though I can't describe how I choose, I can say a few things about my experiences with people on the street asking for money. For me this type of situation provides enlightening examples about the seeming dilemma of how to let go of judging while still choosing without saying yes to everything.

When I listen to someone on the street asking me for something, I try to do it with eye contact and full attention. I often get a sense of whether the person is generally grateful for the little they have, or is one who always demands more, often accompanied by a forceful attitude of entitlement.

Then I can choose to judge those who demand entitlement, or I can remind myself that I don't know what they've experienced and that their viewpoint may make sense given their experiences. I can shift from a negative judgment to a neutral sensitivity of a human being. I can remind myself of the vastness of what I don't know about this person and about life in general.

Sure, I have to choose who to give money to and who to say no to. But I've discovered that I can say no while accompanying it with a respectful caring. Not infrequently, people I've said no to have sincerely wished me well as they walked away.

I've found a way to love life in general and, at the same time, make choices without judgment. It's a sense of neutrality rather than the edginess of superiority I so often used in the past to pronounce people and situations wrong or right and bad or good. With the neutrality of selectivity, the moral fervor of righteous judgment drops away.

In the past, my right/wrong and good/bad judgments made it easy to push people and situations away, to exclude and insulate myself from many parts of life. And now I've realized this as a form of being dominated by the this-not-that exclusionary nature of word-tools. Now I see all kinds of people and situations as part of my world. And it's true, they are part of my world when I don't approach them through my this-not-that conceptual blinders.

I remember being surprised when I first really stopped to listen to a man in a parking lot who asked me for money. It was surprising because I experienced myself hearing a long story without my usual undercurrent of judgment, and without thinking I was too busy because I had places to go and people to see. I gave him my full attention, but not my money. It felt like letting my guard down and allowing a connection with another living being.[19]

And our interaction seemed to benefit both of us even though I changed my plans by taking time to stop, and even though he did not receive what he had asked me for. It was as if we each got what we really needed, a full and alive connection with another human being, rather than what our surface selves thought they needed.

With this man in the parking lot, I felt nonjudgmental neutrality, and a sense of caring and benevolence toward him and toward life itself. This was a first, and it became a marker that has stayed with me.

Again, I can't run around giving unlimited amounts of time to anyone who asks for it. Life is limited. But I can shift away from my me-vs-them judgments that turn others into dirt beneath my feet unworthy of my attention.

---

[19] But in order to listen, I had to drop the chains of my next-next-next and efficiency monster, which I see as arising out of my misuse of word-tools. I had to allow myself to stop the wheels of the strain to continuously accomplish one thing after another, the *should* demands that relentlessly push me to always move forward. In this selectivity situation, instead of rejecting this man without hearing him, I rejected the notion that I have to get to what's next and I have to be efficient. I was simply Being with life.

As I live each moment of each day, I've come to feel the flow of interacting with things and people around me without clinging to the blacks and whites of evaluating every moment. Instead, I embrace the idea of neutral choosing without judgment, and I call it selectivity.

What's in a Pen?

Every once in a while, I expand my feeling of Connectivity by reflecting on a familiar object.

Today, I thought of all the people who contributed to creating the pens I use to write with. There are so many (both people and pens). There are the people who made the metal, the plastic, and the ink. There are the people who designed the pens, manufactured them, and transported them to stores where I can choose the colors and styles I like.

There are thousands, perhaps countless, beings who contributed to me using these pens, because each material element and each stage of the process is connected to its own web of sources that explodes out in all directions.

For example, the metal parts are available only because of the ore from which they were extracted. The extraction could happen only because of all those people who created the mining processes, and all those who created the machinery to bring it forth.

How many more were involved in the creation of the plastics and inks? Plastics come from natural gas, oil, coal, minerals, and plants. Inks in pens include waxes, lubricants, surfactants (compounds that lower the surface tension), and drying agents. And I wonder how many people and processes are connected to the development of each of those.

I've left out hundreds of people who make pens possible. The list also must include those involved with discovery and preparation of the basic materials in manufacturing, business people (accountants, etc.), and storekeepers who sell the pens we use. Perhaps you have thought of many that I've missed.

If we continued connecting from each element backwards, I bet we would find more than we could count.

And none of the materials could have existed without nature itself: earth, sun, air, and water interacting, creating the soil from which the ore and other materials were drawn.

I use this word *pen* and think only of this object I am holding. My words do little to bring to mind all the different people and processes that led to its being. There is so much that goes unseen as I use this amazing object every day.

The this-not-that function of words cannot carry all that led up to the making of a pen.

I notice myself playing the role of a this-not-that type of person as I feel so independent, so separate, and sometimes so superior. I remind myself that this pseudo "separate" me probably involves many more interconnections than the pen. All this lies outside the radar screen of my frozen word-dominated reality, outside the capabilities and range of cognitive symbols.

So again I remind myself that every word I use essentially wipes out the vast array of connections that made it possible. Our word-tools smooth over details that then remain unnoticed, details and connections that are crucial to the whole of reality. Without these details and connections, there would be no pens.

As I try to grasp the wholistic nature of reality, I realize that reality itself has no interconnections – it is simply a whole to start with. But if we now put attention on the interconnections, we can bring back together the whole we first tore apart when we used imagination to create the divisions and groupings we call categories. In a sense we mentally took apart the whole, and it benefits us now to mentally put it back together.

We artificially divided the whole to enable a symbol system that would help us communicate, which means a system that vastly shrinks the experience of actual living so we can more quickly tell someone else about something we see or experience. Now the one word *pen* conveys a general image to you about something I'm referring to. It strips away the full experience and reality in order to produce a frozen sliver that works as a shortcut.

By following words along their webs of interconnections, I come to sense an expansion of my awareness. It's as if I point myself in a direction that can bring back the feel of Connectivity from which it all originates. And then, instead of feeling independent and separate, I feel amazing peace and appreciation. Instead of superiority and antagonism, I sense honoring and gratitude for people, life, and nature . . . and yes, for pens too.

Keeping Score

Spreadsheets have been a major tool in previous jobs, and I've enjoyed many moments of analytical work. Yet even though I used measurement tools in so much of my work, including employee evaluation, I've felt vague discomfort and suspicion about "measurements" for many years.

Seeing that there is life beyond word-tools helped me also see that there is life beyond measurement, and that I use measurement far too often in places where it doesn't belong.

Some of those places include evaluation and judgment (both types of measurement) about "wholes" such as people and life itself, which I also refer to as Source. Since Source is the whole from which all else comes, including our tools of measurement, these tools are simply not applicable. Word-tools based on comparison don't apply to the Wholes from which these tools themselves originated.

Each human being is a whole, and realizing that measurement involves fragmenting that whole made it easier to watch my mind when judgments about people came through. When I'm able to catch myself judging, I notice my inner tension lessen a bit as soon as I put the judgment in perspective. I always feel less stressed when I realize a judgment is just a habitual error of using word-tools. Then if I notice I'm blaming myself for having the judgment, tension goes back up.

But the more I practice, the less that happens; and then more and more I experience watching and noting what my mind is doing as if I were a neutral bystander with my mind standing beside me. I've come to a sense of calm and greater joy, and affection for life, as

I've become more able in catching my mind when it tries to apply measurements and comparisons to human beings.

Just noticing and widening the perspective feels good. Previously even the possibility of this kind of noticing didn't exist for me. I had been blind to the limitations of my own perspective – I was in a way inside my evaluative measurements and inside my mind and I couldn't see anything outside of them. It was as if my evaluative judgments were "me."

Comparison is the devil. And evaluative measurement created to describe Wholes is part of that dark confusion. Comparison, blame, criticism – all forms of word-tool measurement – are destructive when applied to Wholes. Since word-tools are only symbolic representations that carry only slivers of reality, they cannot begin to assess the Wholes from which they come.

In an episode of the TV show *Touched by An Angel* called "Life Before Death", the main character tried to show young Irish Catholics and young Irish Protestants why life would be better for all if they stopped hating and fighting. It showed the Irish youth measuring their "progress" against each other, as if keeping score of killings were part of a game.

The young Catholics and Protestants had only reluctantly agreed to work together on a project. As they continued threatening and arguing with each other, the main character Monica said the following:

> Every one of you has lost someone you loved . . . but the score will never be even. You'll kill him because he killed her, and then they'll kill you, and it'll go on and on and on. For as long as you're keeping score, as long as you both

want to have the last word, the last word will never be spoken and there will never be peace.[20]

I discovered the truth of this as I watched my own inner battles. They were battles of internalized measurements and comparisons that led to blaming, and they damaged my well-being and my relationships with others. These battles were fueled by viewing myself as separate, as if in a vacuum, and by regarding measurements and comparisons as the most believable of truths. After all, aren't measurements objectively true because they can be checked and verified by others?

But the damage of these measurements, the intense and almost continuous inner stress they led to, went largely unacknowledged while I was so busy measuring. Unburying the mental stress I was previously unaware of helped me see the fuller reality of my body. Before this, I attributed physical illnesses to some outside cause that needed fixing by a doctor as soon as possible. But then I began to see I had been doing most of it to myself through the almost-constant tension I created in my body by judging, comparing, and keeping score.

More and more, I am now noticing the tension that comes from score keeping. I notice the tightness whenever I feel negativity and whenever my mind is focused on comparing and keeping score: *Am I better or worse than before? Am I better than him? Is she prettier than her? Am I gaining weight? Is that sensation I feel in my belly a new illness?*

Then I remind myself: *There's the judging, comparing, and keeping score; there's the mental tension that goes with it; and here's the physical tension and problematic symptoms that result.*

---

[20] *Touched by an Angel*, television series episode "Life Before Death", directed by Martha Mitchell, (New York: CBS Productions, 13 February 2000).

No wonder I felt stressed. Ultimately score keeping leads to resisting life through imagining how this or that should be different than it is. Behind the negative thoughts/feelings are stories involving my winning or theirs which depends on measuring against some standard of good or bad. Comparing the "what is" of an action or person against what should be, could be, ought to be, etc. only creates resistance and negative energy inside me. It never leads to contributing to a positive change.

I began to realize that measurement dominated ideals short circuit the inherent Connectivity that is a part of my life whenever I can allow it.

But when I am lost in the process of keeping score, I lose sight of what's ultimately important as the importance of the score overshadows life itself. I resist "what is" through the continuous measurement of comparing and judging Wholes – people, events, circumstances, situations, and, by implication, life itself.

As a young man I thought measuring and criticizing was a good way to encourage change in myself and others. When I think back on that period of youth, I can picture myself strutting around, thinking I'm better because I'm so good at measuring everyone's deficiencies including my own. But now I view measuring people through comparison as a tangled web of error caused by misunderstanding the limitations of words accompanied with denial of anything that may exist outside of the world of words.

When I wage war with "what is" by allowing word-based ideals to dictate my thoughts and actions, I choke off the flow of creativity and of constructive interaction with others. My idealized surface self accuses my whole self of breaking rules whenever it gets the chance. It can't wait to jump to keeping score. And then, using that score as punishment, it blames, disciplines, and therefore stops the spontaneous Being that could flourish.

Keeping score is useful for work within relatively narrow word-based structures, such as those used in computers and manufacturing. But it is grossly misused, at least it was by me, in business and personal relationships. My misuse, fueled by false superiority, relied on separateness and comparison-based judgment, which relied on viewing words as carrying the whole of reality rather seeing them as the limited tools they are: narrow slivers that indicate but hold only a miniscule portion of what's real.

And yet, I can turn this around by viewing measuring and score keeping as signals that work in the same way as a gasoline gauge works in my car. Now, when I catch myself measuring and score keeping, it's as if my gauge is signaling a need to allow "what is." It warns me to notice my resistance and to remember that resistance empties the energy from my tank. If I allow it to function as a gauge that can signal me, it can help me remember that where I place my attention is what matters, that the state of my consciousness is most important in any moment.

When I notice resistance, I can fill my tank with acceptance of "what is". Sometimes I miss noticing because my word-tool mind gets so intensely busy with keeping score that I forget that measurement doesn't apply to Wholes. That's when I notice my tank is empty, and I feel bad. I realize I've been resisting instead of accepting the "what is" of something that's already happened. I remind myself not to misuse score keeping functions, such as "this could be better" or "was better" or "should be better", not to apply them where they don't fit.

When I'm able to stop trying to fragment Wholes through improper use of tools, I begin to look on myself and my surroundings with a sense of nonresistant enjoyment. And then I return to moments of Connectivity, and I feel alive again as a Whole that has stopped trying to oppose itself.

Come to the Moment

I walked out of my house today, stopped, and asked, "Where am I?"

The question opened me to a useful awareness because my answer was that I was in my next-next-next place. My forehead taut, I felt strained about getting to the coffee shop as soon as possible. I was in my slave-to-the-clock mode. Yet, there was no reason for me to hurry or feel pressured.

The question "where am I?" somehow broke through the barriers of the auto-me who is unaware of surroundings because it's always mentally in the next moment not this one. When the question arose, it was as if my frozen reality melted its edges to become permeable to the vastness of this moment on the porch of my house.

I said to myself in a friendly way, *Okay, there's the next-next-next and slave-to-the-clock demands that are part of my thoughts so often.* As I said this, I felt the tension/constriction in my face start to release just a little.

As I came out of this next-next-next stupor, I could stand back from the voice that incessantly drove me to a future point, a future point that masquerades as being all there is. I was now aware enough to take a deep breath and realize there is more than what's next — there is also what's now.

Then it became easier to relax and move toward the car with fuller awareness of the surroundings of this moment. As I stepped off the porch, I felt the snow under my shoes and the freshness of the cool air on my now-relaxed face. I felt my fingers on the car handle as I opened the door, then the wonderful fluidity of the key turning in the ignition.

The more often I connect with my surroundings, with what is around me in the moment, the more life I feel and the better I feel.

When I put attention on, and actually feel, what's around me right now in this moment, my stress-producing word-flow stops or at least slows down.

The question "where am I?" reminded me again that I am more than my thoughts. It helped me notice the demands of my self-imposed pushing to always be a step ahead. The question helped me stop so I could notice I had been in a synthetic-robot mode of functioning.

Once realized, I could set aside the robot and engage with my surroundings as a live human being. I could feel myself fully joined with the whole of the world around me. And I felt so much more alive and energetic than when I first walked out of my door.

Connectivity Example

A man was plowing snow from a driveway shared by me, other renters, and the business next door. The man had been hired by the business, not our rental company. I went out and asked how much he would charge to plow the area for our apartment parking.

The man said his boss had a minimum of $40 which was more than I wanted to pay. As I told him $40 wouldn't work for me and I added, "Well, I really appreciate the way you plow this shared driveway. Can you accept this $5 as a tip?" He said yes and then he said, "Maybe I could do a quick plow through your parking area as an unofficial favor."

Later that day I realized that the most meaningful part of the interaction was our eye contact and the sense of connectedness between us while we talked. It was as if we were two human beings sharing gratitude for being alive, rather than needing or expecting something from each other.

Yes, there were words involved as we talked about the $40 charge, the tip, and the quick plow as a favor. But then there was just a grateful feeling between us as we locked eyes and gave full attention to each other.

There was a sense of whole-person connectedness that seemed bigger, more encompassing than the narrow categories of thinking and feeling. His eye contact and our shared gratitude – this gave me a feeling of well-being throughout that day.

Is there a sense of connectedness that we experience that is deeper and more whole than our word-tools can adequately describe? I have found that there is.

It turned out that the man did far more than a quick plow. He left us with an almost 100 percent clean parking lot.

But again the best thing was not the clean parking – it was not the plowing he did for me or the tip I gave him. It was the feeling of Connectivity. Yes, the exchange of words contributed. But what mattered most was something deeper that was without words.

I felt glad to be alive and to be in a world with other people. It was one of those seemingly minor Connectivity experiences that have contributed to feeling gratitude for life so much of the time.

She Doesn't Know What I Know

I bumped into a friend I rarely see. She has owned her own businesses for twenty plus years, and I have both admired and envied her for this. One day as I was telling her about my writing, I used the word *concept*. She said she wasn't sure what that meant.

I could feel the slight edge of superiority rising up inside. Fifteen years ago, I would have believed that feeling of superiority as a "true measure" or a meaningful difference. I would have seen it as real. *She's stupid because she doesn't know what a concept is.*

Or I would have looked down on her as less educated, "doesn't know much", and so, not of value to me. My judgmental, dismissive attitudes would have affected our interaction because my closed mind wouldn't have allowed me to see her value. I would have used word-tools to dehumanize her as less educated, stupid, etc.

No matter how slight my feeling of superiority, I know it affects the way I interact and my ability to see value. My use of concepts essentially blinds me to the surrounding positives that stand in waiting, if only I can set aside my word-chatter for long enough to see them.

Thankfully, as I have become more aware of my superiority, I am able to discount it as being mind-chatter and as compensation for my feelings of inadequacy. I now see the connections between envy of my friend for owning her own business and the superiority thoughts that arose when she said she didn't know what I meant by the word concept.

Opening up to ways of knowing that are beyond word-tool labeling, and reminding myself of the damage of comparison and judgment that is so prevalent, I am able to see how remarkable every person actually is. And the more I experience that, the more I feel showered with emotions of affection and gratitude for people I had first felt only a rough-edged judgment toward.

I'm not saying that you and I don't know more about specific topics than others. But I am saying that this kind of "more than" is ultimately unimportant. The limitations of word-tools make these kinds of comparisons invalid, except perhaps for specific functions, such as knowledge required for employment. My guess is that we use more-than and better-than value comparisons far more for ego feeding than for purposes of a specific situation. I know that I do. I also know how freeing it feels to notice it and to regard it as invalid and unimportant.

I continue to be amazed at how my curiosity grows when I see my superiority as only a restrictive and limiting response to feeling inadequate. Over and over again I find how smart and wise every person is, and I discover that there are many different ways to be smart and wise.

The life, the experience, and the deep core (source self) of every person is so rich with variety! Having opened my closed word-tooled mind, I am able to see the growing spark in every person, out of which infinite possibilities are available. Each Unique Expressor is an expert in her/his own growth spark and in her/his own reality.

When I was immersed in separation and superiority, I believed in a single objective reality that everyone could know. If people would only try, I thought, they would all come to know the objective reality, the reality that I already knew.

I came to realize that my surface/ego self was ignoring the value of what I don't know in order to feed itself. I rejected the very idea of "not knowing" in order to boost myself above others, as a way to fuel my ego. Once I saw that my reality is not the objective reality for all, my view changed. I no longer believe in an objective reality, at least not in the sense that I own The Truth, but you don't.

Now my reality comes out of Connectivity. It emanates from an outlook filled with curiosity about everything I encounter and with a realization that acceptance without resistance opens channels for change that are activated through Connectivity.

If I function as if I'm separate, as if I exist in a vacuum, my attention is on me-not-them, supported by the this-not-that of the word-tools I've come to misuse so well. My reality is then negative.

But with prime attention on Connectivity, on we, while remembering that I am also there, that I am one with we, I am open enough to sense the value that every Being has. My reality is then positive.

Now I see "she doesn't know what I know" as the destructive ego-tool that it is. A tool that blinds me to value, disallows experiences due to preconceptions, and closes off the possibility of the affectionate gratitude that naturally flows out of Connectivity.

Recognize the "Negative" Inside But Don't Feed It

Years ago my son told me this story he'd heard about a conversation between a man and his grandson. An old Cherokee, teaching his grandson about life, said to the boy:

> A fight is going on inside me. It is a terrible fight, and it is between two wolves.
>
> One is evil – he is anger, envy, sorrow, regret, greed, arrogance, self-pity, guilt, resentment, inferiority, lies, false pride, superiority, and ego.
>
> The other is good – he is joy, peace, love, hope, serenity, humility, kindness, benevolence, empathy, generosity, truth, compassion, and faith.
>
> The same fight is going on in you – and inside every other person too.

The grandson thought about it for a minute and then asked his grandfather, "Which wolf wins?"

The old Cherokee replied, "The one you feed."

During my first fifty five years of life, I fed the negative wolf most. Then I became aware of my habitual way of thinking of negatives as outside me, which led to anger, arrogance, and superiority. And eventually I began to see that all those troublesome problems I had taken as "reality" depended on me to keep them alive. They came out of a combination of my rigid thinking (overreliance on word-tools), my belief that I owned the truth (superiority), and my judgmental flaw-finding habits, including putting attention on why things are wrong and how to fix them.

I discovered that the negatives I'd believed to be in the outer world were sourced and maintained inside me. I had maintained my me-vs-them view of the world based on where I pointed my attention; that's the wolf I fed.

Just today as I drove down the street, I saw a woman walking with a face mask over her nose and mouth. In the Salt Lake valley where I live, we often have winter inversions. My first thoughts were: *That's silly! How is that piece of cloth going to keep the tiny particles of polluted air out of her lungs?*

I was aware enough to catch myself and turn that moment of unconscious functioning into an opportunity. I realized I had judged this woman as stupid, and then I saw how useless that judgment was. I could feel it as coming from my familiar cluster of thoughts: I own The Truth, and I know what is right and wrong and good and bad for other people. I felt a bit of tension in my forehead, as if in response to the tiny barb I shot out at life, as I blamed the world and life for not being quite right.

Then a memory came as a vague recollection of me trying one of those masks years ago when I had a bad sinus infection. More often than not, I find that the very faults I've criticized in others are things I have engaged in or that exist in me. Maybe that's why the barbs I shoot out at the world come back to hit me in the form of tension in my forehead.

As often as I am conscious of it, I practice shifting attention away from my initial judging, criticizing, and feeling superior. Sometimes I find something else to place my attention on – *that woman's hair and the coat she is wearing are pleasing*. More often I make up a story that honors the person's humanness: *perhaps she is a loving mother who takes good care of her children*.

These word-tool formulations point more toward Connectivity. They bring words together in a more realistic way than my initial judgment where I narrowed the reality of the woman by using words to make her into an object of my ill will.

Along with these kinds of attention shifts, when possible I simply break through my prejudices by interacting with the person, often by saying hi and beginning a conversation. Almost every time I do, I'm surprised to see my prejudice replaced by curiosity and good feelings. I feel kinship with the person as I open up to focusing on something other than my initial negativity. Once I shift my attention and accompany that with interaction that breaks through my word-tool walls of prejudice, the internal tension and sharpness melts away and I almost always feel better than before.

Feeling surprise over and over again, after shifting attention, has been an exciting surprise of its own. It was gratifying to discover that the negative voice could almost always be reversed. And I began to realize how meaningless and wasteful my judgments and criticisms are. Shifting, accompanied by just a little openness, became a source of feeling good that began to snowball – and this source is almost always available because there are usually plenty of negatives passing through my mind to shift away from.

So the surprise is that the practice itself becomes its own source of feeling good now and reducing tension. The practice itself is always present and fulfilling in a peaceful sort of way. It becomes a way to feed my positive energies rather than the negative ones.

Even though the negatives are almost always available, the effect of shifting attention has a cumulative effect. More and more frequently, and for longer periods of time, I experience no negatives to shift away from.

Some spiritual teachers talk about the need to face your demons, to confront the negativity and weaknesses in yourself. This confuses me because I've found such tremendous benefit in shifting attention away from negatives rather than toward them. My view is that taking words seriously enough to apply *demon* or *weakness* to myself is an instance of forgetting the limitations of word-tools.

And right now, as I write this, I notice I can shift away from my view about those spiritual teachers. I can reinterpret what they mean by *face* and *confront* demons. Maybe it was facing demons when I caught myself judging the woman with the mask and then remembered that I too tried one of those masks years before. My recognize-and-shift might be what these teachers mean when they suggest that we face and confront our demons.

But for me, it doesn't carry the discomfort of facing and confronting a negative in myself; I haven't experienced much suffering from noticing my negative judgments and then shifting away. To me, it's been just one positive after another, including remembering that I too used one of those masks, including that if I see I'm blaming myself for being a hypocrite, that's just another negative to shift away from. I am simply glad I experienced another moment of the process of shifting away from blaming anything.

Generally, the more I dwell on negatives, the more I feel bad about myself and others. When I churn a negative thought/feeling, it seems to feed on itself as my mind seeks out more interconnections that are painful, doubtful, worrisome, or anxiety provoking. It is as if my attention on them pulls up a web that expands into a tornado of bad energy that grows wider and wider as I churn it. I find it spins around until it emanates out toward everything in reality. It becomes a complex logical structure with all sorts of evidence to support it from the same word-tooled realm of negativity that started it.

I've repeatedly seen that my criticisms of people and situations increase after I've judged/criticized myself. After negative self-judgment sneaks in and begins to multiply, I notice that people all around me seem to be inconsiderate, irritating, or incompetent. At times this turns into an expanding whirlwind of bad feelings, with no specific target, that can last hours.

When that happens, I consciously practice shifting attention away from my negatives and toward something neutral in the moment, or toward something that makes me feels just a little better. I look at sensations in my body or at sights of nature around me, and these shifts usually bring up hints of gratitude for living. Even if the sensations in my body are pain, I view them as signs of my body's interactivity and of me being alive.

The practice of shifting attention feeds the best in me. Feel Good Now is like watering and fertilizing the garden of my inner environment so that my seed can bloom with vibrant colors of life rather than droop with blotches of disease.

My direct influence boils down to where I point my attention. I shift, and then I watch to see if my feelings change. It's not that I'm forcing myself directly into a positive feeling state. Thinking or feeling positive is an indirect happening that comes from watching my thoughts, then from seeing unconscious judgments as they are brought to light so they can flow through me and back to the meaninglessness from which they came.

This is what I have control over: where I point my attention. This is how "the one I feed" points to a reality where there is no longer a need for a terrible fight inside me.

A Sense of Unfiltered Neutrality

Today I noticed my mind active with word-tools. As I passed by trees, buildings, and people, labels were streaming through my mind. It's as if everything my gaze swept across got pushed through a concept/word filter. There was no stopping to simply look, with a quiet mind, to fully take in what I was seeing. I was in such a rush to tie a little tag onto anything I laid eyes on. *That man looks sad. That bush looks like it's* dying. *That woman seems* vibrant *and* beautiful. *That tree is like a* huge umbrella *over the front yard of that house.*

As a child, I liked using a strainer in the sandbox. I would sift the sand so the smallest granules would fall through the holes in the screen of the strainer, then back into the sandbox. The larger grains of sand stayed on top of the screen.

Sifting sand works like the groupings made by word-tools. The unique nature that's discarded in forming the grouping is like a fine grain of sand that falls back to the sandbox. The conceptual grouping is the larger grain that stays on the surface (the screen of the strainer). The uniqueness is lost – it gets left behind with the whole of the reality (the sandbox) – as our word-tools are unable to carry it.

So today, after I noticed my mind active with labeling, I asked: *What's an experience I've had where I set aside my conceptual strainer/filter and simply looked around without labeling, without dividing small grains of sand from large ones, with no separating, and no judgment?*

My first reaction was: *I don't know anything about that yet – there are no examples because I haven't experienced it.*

But then a statement from Tara Brach popped in: "I don't feel bad or good *about* myself; I just feel good."[21]

When I first heard her say this, it hit a chord deep inside me. *Bingo. That's the way I feel when my mind is not cluttered with active word-tooling.* This "I just feel good" is like being in a state of flow with no resistance to anything around me, and for me it is the sense of being connected to Source.

Then I thought of something I wrote many months ago in my notebook: "Don't focus on the person you want to be. Focus on feeling good now, and the person you want to be will flow naturally, growing out of that Being that feels so good."

This suggests a state of neutrality where I let myself grow freely from my seed, without the cognitive directness of the push from a structure that conceptual force can bring. It points toward a way of "being" that screens out nothing and thereby allows rather than directs a process of becoming.

When I write by hand in the mornings, I dump out a plastic bag filled with about fifteen different colored pens and highlighters. I like the variety of ways this gives me to mark the pages of a book. And when I write in my notebook I can use a different color for each unique note. So I can put many different notes on the same page and easily see each. It helps avoid the run-on look that would result if every note were in the same color.

Why am I telling you about my colored pens? Well, when I was putting them back in the plastic bag this morning, I felt Connectivity and a nonjudgmental gratitude, a positivity toward the pens and highlighters.

---

[21]Tara Brach, *Radical Acceptance: Embracing Your Life with the Heart of a Buddha*, audiobook read by Cassandra Campbell, Chapter 3, 10:20 (Tantor Audio, 2012); in print format Chapter 1, page 9 (New York: Bantam, 2004).

It didn't feel like one side of a negative/positive dichotomy. There was no sense of feeling bad or good *about* the pens, no sense of comparison or ranking inside me. No conceptual filtering. There was only a calm, full-of-peace, joyful appreciation for these objects here and now. I just felt good in relation to putting my colored pens back in the bag today.

I've heard the terms *presence* and *stillness* from spiritual teachers Eckhart Tolle, Byron Katie, and others. For me, these words fit the Connectivity to Source that I sense during these occasional instances of unfiltered neutrality.

So even though my mind tells me I've rarely experienced neutrality, it's happened more often than my mind cares to admit. I wonder if I've experienced many more of these moments than I remember. Perhaps these neutral moments had been sifted out of my memory because my attention was dominated by the larger grains of sand, by the world of the conceptual, by the immersion in word-tools that doesn't allow the uniqueness or the flow of life to remain.

I only know that I enjoy letting go of judgmental tension. I enjoy these moments of unfiltered neutrality as "I just feel good" while I interact with my surroundings.

Disciplinary Inner-Control System

Some say everything that's wrong with the world can be summed up by one problem: people who have no remorse or regret for doing something bad. It's attitude of "Yeah, I did something bad, but it doesn't matter, I don't care". The answer often proposed is that these uncaring people need to be punished or disciplined so they will feel remorse, regret, or guilt because that's the only way they will change.

For me, remorse, regret, and guilt carry a kind of self-blaming. It takes me into feeling "bad". My surface self says it's good for me to feel bad because until I do, I won't be good. When I apply this punishment-based view to myself, I find it takes me nowhere good. Actually I begin to care even less about being good.

Recently I talked with my mother on the phone. At the beginning of the call, I was not sympathetic or accepting when she said she was feeling sick. My surface self/ego jumped to labeling her as "a victim who goes on and on" because "she's always feeling sick or moaning about some discomfort, weakness, or injustice."

About five minutes after this unpleasant, conflict-ridden call ended, I realized I had done the "bad" thing I've been writing about in this book: I used word-tools to label her as a *victim*, and then continued the interaction as if that label were the whole story of what she is. It affected the way I spoke to her, including my tone of voice and words, which then affected the way she spoke back to me.

During the call, I remember thinking my mother was the cause of the unpleasantness we were experiencing – I was blaming her for what I had started. Soon after the call, I realized that my labeling her a victim is what actually set the stage for the unpleasant interaction. When I placed that label in my mind as if it were *the* truth about my mother, I closed out the possibility of a connection between two human beings. I started a back and forth between two word-tool warriors. All my talking was being filtered through the label *victim*; and all hers was in response to my blameful label. I had restrained my mother and our conversation by holding that one word *victim* in my mind.

So I called my mom back and apologized for jumping to label her as a victim the way I did. She was crying a bit but thanked me for calling.

After that, I realized that if I could go back to the beginning of our call, I would have liked to have said, "I'm sorry to hear you are feeling sick. I hope you feel better soon." A couple of days later, I called to tell her that. We talked for two hours. I felt grateful to hear my mother talk about family history, even though it was filled with her own judgments, labeling, sorrows, and life difficulties. When the *victim* label crept up in my mind, it was as if I said back to it: *I know how limited you are; I know you are not the truth; and I am aware of the value of what I don't know. Let me be open and actually hear this person rather than close her out.*

Did I feel remorse, regret, or guilt about labeling my mother as a victim? Yes, I felt just a bit of self-blame creep in. But mostly I felt the fullness of a desire to tell her what I would've liked to have said. Mostly I felt a sense of Connectivity with her and the world around me, a no-guilt sense that invites healing without self-punishment.

What if I had walked away from the first call thinking something else: *I know I hurt her, and I know that my labeling created conflict during our call. But it doesn't matter. I don't care.*

Wouldn't some kind of self-blaming help me get back on track? Wouldn't self-blaming and punishment have made up for the hurt I had caused? Isn't self-punishment a good and just thing to do?

My experience says no. I've found self-blame and self-punishment to be a demotivator; it's not something that invites me to do something different. Sure, making myself feel bad can push me into doing something different in this minute. But that pushed reorientation doesn't last long term. Dragging myself down never helps with allowing for the kind of growth that is foundational to a lasting reorientation.

And yet, I grew up believing that self-blame and punishment were the right things to do to compensate for a wrong.

But if I look a little deeper, I think I believed this only because it was prevalent in society and because I saw it as a part of being logical, moral, and reasonable. All of this was rooted outside me, even though I had adopted and brought it inside. It's as if I placed it inside of me with quotes around it: *Okay, I'll go along with this. It must be true since so many people approve of it. Isn't compensating for a wrong a necessary part of justice, logic, and wanting to be moral?*

Although I went along with this, somehow it seemed there was something wrong about self-blame and punishment. I thought and felt it only in word-tool format . . . it seemed logical and moral. It fit my in-the-head judgment structures. But deep down, and in a whole-self way, I never sensed it as constructive or as an idea that was worthy of embracing.

Through Connectivity, I've found an alternative to blame and punishment. Connectivity, an awareness of endless interrelatedness, invites without any blame and punishment to examine what I did and to possibly envision a change in what I'll do next time.

Blame and punishment are disconnectors. They rest on the belief that I am separate, as if in a vacuum. They hold the ideas that "me in a vacuum" should compensate for hurt I caused "someone else who also operates in a vacuum".

Connectivity on the other hand flows from feeling affinity for all that is real, because I am inextricably with it. There is no "me in a vacuum" just as there is no "you in a vacuum". As I began to sense Connectivity, I realized that there simply isn't an only-me; only-me isn't real: *If there is only me, there is no me.*

Yet blame and punishment rely on beliefs of only-me. If I am a separate only-me and my mom is another separate only-me, then it fits to call her a victim and it fits to blame myself for that afterwards. The judging, blaming, and punishing never stops.

Related to widespread use of self-blame and punishment, I am grateful for the words of psychotherapist Karen Horney as she discusses the concept of a disciplinary inner control system:

> But there is a wide divergence of opinion about the desirability or necessity of a disciplinary inner control system for the sake of insuring moral conduct.[22]

This hit home for me because I had never heard anyone use these words to question the kind of judging, blaming, and punishment that causes so much suffering and unhappiness. The constraining judgmental monitoring of my disciplinary inner control system has never encouraged me to "do the right thing". It only encouraged a *should* followed by blame and punishment.

---

[22] Karen Horney, *Neurosis and Human Growth*, Introduction: A Morality of Evolution, page 14; (New York: W.W. Norton & Company, 1991).

Even if I complied with the *should*, I would do it with a resentful rebellion that was hidden so deeply that no one could see it, including myself.

Later, in the same section of her book, *Neurosis and Human Growth*, Horney continues with the following:

> There is no doubt that such disciplinary methods can succeed in suppressing undesirable factors, but there is also no doubt that they are injurious to our growth. We do not need them because we see a better possibility of dealing with destructive forces in ourselves: that of actually *outgrowing* them.[23]

This may provide an answer for those of us who've ingrained the idea that blame and punishment are necessary functions in our world. Allowing ourselves to grow is effective. Pushing ourselves into a *should* through use of a disciplinary inner control system is not only ineffective but damaging.

For me, outgrowing destructive forces began naturally once I experienced approaches to living that were not dominated by word-tools. I sensed that I am more connected than separate. I realized that the this-not-that limiting nature of word-tools doesn't support using them to blame and punish. I saw that words are merely tags/labels, not the truth-tellers I had thought them to be. Experiencing Connectivity rather than the illusion of separateness, in light of the limited nature of words, set me free to grow, including outgrowing any destructive forces that may exist.

The truth is not that my mother is a victim or that I am abusive and hurtful when I approach her that way. It's that because we are all linked, tied, connected in so many ways – and realizing that word-

---

[23] Horney, page 15; Horney also uses the words *inner straight jacket* in referring to these self disciplinary methods.

tools make this Connectivity difficult to see – I want to, not have to, contribute to allowing myself, my mother, and everyone I encounter to grow (and outgrow) as the natural Beings we all are.

Blame, punishment, and disciplinary inner control are replaced by growing that is allowed and nurtured by we interconnected Beings of life.

I babysat my friend's puppy this past weekend. His name is Snoopy and he's a gentle playful white-and-gray colored poodle-like dog that weighs only about ten pounds. He looks like a toy at times and the lighthearted bounce in his walk shines with a happy, prancing quality. I've taken care of him many times, but this time I really noticed his eyes watching me. I would look back at Snoopy, and as we held eye contact, I felt as though we were in a deep, full, loving embrace.

This weekend, Snoopy and I sat outdoors next to a city street as I drank a cup of coffee. People were walking past on the sidewalk, and cars moved down the street. Snoopy interrupted his sniffing of the grass and surrounding trees to watch the people and cars. Almost every time, his tail was wagging.

Today I sat outdoors alone at the same café. I thought about eye contact with Snoopy and about how he watched cars and people as they passed by. As I watched people today, I noticed that some looked straight at me, made eye contact, smiled, and said hello. Others did not.

Then I thought back to the weekend again and remembered that Snoopy showed no sign of bad feelings when people did not respond to him. His tail appeared to be just as happy even when people walked on by without attending to him. He simply looked toward the next person passing or the next bird, squirrel or car, or returned to sniffing anything on the surrounding grounds.

Snoopy showed no signs of rejection, disappointment, or sad "little deprived puppy me". He continued to respond to passersby with eager curiosity and happily shifted attention to the vibrancy of the other surroundings when no one was present.

There was no word-tool labeling, no judging, and no comparing. Just the simple joy of watching and Being.

When I'm flowing with Feel Good Now, rather than trapped in evaluation and comparison, I too sense a kind of joyful neutrality toward people, and a warm affection toward my surroundings.

Puppies aren't concerned about evaluation, comparison, or any type of measuring-up. They simply and playfully enjoy the world around them. And when my word-tool thought stream is quiet I experience something like what I think Snoopy does.

So I enjoy these images of Snoopy looking at the world with tail wagging. It's a natural state of Being without effortful trying, or of following an instruction or feeling the push to plan or look to the next action. It's simply a state of Being joyfully in the moment.

One day last week as I felt this state of Being, I was riding a bicycle to the coffee shop. As I rode past a man who was walking, I said hi. His face lit up as our eyes met and with a warm, genuine smile that felt like a big hug he called out, "Hi! How are you? Have a really good rest of the day!"

His warm energy made me want to jump off the bike and "hug him back". These are the kind of Connectivity moments I've found to be available everywhere now that I'm open enough to let them come to the surface. And like a puppy, even when I don't find moments with this much joyful connection, "my tail" is still pretty happy because I know there is so much more in my surroundings to find, if only I can allow and open up to it.

Lack and Longing

In "Feel Good Now" I noted how easy it's been for me to slide into feeling lack. This happens when I think of something that feels good at first, but soon turns into a bad feeling because I no longer have that amazing partner, house, or job. Something that felt good when I first thought of it quickly turns sour when I shift attention to not having it now. *It was so great when my girlfriend and I were together! (Happy!) But then she broke up with me . (Sad.)*

The word *longing* came to mind the first time I noticed sliding into those thoughts about lack. Longing is a feeling I am very familiar with.

It feels so good to think about the woman I love. But it feels bad if I then bring in the thought that I may never see her again. Shifting attention toward a positive (wonderful feelings) can easily turn negative (wishing for, but no longer having).

The same pattern can arise for house, job, vacation, weekend, music concert, hamburger, or salad. Any favorite from the past can bring up a feeling of lack and longing. A positive back then (*Wow! That was the best xyz ever!*) becomes a negative in this moment now (*But I might never experience it again.*) What felt good then, feels bad now. Life is all downhill from "the best ever".

At some point I realized that longing was a special type of comparison that I created. The thought of a past favorite transforms itself into comparison: *I had that xyz before – I don't have it now.*

I began to watch for the pattern of "I had it before, but I don't have it now". As I continued to watch, I realized that I didn't *have to* think it. I didn't *have to* put my attention on it. The comparison that led to my longing was a story I made up. It was something I invented from two thoughts, a before-thought and an after-thought, pivoting on a hinge called *loss*.

> *I loved being able to kiss her when we were together – now I don't have that. And I miss it.*

> *I loved the light and space in the home I lived in before – now I don't have that. And I miss it.*

> *I loved going on vacation trips with a travel companion – now I don't have that. And I miss it.*

It was like imagining fractions made up of two thoughts:

$$\frac{\textbf{I had it}}{\textbf{Now I don't have it}} = \textbf{lack} => \textbf{feel bad}$$

As I sit here writing this, I feel the pencil between my fingers, the paper beneath my hand which has ripples from pencil marks on the other side. The air on this 100°F day feels hot and moist. The chair that supports me, the coffee cup and plate in front of me – all this is real.

As I experience these sensations of living, I see more clearly that the freeze-framed images of lack are artificial, synthetic, and symbolic. The thought-fraction comparisons leading to longing are not real, but the experience of living, ever flowing sensations I'm having right now are.

We look out and create word-tools as symbols to represent what is real. The problem for me happens when I confuse the symbols with the reality. With my thought-fractions, I've confused products of my imaginative use of those symbols with what is real.

The pencil, paper, air, chair, etc. are in a sense alive with me in this moment, with me here and now.

My thought-fractions are fantasy comparisons, unreal symbolic formulations that never feel good. Being made up of word-tools, they are combinations of stopped movement, of snapshots from memories past and images of frozen fear-based guesses about the future. Through combining concepts, my fractions seem to expand the power of word-tools. Actually, they only expand the intensity of distorting reality through misuse of a tool.

This kind of memory of the past is imaginative. It's not a state of being with what's happening in life now in this moment. It is me disallowing what could be by being too heavily immersed in what was before. This imaginative pointing of my mind's attention to the past is merely a reflection of highly limited representations, not an alive state of Being.

When I'm immersed in the content of remembering, I'm limiting myself to my surface self and the surface world. I'm lost in the 10 percent of the iceberg that's above the water, forgetting about the 90 percent below.

What is now is what is here now: the pencil, paper, air, chair, etc., and my awareness.

But when I imagine a relationship between "I had it before" and "now I don't", my attention is drawn away from the reality of this here now and toward that imagined image made up of thoughts and feelings, all generated by my symbolic word-tools. That relationship I invent is a comparison that torments me whenever I pretend it is worth creating and worth attending to.

Just as I so often misuse word-tools, making them seem to be more than they are suited to be, here I am misusing memory.

If I'm going to make up stories, why not make up stories that feel good rather than bad?

Scientists have found that everything and everybody emits energy.[24] The pencil, paper, air, chair, etc. all emit energy. They are reality. Their energy vibrations go with reality. Their constant energy emissions are Arm-in-Arm with what is.

My thought-fractions are comparisons created by manipulating word-tool products. They are *what isn't*, and because of that, they go against reality. I found that lack is an empty pit created by combining artificial symbols, a state of not-having that I invented out of something past and an arbitrary now. I can show myself that "now I don't have it" is arbitrary by realizing that I could replace the "it" with countless other imaginary "not haves" – there are countless things I don't have.

My surface-self mind argues that there aren't countless things that I had before. But since I'm inventing lack, I can just change the top part of the fraction to "I could have had it". Or "I could have had it, but I don't". Or another one I've seen is "I wish I had it, but I don't". Or "I worked so hard and deserve to have it, but I don't".

Using any of these as the top part of the fraction while combining with the "now I don't have it" image on the bottom, I create a relationship that is more complex than either image alone. I form a mental *what isn't* which is not as easy to see the nature of. And because it's a *what isn't*, it emits vibrations that run opposite and against what is.

[24] "Remote Sensing," NASA Earth Observatory, accessed August 8, 2017, https://earthobservatory.nasa.gov/Features/RemoteSensing/remote_02.php

That's where the bad feelings, the suffering comes from. My thought-fractions emit energies that oppose the flow of what is real as they resist "the now" of living my life.

By making these fractions, I've made my mind into a tool of feeling bad. If I misuse my mind and its word-tools in this way, without regard for their limitations, my mind becomes like a mad scientist who ties me down and tortures me.

The energy of lack and longing is not a friend of feeling good, because it's not a friend of what's real.[25]

[25] Note: Thanks to Bentinho Massaro for the insight that *lack* is not harmonious with the energy vibrations of reality. I heard him discuss this in Tami Simon's interview in the Sounds True audio book *Waking Up – What Does It Really Mean?* published May 1, 2015.

This Breath Is Different

During a guided meditation, I heard the narrator invite listeners to notice how each breath is different from the last.

I thought, *That's weird . . . how will I see a difference between one breath and another when breathing is essentially the same process? What is there to notice?* For me, breathing was something I'd rarely focused on until recently. So I wondered, what's so different about this breath?

I'm so rebellious. I began trying to make each breath the same. But gradually I noticed subtle differences such as breathing in more or less air, longer or shorter time between inhale and exhale, and the speed of drawing in the breath and then letting it out. Eventually I realized that even if I could make one breath similar to the last, they were still different.

I started thinking about trees along with other things I see every day. My previous view was *ahh, there's a tree* and it was always accompanied by the underground idea that I know what a tree is. Same with flowers and people. Each one is just another member of my conceptual grouping, my category. It doesn't occur to me that each thing is more than the symbolic representation of its name, more than the word-tag we put on it, more than this artificial grouping we created.

What about the full reality of each tree, of each flower, of each person?

Living totally from my head-based surface self I had wiped out the vibrancy of experiencing life directly in reality. I had accessed life only through the filtering of word-tools for so long that I didn't even want to accept that there was uniqueness across many breaths, many trees, many flowers, and many people. It seemed so much easier to view them as the same and I appeared so much smarter when I did.

I had been so overtaken by the power of word-tools, that I forgot the whole of reality from which those tools came. When I'm riding the high horse of how smart I am, I miss the uniqueness of life experience that gave rise to that word-based "smartness."

How amazing it feels to bring back so much of that life experience I had missed by just noticing that this breath – and this tree, and this flower, and this person – is different from the last!

Now every day, I feel a sense of awe at the amazing vibrancy and uniqueness I see, smell, feel, taste, and hear. And although I missed this vast richness in the past, that doesn't really matter because I'm experiencing it now.

I now get so much enjoyment from the "color" and energy of each unique experience! It's a kind of enjoyment I couldn't access when I viewed everything through the filtering of conceptual groupings: *That's just another breath, tree, flower, person; I already know what that is because I know the word we use as a name for it.*

Words/concepts have been a been-there-done-that tool to support my superiority. Once I allowed myself to notice this dismissive, superior outlook, I was gradually able to be aware of it more often. Realizing that the "I already know all about that" was just a byproduct of being lost in concepts, I noticed I had confused skill at labeling things with reality itself. I had knowledge about a breath or a tree because I could name it and there was nothing more to learn about it.

Finally I began to sense the physical tension that came with the "I know all about that" state of mind, mostly in the form of tightened face muscles. I am grateful for awareness of the limitations of word-tools and the value of what I don't know. Using these as reminders to become more widely conscious helped me first to notice then to shift away from tension causing states and move toward a new freedom – freedom to breathe a new breath, to look at a new tree, to experience a new flower, and to sense the Being of a new person.

Traits and Characteristics Distort Reality

I was walking into the coffee shop one day when this hit me: *Wow! I don't think I believe in traits and characteristics anymore! How can this be? Am I crazy?*

As I wrote this, I noticed that the "Am I crazy?" is me threatening to put a trait/characteristic on myself. We do it all the time, don't we? Well, at least I do. He's *strong*; she's *beautiful*; he's a *grump*; she's *stubborn*; he's a *cheat*; he looks like a *computer guy*; she looks like a *model*; she is so *kind*; etc.

How have I come to regard this kind of labeling as bad? I've begun to notice that whether I do it to myself or to others it narrows my orientation. It puts a person into a word-box that limits my openness to what I would see if I had not set my mind in prejudice mode. When I say to myself *he is strong* or *she is beautiful* or *I am arrogant*, my attention gravitates toward that trait or characteristic and nowhere else. I've confined the person to that one word-tool bucket.

When I label someone this way I create a preconception, one that has the same limitation as all word-tools: a this-not-that restriction that gets locked into my mind as soon as I use the word. Isn't it generally acceptable to use traits/characteristics to describe ourselves and others? And yet, what we are actually doing is presetting a viewpoint about that person in the same way that typecasting, stereotyping, and prejudice do.

I now view my use of traits and characteristics as not only useless, but also distorted. When I label someone with a trait or characteristic, I remind myself that I've misused word-tools.

A word is a device that allows and even invites prejudice. When my mind says "he's *strong*", it pulls my attention toward that one aspect as if it took precedence over all others. When I label him *strong*, I leave out the complexity of the whole of this person. I slant my view toward that single freeze-frame. I could instead say, "There are so many facets about this man that I don't even know, but in this moment as I look at him, one trait I see is that his muscles look strong". This takes more words, but it provides my mind with a wider context than "He is a *strong* guy".

Even if a person regularly behaves in a certain way, describing that person as "being" that characteristic narrows my own ability to be open when I interact with him or her. What we call a personal characteristic is actually only a tiny sliver, an opinion that holds almost none of the immense interactive environment from which it was extracted. The snap-shot we call a trait or characteristic doesn't exist in a vacuum; it exists as part of a whole that word-tools can't carry.

I remember the guy I often saw at the gym whose identity I limited with the characteristic *grumpy*, and the roommate who I initially shackled with the label *messy*. I notice that my labels shackle me at least as much as they shackle others. Just to be clear, shackles are those heavy metal loops put on hands and feet, connected by chains that limit movement to a very narrow range. That's exactly what word-tools are so well suited to and I've used them that way most of my life to limit my movement, my viewpoints, and my range of allowance. Just like shackles, when word-tools limit what I do or narrow what I see they also create the stress of internal tension.

At the same time I'm using words to shackle myself, I am also using them to put myself above the person I'm labeling. Through the label, I take the position of judge or God who thinks he has the wherewithal to define the nature of that person. When I take time to dig deep enough, I find the label functions to validate my illusion of being superior. Then digging deeper still, I see that I needed that validation to compensate for feeling that I am lacking, that I am small or inadequate.

Lack is compensated for by superiority, just as "not enough" is compensated for by "more than enough." They are opposite sides of the same coin, at least in the way they work in my mind.

For example with the man at the gym I called *grumpy*, I later noticed I viewed him as masculine, which is a characteristic I see myself as lacking. Likewise, I came to realize that calling my roommate *messy* was a reaction against my own self-critical *shoulds* about keeping a perfectly clean house, something I haven't ever done well anyway, at least in comparison to the many people I've known.

I find my mind gushes with traits and characteristics when I feel as though I'm not enough or not measuring up to "what I could be". And most of us have been conditioned to hesitate admitting to these types of feelings. We are trained not to talk about them even to ourselves.

Once I've assigned a trait or characteristic, I've closed the door on the possibility of facing those feelings. At the same time, as I approach any interaction with that person, my mind is closing out anything that doesn't fit that trait/characteristic. I've limited and constricted what is possible between me and that person by taking my word-tooled thoughts too seriously.

Anything not supported by the trait/characteristic becomes inconsistent, and in response I immediately dismiss it. The vast realms of the non-grumpy and non-messy that would be possible for me to discover without those labels become nonexistent to my mind. The same thing happens in the other person's mind if they have labeled me. And we end up with two sets of preconceptions interacting. Interaction between two people gets replaced with interaction between two sets of ideas.

Yet my mind tries to justify these labels, these traits and characteristics, as patterns I observe in people. Actually they are just another way I stay lost in concepts. My use of what we call traits and characteristics works to avoid facing myself and others as the whole beings we actually are.

Much of the time, after I notice I've labeled someone, I also notice I'm blaming myself for labeling them. All of the sudden I am criticizing myself for being *rigid*, *closed*, *prejudiced*, and *egotistical*. That's my mind continuing the same process I've been conditioned to operate with when I use traits and characteristics.

But it's the noticing that's important, noticing I did it toward someone else and then noticing my mind's habit of doing it toward myself. I also notice how word-tools narrow and distort my functioning by reviewing their this-not-that nature: *man* not *woman*; *bird* not *cat*; *tree* not *building*. I simply look around to bring to the forefront the incredibly tight constriction that is built into every word unit. This is a kind of noticing that eventually leads to change.

Then when my mental chatter puts out traits and characteristics, I'm more apt to remember not to continue misusing word-tools by taking them too seriously. Yes they stream through my mind. But do I have to embrace them as truth? No I don't.

I continue by reminding myself that blaming is not only useless but damaging. Then the challenge is not to blame others who actually believe it is good to blame. I continue to remind myself of the narrowed constriction I create in myself whenever I label and blame.

So how can I think about and interact with the "grumpy guy" and the "messy roommate" without using traits and characteristics?

First I bring to mind the value of what I don't know. That helps me open up to becoming aware that the grumpy guy may be better characterized as quiet, or scared, or a hardened man who has suffered abuse and is displaying a tough-guy image to compensate for feeling hurt or inadequate. And, perhaps the messy roommate is better characterized as forgetful, busy, preoccupied, or not bound by the *should* of keeping a perfectly tidy house.

These steer my mind toward a wider view. They allow me to carry a more open outlook, one that sees the person as a flowing, changing, living human Being like me. Words like *quiet*, *scared*, *sufferer*, *inadequate*, *forgetful*, *busy*, *preoccupied* – these are traits that are usually less blaming, and less likely to feed my superiority. Yes, they are still traits and characteristics. But they are not as constrictive in a this-not-that kind of way. They open me up to a sense of compassion more than to a superior position of judgment.

As I think back on the guy at the gym, I remember that as soon as I saw him my mind would immediately say, *Oh, there's the grumpy guy*. I wonder if that affected my facial expressions and general energy toward him. Perhaps *my subtle expression and energy flow* affected how he acted toward me which included him putting out more of a tough-guy image. Likewise, when the term *messy* was on my mind with my roommate, I'm guessing that affected my body language, tone of voice, and reaction toward her.

As I've watched my labeling over the past few years, I've seen that what I called *grumpy* and *messy* arose from complex interactions that I played a major role in. When I label someone using a trait or characteristic, it's as if I'm setting a stage that I too am standing on, but I am ignoring and even denying my role. Instead of facing my part in setting the whole thing up by using traits/characteristics, I function as if I am separate and operating in a vacuum. It's as if I'm sitting in the audience as a critic with my surface self flinging out labels which are actually just an excuse to see myself as superior.

So as I practice applying my newfound view of traits and characteristics as a misuse of word-tools, I find it challenging and enjoyable to use words in ways that open to a wider scope. That is why I love this pop-in:

> *Use words in such a way as to highlight the Connectivity*
> *from which they come rather than the separations*
> *to which they lead.*

I've found a lot of satisfaction from practicing using words in this way as I avoid believing the validity of any traits or characteristics that may pass through my mind.

Note: I finally said hi to the "grumpy" guy at the gym. We had an enjoyable conversation, and then became friendly acquaintances rather than an isolated pair of strangers. And guess what happened with my "messy" roommate? During our last year in the house together, she became far tidier than me. I was definitely the messier one in the end. Whatever label I put on another person, I eventually find it in myself.

Fabrications vs Life and Nature

Part of being lost in concepts for me involved never really connecting with people, animals, or plants – I basically had no time for anything natural unless it served some productive use. For something to be of value, it had to be a means to an end, it had to be useful for some purpose I wanted to accomplish. Anything else was not worth my time.

Sure, I connected with people in a robot-type way by granting a quick hello and taking time to listen to someone if I could see potential for gain. I would take a few minutes while I analyzed, judged, and advised, and then I would move on to something more productive. I always aimed to maximize the utilitarian gain in any interaction and to complete as many tasks as possible.

Yes, I would occasionally stoop down to say "nice doggy" or smell a flower, but always with the idea that it was all just fluff, not the really important stuff of life. And I would warn myself not to let this kind of "fluff" get in the way of what was really important: productivity.

I functioned as if everything was an object-like thing either to gain from or to avoid as a threat. I viewed everything, including living things, as spiritless stuff, as if assembled from parts in the same way as a computerized or mechanical toy.

Tables, chairs, cars, buildings, desks, TVs, phones – all were objects to be used for something. To me, the living "things" of people, animals, and plants were the same. And I was one of them – a robot-type entity that needed to be useful in some way, whose purpose was getting things done, to use and be used by other robot-type entities to get things done.

I spent years with this code of conduct: to achieve, accomplish, produce. And yet, something was missing.

I sensed "something missing" during a lonely time in my life when I made eye contact with a store clerk at a hardware store, and I sensed it when I felt vulnerable rather than superior in a business meeting at work that included all levels of employees. These moments of non-purposeful connection touched something deep inside – they were seemingly meaningless encounters, but they felt good and stayed with me as wonderments and markers.

While I was robot-man I saw everything through the this-not-that word-tool lens of separation. Everything was just a product of distinct fabrications assembled from distinct pieces.

For such a long time, I rejected any idea of some sort of inner energy. I refused to seriously consider anything nonmaterial in the same way I refused to take seriously anything noncognitive. Possibilities such as soul or spirit were out of the question. As robot-man, I viewed everything as just this-not-that fabrications assembled from pieces. My view fit perfectly with my detachment from the natural world.

Then I gradually began viewing living beings as different.

I began to sense that life offered more than what word-tools and material stuff could provide. As I began to feel this inside myself, I also discovered a distinction Alan Watts wrote about:

> The seed grows into the plant by an expansion from within, and its parts or distinguishable organs develop simultaneously as it expands. Certainly, the growing seed is gathering nourishment from its environment, but the process is no mere sticking together of the nutritive elements, for it absorbs

and transforms them, and one sees nothing like this in the manufacture of an electric motor or computer.[26]

The difference between "mere sticking together" and "absorbs and transforms them" went well with my new experiencing of a sense of Connectivity. Connectivity feels like absorbing and transforming all that is around me as I come into contact with it.

Alan Watts continues describing this difference by writing:

We must make a distinction between an organism which is differentiated and a machine which is partitive.[27]

As I became more aware of this distinction, I was surprised to notice that nearly everything around me was fabricated! Living in a midsized city, it seemed as if I were completely surrounded by fabrications. As I drove down the street in my "partitive" car, I saw buildings with windows, doors, balconies; I saw billboards and traffic lights; I saw telephone poles and power lines; I felt the steering wheel of my car and my car's seat under my buttocks. All of it, except of course my buttocks, was formed by putting parts together.

I saw how easy it had been to see a person, a dog, or a tree and view them also as fabricated objects like all the rest.

But now when I see a living organism, I occasionally remind myself that it grew from the inside, and that it absorbed and transformed the nutrients it used to sustain its life. I remember that a living organism isn't a product of the fabrication process that can seem so prevalent: putting parts together and being molded by an outer force.

---

[26] Alan Watts, *Tao: The Watercourse Way*, Chapter 3: Tao, page 50 (New York: Pantheon Books, 1975).
[27] Watts, pages 50-51.

I began to view living organisms as having an animating force of some kind, an inner energy that grew the organism rather than an outer one that molded it. I began to realize that living beings function as wholes.

And for me this made the artificiality of word-tools easier to see. I more often remembered that word-tools are symbols we create, and that they specialize in breaking things up into parts. Every word represents a this-not-that bucket that attempts to symbolically break a whole into separate parts.

How very different is a living being – something which grows all at once and as a whole with many "parts" simultaneously developing and forming inter-connectively from within.

And keeping this in the forefront of my thought, at least once in a while, helps me experience this wonderful difference. It helps me to occasionally sense the inner energy of living beings, both inside myself and as it flows back and forth as I interact with people, animals, and plants.

Loving Is Better Than Being Loved

A couple of years after my second divorce, I began to feel more connected to people. Feeling affection for others and compassion for difficult times they may be having, I found that I wanted to express that affection and caring. There was no reason – I simply wanted to express positive feelings.

There was a friend at work who loved the bubble tea I could easily pick up at my morning coffee shop. I began leaving a bubble tea on her desk almost once a week. She would sometimes request it. I remember being aware that I was spending money. I remember having thoughts that I was "being used by her". But when I connected to my feeling for her, and for people in general, the thoughts of being used dissolved.

Recognizing birthdays for people at work, giving special gifts to my roommate, and buying lunch for friends became an outpouring of giving that felt like a natural flow. The Connectivity I felt about the enjoyment, the moments of smiling and surprise, were like fuel.

I admit that there was a bit of surface self/ego in this. Many of these friends were beautiful girls, and I took pleasure in the association. Now, I still enjoy beautiful girls, but it doesn't really matter much if I am "with them". And I sense a more neutral attitude toward using the category of beauty for people.

These experiences were a mixture of what could be called "good" (the flow of generosity) and what could be called "bad" (the ego boost from being around beautiful girls). But overall, I think the mixture was beneficial in showing me something about being alive.

I had never before experienced the feeling of giving without expecting or wanting something back. This gave me that experience. And even though there was ego involvement that I don't view as beneficial over the long term, I experienced feelings of affection and gratitude just because of the very Being of these friends. Yes I also appreciated their smiles and joyful responses, but these seemed secondary.

For the first time, I sensed an outflow of giving without needing back, without tit for tat. I felt the benefit of giving as an internally driven movement. It felt disconnected from the world of trading, the give-in-order-to-get view that I'd always carried.

I felt as though I'd discovered a secret. As long as I didn't stifle this giving with thoughts of money or being used, I was feeding my positive energy in a way I'd never known. I began to understand why people volunteered their time to help people. I sensed that love flowing out is far more important than love flowing in.

That was also the time of life when I realized that the same applies to romance. Love flowing out is far more important to my Being than the wished for result of getting together "permanently". Experiencing the flow of love was more important than being loved back. Because just the experience of the flow itself somehow gave me much more than the feeling of being loved.

The role of my word-tool based thinking in this are many. Part of me says that this can't be good if it has the ego involvement of impressing or buying the affections of beautiful girls. The joke is on these viewpoints – although there was some ego involvement, I did not sense the drive to impress or buy affections as a primary motive. I felt mainly a flow from within, an internalized circle of generous affection and of allowing the good feelings to come out and around. It was a form of being like the shining of the sun or the glow of a beautiful flower – simple giving and that's all.

Ideas of buying friendship or being used or using them – all of these were common word-based thoughts that flowed from my me-vs-them, suspicious illusion of separateness. I discovered that these thoughts were no longer real . . . at least not in me. Instead of those thoughts, I was sensing and experiencing Connectivity, and it felt so much better than the ideas I'd held previously.

I am grateful for these experiences of the shining, glow-like flow, and of becoming more aware of the functioning of my surface self/ego. It's as if this one set of experiences carried two different lessons.

One was a lesson of what Being and connection to Source felt like. I sensed the internal benefits of shining without external reward. Another was a lesson about the workings of my surface self as my mind put out accusations of using and being used. I learned how to spot this part of my functioning just a little quicker.

Do I enjoy responses of smiles and appreciation from others? Yes. Do I enjoy feeling loved by others? Yes, absolutely. But experiencing love flowing out in these ways somehow led to feeling an enduring well-being that diminished the need for a "payback". It was an experience that put the feeling of neediness and "little me" in the background, and a sense of goodwill through Connectivity in the foreground.

Narrow In Order to Expand

I view a wise person as one who realizes a wider view. An obsessed, fixated, moralistic, and closed person is one who gets stuck in tools of narrowed focus: word-tools/concepts/language. I've come from a place of being stuck most of the time. I was closed off from realizing a wider view because I saw words as so much more than tools.

As I drove down the road each day, I was quick to call other drivers *bad* because they slowed me down or pressured me to drive faster or cut in front of me. Why didn't they make me and my convenience their top priority? Like many two-year olds, I viewed everything outside as if it should revolve around my desires and convenience. It amazes me how frequently my egoic surface self still reacts with this type of inner mind chatter.

A muffin was *bad* because it wasn't as moist as I like. And as I narrowed my focus to the dryness, I missed out on the flavor I may have enjoyed. Immersed in the isolated word-tool bucket called *dryness*, I could see nothing else.

As I practiced breaking free of the confines of bad drivers and dry muffins, I discovered that life could feel lighter. I realized that drivers had feelings and that their own life situations were as worthy of respect and compassion as mine. I found I could widen my view of muffins to include flavor, texture, and color; and that I could enjoy these even when I didn't find the dryness level enjoyable.

The wisdom deep down inside me had waited, and finally I was peeling away layer after layer of narrowing word-tools.

Now as I continue to watch these negative stories passing through my mind, I replace them with a different kind of story-making. Stories with "others" as human beings like me, rather than as irritating objects that are always in my way.

Those wider stories free up energy previously used on criticism and blaming. I let go of inner tension as I view other people as like me, as beings who want to feel free to live their lives too. I honor the fact that they don't put me at the forefront of their existence. I feel a sense of Connectivity. And that leads to a wider outlook toward the outside that springs from uncovering what's been inside all along.

Eventually I realized that the whole purpose of narrowing my focus is to benefit me, other people, other living beings, and the environments where we live.

More and more, I see that everything I do is to assist with the flourishing and nurturing of living beings and this planet which supports them. And I am one of those beings, but I am not solo, not in a vacuum.

When I carry a view of Connectivity, I feel open to life with a sense of embracing existence and Being wherever I encounter it. The function of narrowing my focus in order to "get things done" is a mere tool, just as words and everything made of them are merely extractions in relation to this whole of Connectivity, the whole of reality.

Word-tools by their nature are narrowing devices. But their purpose was originally to expand by providing shortcuts to help us communicate more efficiently. When I misuse them by trying to make them do more than they can do, I create resistance to the expansion that life offers. For example, when I judge people as bad/

good, I miss the core Being that lies deep down in them, including those who drive badly and sell dry muffins. I miss out on life when I get lost in the narrowing. I forget that the purpose of narrowing is to widen and expand. It's to serve life, but not any one life as if it exists in a vacuum.

Grouping across many in order to narrow the attention to a this-not-that difference can be constructive, but only when I use this tool in awareness, and only when it serves the interconnected whole from which the grouping came in the first place.

This includes me as A Whole of The Whole. The synthetic separation that word-tools make seemingly clear is actually less real than the reality of the whole of Connectivity. That separatist clarity that seems so real, resides only in the network of the symbols that lead to that impression. What seems real in our world of artificial symbols is not real to the whole of "what is". Connectivity is reality. Separation is a byproduct of our synthetic word-tools, essential to cognition but not to the Being of what is real in life.

The whole from which words come cannot be described by them. Words represent merely slivers, extractions that indicate, but word-tools omit most of the "what is" of the whole of Source.

Resistance, Force, and Heroism

I've noticed these beliefs in myself and in people around me:

- Worrying is what gets me to do things; *musts*, *shoulds*, and obligations are what make things happen. I wouldn't do what I need to do without these types of pressures.

- I must punish myself when I feel sorry for something I've done so I will be motivated to behave differently next time. To blame and criticize myself, or to deny myself things I like, is a way to correct and improve.

- The best way to achieve anything is to tighten into a state of self-discipline, become inflexible in order to insure a firm commitment to follow through, i.e., put the doing of an action above the being of living – these approaches get results.

- Getting upset or agitated motivates change.

- If I worry, fret, and analyze, it helps me figure out what I should have done, or what I should do next.

These ideas of making things happen through pressure, blame, discipline, and stress continue to lurk around inside me. So do these spin-offs of the ideas in the form of mind-chatter.

- I should have, but I didn't.

- I don't want to, but I should.

- I regret that thing I did or didn't do, so I must punish myself by feeling bad.

- Hard work and discipline is how things get done.

- If I don't discipline myself with a time deadline, a high standard, or a goal, then I'll just sit around being lazy and do nothing.

- Analysis and struggle is the way to get the answer (and it's always a word-tool based answer because that's the only kind allowed).

All of these – the beliefs and the mind chatter – are different angles on how I've been conditioned to get myself to achieve and accomplish. And they all create resistance inside me. Each is a thought that goes against "what is", or two thoughts that go against each other, tangled with emotions that get pulled in. But the fundamental is the "against"; that is the crux of the resistance I find inside me.

Once the resistance is set, what follows is a need to push through it. I must overcome whatever goal or *should* or obligation is weighing down on me. It's as if I've created reasons to push against and force life rather than to allow its natural happenings.

In my mind, many "noble" ideas accompany these resistance-creating views: determination, not giving up, and sticking with your dream no matter what. And these bring the feeling that I need to push through and use force in some way. Aren't these "noble" ideas something to be admired? Isn't this what heroes are made of?

But why create something I have to push through in the first place? Why create something that requires force in order to get through it?

I know I've incorporated these points of view from parents, teachers, media, and many other sources. I also know that I indirectly choose my own beliefs, gradually, aided by where I repeatedly put my attention. So, why continue embracing beliefs that lead to seeing things as hardships, obstacles, and burdens?

I for one seem to have internalized the idea that creating resistance, and then pushing through that resistance, is good and heroic.

But, instead of painting "life is hard" on so many situations in one broad brush, why not shift attention away from these stress-producing thoughts? Why not drop the need to create resistance and release myself from the role-play of "good and heroic"? Why not allow rather than resist the "what is" of reality? Why not look for the positives in the worst of situations, as I accept and allow what is, even if the only positives I can find are learning and potential growth?

When I choose resistance-creating views, I end up believing that force is necessary in order to deal with life situations. And then yes, I also create all kinds of heroic roles I can step into. But all the while I miss the fact that I created the resistance in the first place, perhaps just so I could feel like a hero for a while.

Whenever I function with this resistance/force/hero scenario, life seems like just one damn *have to* after another. What's more is that I often feel a touch of guilt about the force I apply as I am being a hero. But it's easy to gloss over that by saying that I did the right thing even though it was hard to do. Being a hero is difficult, but "the right thing" has to be done, doesn't it?

Pushing through one *have to* after another becomes the way of life, while enjoyment takes a distant second place on the priority list. Heroes have a hard job – they can't just enjoy life, they "have to" push through all the resistance in this world.

I'm glad to say I've finally begun to see through these troublesome ideas. There is another way to live.

I found that I can reduce resistance, or not create it in the first place. I can shift attention away from flaw finding. I can practice watching and questioning my judgment/blaming and eventually come to see it as just mind chatter that's best not taken seriously. I can remind myself that "what I don't know" is a valuable source of learning, growing, and experiencing. And I can follow my own internal positive energy flow with Connectivity as grounding.

And, when I sense what seems to be an overpowering resistance inside me, I can even accept the "what is" of that resistance. Once I create it, it's a reality for me. But only in that moment. I can then shift my attention to creating something different, not always immediately and not always directly, but in ways that have a cumulative effect on my general state of being.

I express this cumulative effect as Connectivity. It's the sense of taking action from an all-embracing place that connects to all that's around me, rather than from my word-tool/belief-filtered drives that lead to so much tension and hurt.

But if I rebel against my own resistance in me when I notice it, if I fight it with additional resistance, I remain stuck in the loop-around trap of rejecting what is. And then it only gets stronger, more intense, and stays longer – I generate more resistance when I resist the resistance I already created.

So instead, I stop, take a breath, and "look" directly at the resistance, rather than judging and trying to reject it. And then it dissolves much more quickly. I caution myself that blaming and judging is just piling more word-tools on top of a problem that was initially caused by word-tools. I release the resistance through awareness, by acknowledging it and moving on. And then there is no need for force or heroism, just Being and enjoying are enough.

For me, resistance and force, along with a belief in the goodness of heroism, are partners in unconsciousness, in being lost in concepts.

They come out of my egoic need to feel superior, which is a way of trying to compensate for something else that I resist: feeling as if I'm inadequate, needy, and not enough.

Real heroes don't need what is commonly admired as the goodness of heroism. They don't seek or gain significance from the status of being a hero. They don't need to compensate by categorizing or conceptualizing themselves.

Real heroes act in response to an immediate need through Connectivity, rather than by creating resistance that then needs to be "heroically" pushed through. That is why so many heroes say, "I just did what anyone would do. I responded to what was needed, that is all." These are natural heroes, the reality-based human beings who have no need to create resistance in order to then force their way through it and be identified as heroic.

Connectivity With-All and With-In

My transition toward Connectivity started with the ending of a
sixteen-year marriage and with readings from Karen Horney's
writing. Dr. Horney's writing introduced me to something I'd used
most of my life but never given a name to: the tyranny of the *should*
and the concept of an ideal self (an internal critic).

My ideal self included what I should always be but wasn't:
completely rational, logical, objective, calm, productive, fair, and
much more. It was an ever-present internal punishing agent,
demanding and ruthless. An imagined critic with one function:
telling me I was wrong, stupid, inadequate, lacking. It formed a split
that created an "I hate myself" circle with my ideal-self hating my
real self because I never measured up.

My real self just wanted to be "me", spontaneously open to sensing
and enjoying life as it came. The ideal self wanted to impose
restrictive demands and attempt to control situations by telling life
what it has to be before even encountering it.

Before finding the labels "tyranny of the should" and "ideal self",
I had tried for years to disengage these structures and reduce my
self-hate. I wanted to stop beating myself up. I wanted to become
more aware of what made me feel bad so much of the time. But
my efforts were primarily cognitive; I was too stuck in the *shoulds*
and couldn't see through them by using the same structures that
gave them power to hold me: concepts/word-tools as the only way
of knowing.

I wasn't getting anywhere using thinking/cognition. I wasn't able
to change negative feelings about myself and my life through direct
means. My typical ways of trying such as setting goals, creating plans,
analyzing, and sticky notes with reminders, simply didn't work.

Although some of these may have contributed just a bit, the lasting reduction in self-hate came indirectly as I began to feel more Connectivity with other people. For me, connecting with the outside helped me reduce the separation I'd created inside.

I realize now that they are mirror images: my interaction with the outside, which was dominated by enemy mode, reflected the battle going on inside which was ideal self vs real self. The separations I thought were so real between me and others were a reflection of the separation inside me.

Connectivity with other people seemed to be aided by a couple of different shifts in perspective. One was realizing that other people's problems were similar to mine, no matter how different they seemed on the surface. Another was showing myself that judgments of other people never accomplish anything except tension and unhappiness inside of me.

I began to see my criticism of others as surface stuff, and at the same time I realized there is always a deeper core underneath that surface stuff. I also saw that my judgments of other people were just forms of Flaw Finding and Crazy Thoughts.

Noticing I could find flaws everywhere and anywhere, and noticing the frequency of my crazy thoughts, helped me recognize the ability to direct my attention. If I could find these anywhere and frequently, I could find positives anywhere and frequently too. If I could direct my attention to that store clerk's *incompetence*, I could also shift my attention to the friendly energy she carried as she apologized for the wait and thanked me. But when all my attention is locked-onto the *incompetence*, I'm unable to see the friendly energy, the apology, and the thanks. The *incompetence* label simply doesn't allow anything else to enter its this-not-that bucket.

As I looked beyond other peoples' surface characteristics, I began to look beyond my own, and to sense the deeper selves that sat peacefully beneath the surface problems and "faults". It's as if the deeper selves were all waiting to be unearthed and recognized as connected.

All these word-tool mental pointers were helpful. But internalizing Connectivity came less from word-tools and more from feeling. Feeling the simplicity of Being around other people made me want more of it. The feeling of simply Being with someone had been almost nonexistent when I was 100 percent dominated by word-tools. But as I loosened my grip on conceptualization as a security blanket and shifted away from continuous mental judgment, gradually feelings of acceptance, liking, and even affection arose and became a more frequent part of each day.

For example, while in my car at a traffic light, I watched a very obese woman cross the road in front of my car. I started with the usual initial reaction of negative judgments. But as I continued watching, I thought of her being a little girl growing up, and wondered about challenges she had faced throughout her life. I wondered how it might be to look into her eyes and get to know her, and how it might feel to hug her and be tender or to laugh and have fun with her. By the time she reached the other side of the road, I was filled with affection. Through that shifting process she became a human being like me.

My affection was clear, alive, and flowing over. Its intensity shocked me given my reactive judgments when I first saw her. I couldn't believe (cognitively) that my feelings could change so quickly. And yet they did – the transition inside me was real.

By shifting my thoughts, my feelings changed, all in the short time it took her to cross the road. I felt connected to a human being, rather than immersed in judgments that turned this woman into an object to look down on.

This experience, along with many others like it, brought a sense of "with-ness". Seeing through the temporary surface nature of my negative judgments helped bring to light the unreality of my misuse of word-tools and the mental/emotional goings-on that come out of that misuse.

I practiced shifting while looking at people of all shapes, sizes, nationalities, sexual orientations, degrees of cleanliness, and every other negative concept that struck my mind. Again and again I shifted attention away from evaluative labels that first came to mind, toward positives based on sensing the Being that was deep down, even if those positives and that Being were not readily apparent.

I reminded myself of the still, quiet eye contact with friends and acquaintances that formed experiences I call Grateful Being. These experiences brought a sense of connection so deep that it felt like my source self was embracing the source self of the other. It felt as if we were touching the Whole of Source and honoring life itself by means of our connection with each other.

So for me, connecting with people was an early and significant step. Connecting with my body and the natural environment came next. This may be unusual. I can imagine people who are lost in concepts connecting with their body and nature first, and with people after. Then I remind myself that there are many roads to the same reality and that each of us finds our own road.

Once while sitting in a coffee shop, I thought, *Isn't every person here an exciting expression of a combination of word-tools and the Being that is life itself (Source) which underlies them?*

That day, without talking to anyone in that coffee shop, I felt deep gratitude and appreciation for the existence of every person and every thing.

As I felt more and more Connectivity with all sorts of people at work, walking in the streets, at coffee shops, at the gym, anywhere and everywhere, I began to notice more and more Connectivity within myself. It was as if I were mending the wounds of my own internal split, through mending my attitudes/outlooks toward the "outside" including people, nature, and the earth. It created a feeling of *being with* people and my environment that I'd never experienced before.

By creating more wholistic interconnections outside while letting go of we-vs-them enemy thoughts, I discovered a more wholistic, interconnected flow inside. I began to better manage my internal we-vs-them thoughts, including the ideal self vs real self thoughts that made me an enemy to myself.

I can still recall exactly where I was when I had a surprising awareness that really shocked me: *Wow! I don't think I've criticized myself for the past day or two!* My self-hate and *shoulds* had diminished. That was the first time I remember consciously noticing freedom from the self-critical, *should*-based inner voice that had dominated most of my life. It felt so good to begin to sense that it was possible to experience a day or two without feeling criticized. The battle between the ideal me and my real me had lessened just a bit.

I uncovered Connectivity with-in after opening up to Connectivity with-all, which included with-all people and with-all my surroundings.

I don't think I could have experienced this opening up to Connectivity by directly wanting, striving for, or willing it. My direct control rested in shifting attention, which then led to more constructive and connected interactions. And this shift of attention included being more conscious of my words. I had begun to: "Use words in such a way as to highlight the Connectivity from which they come rather than the separations to which they lead."

All this generated enjoyment of people who are different on the surface. And then it seemed to flow over into enjoying different voices inside me, including my real self that became much more playful. It even included telling my critical ideal self to "shut up" occasionally. (You'd have to hear my tone of voice to know how affectionately playful my real self sounded as I said it. Even though *shut up* can seem negative, the *shut up* I used carried a cute, almost flirty tone without any negativity.)

It makes a difference to me when I cognitively view reality as a Whole, as a web of interconnections. But *feeling* that web is what made the biggest difference to my life. The feeling, not the cognitive viewpoint, is what uncovered Connectivity as a reality for me. My sense of peace, joy, and flow with life has become so much more through Connectivity with-all and with-in.

Bursting a Bubble

I watched a girl as she walked into the coffee shop. She was waiting in line to order; I was sitting at a table reading and making notes. I noticed as the chattering voice of my surface self/ego said:

- Wow, she is so beautiful!
- I really like her hair!
- She has a feminine, attractive way about her.

Then I felt a sense of distance and separation with a touch of fear in the background of my mind. It was as if, with my words, I had put her above me. Just the words *she is so beautiful* seemed to make her unapproachable. I could feel my thoughts of admiration keeping me away, insulated, and detached from this life situation.

I reminded myself that these words/labels/thoughts were just surface aspects. I realized again that none of these synthetic word-symbols carry the reality of the whole of this person. Perhaps these reminders helped me with what came next.

While she waited for her order, she moved nearer to my table. At one point I looked over and caught her eyes. I said hi, and we began to chat while she waited.

All at once I felt a sense of relaxation as the distance and tension faded away. The change surprised me given how tensely separate I had felt just seconds before. It felt good.

It was like the bubble of categorization had burst. The words my mind used as labels made her distinct and separate, as if she were a totally different kind of being. The thoughts felt like constraints that held me back from being alive in those moments. Then when I saw my words for what they are, as only highly limited symbols, there was an opening which led me to look up, catch her eye, and begin to chat.

The this-not-that functioning of my word-tools (*so beautiful*, etc.) encased her in a bubble. The walls of this bubble seemed impenetrable due to the definite, closed nature of how labels work, combined with an underlying thought that her beauty was above me.

But as soon as we started chatting, I felt the boundary melt away; the fear, the separation, the unapproachability began to dissolve. As the constrained feeling of separation fell away, it was replaced by the enjoyment of talking to a human being, not to some unapproachable, detached beauty queen.

Once I had discounted the word-tools and said hi, it was as if she had been transformed into human being in just a few brief moments. I felt a Connectivity not previously allowed by my belief that words are to be taken seriously as truth-tellers.

Discounting my labels also removed the false certainty and superiority that using those labels carries. The woman struck me as beautiful. But, she is not objectively beautiful because some people would hold a different opinion. Some would say, "She's not my type, not attractive to me."

It's interesting that my words placed her above me, and at the same time, placed me above her. I wonder if that's the nature of feeling superior. Perhaps the other side of feeling superior is feeling less than.

It does not serve this girl or me to put her in the confined space of the bucket called *beautiful*. With this experience, I sensed for the first time that even positive labels mentally turn people into objects. It's a disservice to both her and me if I put her above or below by using word-tools.

Once we'd burst the bubble I created and started chatting, I simply enjoyed being me. And it seemed as if she enjoyed the energy of freedom to talk without the tension of classification that she may have so often experienced. As the surface-based synthetic categorization *beauty* dissolved in my mind, our beauty as two human beings could wake up to an enjoyment not previously allowed by my word-tools.

It became simply one human being experiencing another, without the preconceived labeling I am so used to using . . . oops, I mean so used to misusing.

From Rigidity to Life – the Movie Chocolat

There is a movie called *Chocolat* that tells of people in a small town who are stuck in rigid rules and frozen ideas from the past. What's great is how this movie shows these people gradually letting go of their rigidity. By opening to other ways of knowing and Being, they uncover a sense of joy that had been covered up by their beliefs about how they thought life *had to be*. Ultimately, all these beliefs are in the form of word-tools.

A pastor delivers the following sermon near the end of the movie – it illustrates some of the ideas behind loosening the chains of their rule-bound living, and the readiness to feel more and be more.

> Do I want to speak of the miracle of our Lord's divine transformation? Not really, no. I don't want to talk about his divinity. I'd rather talk about his humanity. I mean, you know, how he lived his life here on Earth. His kindness. His tolerance.
>
> Listen, here's what I think.
>
> I think we can't go around measuring our goodness by what we don't do. By what we deny ourselves. What we resist. And who we exclude.
>
> I think we've got to measure our goodness by what we embrace. What we create. And who we include.[28]

Monitoring, measuring, and excluding is what word-tools support so well. The this-not-that nature of word-tools reinforces exclusion and fosters belief systems that confine us to the past or consume our attention with the future.

Our word buckets admit only one type of "this." They exclude all else.

---

[28] *Chocolat*, directed by Lasse Hallström, written by Joanne Harris and Robert Nelson Jacobs, (Santa Monica, CA: Miramax, 2000), DVD.

That's the consequence of a system of shortcuts – we use them as an alternative to the effort of physically pointing and saying: *Here's what I experienced firsthand. I wonder what it will be like for you to experience and to come to know this on a firsthand basis.*

We forget that words leave out so much of what could be experienced firsthand! They leave behind the uniqueness of every "this" they admit into their category grouping. As a dog, cat, or human being in reality, the criteria for joining the conceptual group is that you give up your uniqueness.

Words simply don't connect us to life unless we use them as the limited tools they are. Instead, these this-not-that devices detach us in a way that separates us from experiencing life firsthand. And in a way, each word establishes a hidden sort of resistance to everything outside of its narrowly defined bucket.

Words support us in resisting "what is" when we misuse them *without acknowledging their limitations*. Without this acknowledgment, a concept/word-tool carries the resistance embedded in its this-not-that nature.

As I've been able to take first steps toward using words with awareness of their limitations, I feel so much gratitude. I am grateful that words allow me to break things down into manageable pieces for my mind to work with. And I'm grateful I can use words as tools for pointing toward experiences I want to tell other people about. I wouldn't be writing this book if I didn't enjoy words so much.

However when I misuse them by granting them a power they don't actually have, I find myself being rigid, resisting "what is", and excluding life and other people as if I exist in a vacuum. I experience suffering rather than enjoyment. I am not happy. I do not "feel good now." Words are tools that can serve me and those around me, if I use them in ways that contribute to our lives. Words serve me when I use them in a way that aligns with Connectivity.

I've written in other sections that "If there is only me, there is no me." Creating the illusion of isolation by embracing exclusion doesn't resonate in this reality of interconnectedness.

Despite saying that words are best not taken too seriously, I've found that my choice of words makes a difference. Words such as *embrace*, *create*, and *include* help point me in an expansive direction, one that is more likely to allow me to realize and stay in tune with the Connectivity of life.

To me, the movie *Chocolat* provides an enlightening portrayal of people gradually loosening their rigid viewpoints of *deny*, *resist*, and *exclude*. It shows them releasing themselves from being held by the demand that life be funneled exclusively through the confines of conceptually filtered beliefs. As they sense something more than rules and traditions, they also discover inside themselves an enjoyment of pure and direct living, an enjoyment they could now be allowed to experience without the need to justify it with word-tools.

Life is the starting place. Words and all their combinations come out of the Connectivity of life, they come from Source. And when people begin to realize words as only one of many tools, as only shortcuts for pointing, as only symbols for indicating, it may become easier for them to put primary attention on "what is", on the reality that words are only tags for.

I loved watching the people in *Chocolat* as they restored the uniqueness and Connectivity that words can't do justice to, and along with that, the vibrancy of living without the shackles of their this-not-that exclusionary beliefs.

Indirect Not Direct

The more I "try really hard" to get things done, the less peace I feel. I become more focused on straining for an end result than on the activity itself. With the order that I "must get this done" as I drive myself toward the finish line, there is little energy left for enjoying the doing. It feels like going through the motions in a way that's enveloped in stress. And I find this is often tied to outside demands, to what people tell me I should want, rather than to what's really inside me as my deepest want.

For most of my life I believed the way to do things was to *make* them happen. If I tried hard enough and learned what I needed to know, I could get the result I wanted by using effort and will. I thought that "not giving up" meant rigid determination and forcing things, and even getting angry and abusive if people got in the way of progress.

Seeing the world only through ideas, I often try to convince others that mine are best. It never works. Even if they seem to agree, when I push to persuade them, they can't help but walk away with at least a little resistance. My pushing closes off receptivity.

Same within myself. If I try to push an idea or activity on myself, it doesn't work because I push back, I rebel. Strong arming only causes poor quality in what I do. If I try to force my writing, the result is usually artificial and academic – it's disconnected from the reality of living. Most of the writing I find myself "trying really hard with" gets tossed out.

I occasionally take care of my friend's dog, and I've found that tensing up and sharpening my voice when I call him doesn't work. Using a stern voice loaded with the expectation of direct obedience doesn't get reliable results. But building a bond with him, coaxing him with acceptance and gentleness, with no stress in my voice or my body (i.e. without trying to *make* it happen) – this works far better long term. It's not 100 percent effective. But it *brings us together* much more frequently than my more forceful and direct attempts to get him to come or to stop chewing on something. And it's so much more enjoyable.

In a similar way, my occasional angry outbursts at people are tied to trying to directly control what happens. Over and over again I see that the tension/stress of trying to force life to happen in a preconceived way just doesn't work.

The definiteness of word-tools which comes from their this-not-that rigid nature is part of what makes me think I can directly control an outcome by tensing up, by forcing, by trying hard to make it happen. Words form buckets that I then expect outcomes to fit into. They are cut-and-dried exclusionary devices. The word *tree* includes only trees and excludes everything else. I've experienced the tension of this exclusion. When I notice words flowing through my mind, while on a walk for example, I feel tension in my face. When I quiet my mind-chatter, the tension settles and dissipates.

I heard or read somewhere that trying to force the petals of a flower to open before they are ready doesn't work. It doesn't fit the flower's growth pattern, which arises out of the nature and complexity of its seed and its environment.

As I realized the limitations of word-tools, and my frequent misuse of them, I became more comfortable with my limited control. With a friendly, affirming nod to the vastness and value of what I don't know, I can more easily let go of controlling outside events directly. And I more fully realize that my control lies with my ability to point my attention.

In other words, I've come to see that while I can influence, I cannot make happen, force, or push a result. When I try to, the result comes out unnatural, faked, and pressured. If I'm open enough, I see that the poor quality of the forced result makes it not worth doing; it works against the purpose of acting toward that outcome in the first place. Forcing a dog or a person to do something may work in the moment. But the long term purpose of joining with this Being in action, including when this Being is myself, can only be damaged by that kind of directness.

Here's something else making it difficult to let go of control: the idea that events have a single cause. I'm weaning my mind away from the compulsion to always look for a single cause. Here too, word-tools play a role. A word retains the *one this* while ignoring the complexity of all the rest of reality, that is, of all the *thats* excluded as part of the process of forming the word. I remind myself again how limiting our this-not-that symbols are.

My immersion in the *one this* along with my engrained impulse to look for single causes easily leads me to think I have direct control when I don't. Word symbols are absolutist, e.g. only *trees* are allowed. In that sense, words are rigid as they have no ability to overlap and no flexibility. They lend themselves well to forgetting the multi-caused Connectivity that surrounds us. Perhaps I should say "multi-influenced", because what I experience with Connectivity is less direct than the willfulness involved in thinking I caused something and made it happen.

For example, it seems that whenever I think I've determined the single cause of a body ache, I notice the ache coming back again months or years later. At first, I'm so happy that I found "the one cause" as I consistently apply this solution that initially worked, believing I now have direct control over the ache. But sometime later, I find that my control didn't last as I begin to feel that ache, or some similar pain, again. After twenty plus years of thinking I found the solution for this ache or that, I finally realize there are too many interacting causes for my cognitive mind to handle. Sure, I wish I could find single causes and direct control. But reality continues to show me something different.

Believing words to be powerful beyond their capability lends itself to longing for a predictable and direct form of control that simply isn't real. But my mind continues to argue. I put my hand on the faucet and turn on the water as I ask, "Isn't that direct control?"

This incredibly simple act of turning water on, initiated by pointing my attention, is different than most efforts to control relating to people and events. People, events, and body aches involve a multitude of interconnected influences from countless sources. Even turning on the water, although it appears I have direct control as I enact a "single cause", involves so many connections not typically in our awareness. If the main line at the street is shut off, or if the water company suddenly stops functioning, there will be no water. If those interconnections are not maintained, the direct control of reaching for and moving the handle of the faucet will not make water come out.

And yet my mind continues to cling to single causes – the belief that I have direct control in making things happen, fixing things, and then keeping them working forever.

As children we are surrounded by people who emphasize the value of word-based education. We feel we must gain great quantities of word-based knowledge in order to live. We hear Francis Bacon's famous statement that "knowledge is power". Many of us are taught that the only kind of knowing is word-based, conceptual, cognitive, and we easily dismiss consideration of any non-word-tool type of knowing. We may have never realized that words are only one of many different types of tools, and that like a hammer or a screwdriver, each tool is suited for something specific.

One of the first times I recall thinking outside the box of word-tools was after I read the following quote from psychoanalyst Karen Horney. In discussing a child's development, and after acknowledging that a child learns and acquires skills as he/she grows, Dr. Horney wrote:

> But there are also forces in him which he cannot acquire or even develop by learning. You need not, and in fact cannot, teach an acorn to grow into an oak tree, but when given a chance, its intrinsic potentialities will develop. Similarly, the human individual, given a chance, tends to develop his particular human potentialities.[29]

I've discovered that I stifle my growth when I fail to acknowledge the "forces in him which he cannot acquire or even develop by learning". I cannot grow naturally when I try to apply direct control. It's like trying to force my petals to open before they are ready.

Now I view myself as a growing thing, like a seed that can develop "particular human potentialities". But to do that, I have to allow things to happen rather than tensing, straining, and struggling to *make* them happen.

Connected to the passage above, Dr. Horney goes on to say: "Like any other living organism, the human individuum needs favorable conditions for his growth".[30]

One of these "favorable conditions" is allowing things to come together in Connectivity. But I can't know or express this Connectivity with words. Words simply can't carry enough information. They can only indicate, and they can do this constructively only when I remember their limitations. When I

---

[29] Karen Horney, *Neurosis and Human Growth*, Chapter 1: The Search for Glory, page 17 (New York: W.W. Norton & Company, 1991).

[30] Horney, page 18.

forget this, I revert back to trying to force life to fit my preconceived images, which are made up of word-tools. If I hold too tightly to my word-tool reins, I constrict life as I interfere with favorable conditions for growth.

As I allow my growth, my direct action lies in watering and fertilizing my "garden" environment. And again, as I care for my environment, I cannot *make* a particular result happen in the exact way I want. I can't force myself to meet a specific, predetermined outcome, and I can't rush the process of blooming, at least not if I want the best of what can grow through me.

Nurturing my environment through where I put my attention is where my control lies. If I put my attention on being around people, I may find new friends. If I put attention on learning a new subject area, I may get a college degree, and then a job. But I may not. I cannot *make* those end results happen, not without diminishing quality and not without a diminished awareness of Connectivity. Any specific result isn't guaranteed ahead of time. Yet where I place my attention is influential, especially when I am in tune with Connectivity.

I can't make things happen directly, but I can influence and nurture. And if I allow the natural processes to unfold, an outcome I could enjoy is more likely to come than if I did nothing. Whatever the result, it will be one that fits me in my environment, within the Connectivity from which I grow.

When I more often put my attention on the best in people, and honor the value that's inherent in life itself and in all things; when I remind myself of the limitations of word-tools, and remember the vastness of what I don't know; then I can nurture my environment in a way that allows for the whole of reality, not just the disjointed slivers carried by my system of word-tools.

If I open up to and allow the flow of "the forces in me which I cannot acquire or even develop by learning", I place my attention and move through life in a way that leads to natural growth for me and others. As I realize that word-tools are not the only way to know, and as I let go of trying to make life be what I want it to be rather than what it is, I regain Connectivity to the whole of the environment from which I grow. And this is something that happens indirectly, not directly.

My Stories about Their Stories about Me

I wonder how many people wonder what others think of them and then make up stories about what those others think. I've been in this circular loop since I was a young boy, starting with guessing what my mother was feeling, and then worrying that I had somehow caused her to feel that way. Guesses about other people's unexpressed thoughts/feelings have disturbed me all of my life.

Does the this-not-that nature of word-tools contribute to this inclination to guess what others think/feel about me? I see some connections.

Words come after life experience not before. Pulling words out of experience creates frozen snapshots, thereby separating the words from the moving whole of life experience. Word-tool separation encourages a me-not-them outlook, and that sets the stage for wondering what they think of me. If am so separate from others, I'd better worry about what they think/feel about me. If I see myself as separate, I will be afraid.

Through Connectivity, I've seen that I'm not as separate as I may appear to be. My reactions to people around me in any one moment are different depending on what those particular people are doing, saying, and expressing in that moment. What I am in any one moment ties directly to other people and what's around me in my environment. There's no way to escape this reality. My "I am" is a connected "I am".

I've also seen that even though it is apparent that people are uniquely different, I am like a seed surrounded by a multitude of interconnections. Once I allow attention to flow to Connectivity, I find the essence of any one person as a force of like-me-ness that overshadows the separation our word-tools suggest. I remind myself that this-not-that word-tools can't carry Connectivity.

Yet my mind attempts to defend separateness as a reality that words accurately represent. And it continues by claiming that words carry Connectivity through the general categories we use, that is, through the genus of a definition. A dog is a type of *canine* (genus), which belongs to the grouping *mammals* (wider genus), which is a type of *animal* (wider genus), which belongs to the category *living things* (wider genus).

But if I carried these general categories in the forefront of my thinking, why would I walk around with enemy-mode viewpoints arising from seeing myself as separate? Why would I try to snatch the first place in line, or quickly grab the open lane in traffic, before somebody else gets it?

If word-tools carried Connectivity, I would not react as if other people were my enemies. I would not view every "other" as something to defend against, attack, or compete with.

If word-tools carried Connectivity, I would view someone else's positive experience as I view my own. I would feel gladness about someone else getting first place in line or winning a competition, just as I would feel glad if I were to do the same.

Why? Because "me" would be with "we". If my main tool of thought and communication carried Connectivity, it would be clear that I don't exist in a vacuum. But our limited word-tools exist in artificial vacuums, in the form of frozen snapshots, in the separation of the this-vs-that, in the pretense of describing what is real while holding only the miniscule label of what a tag on a string gives a name to.

Despite the function of a genus in a definition, my experience is that word-tools don't carry the reality of Connectivity, at least not in the way I and most people use them.

But I find I get closer to Connectivity when I exclude words that point toward judgment, evaluation, and comparison. To my surprise, at times when I'm speaking to someone, I experience an almost natural avoidance of words that carry these types of judgmental measurements. Instead of saying "He's a really bad guy!", I catch myself and say "He's hitting that woman, and she appears to be in pain – what can I do to change this situation?"

Connectivity can't be carried in a mind that holds tight to an outlook of separation and a superiority that embraces judgment, evaluation, and comparison.

When I'm grounded in Connectivity, my stories about what others think of me don't churn round and round because they aren't present. If I catch myself wondering what others think of me, I remember that my own judgment stories aren't to be taken seriously, and neither are theirs. The nature of words simply doesn't allow them to carry truth in a way that threatens me. For the most part, what others think of me is insignificant, just as what I think of them is insignificant.

Here's what's significant. As frequently as possible I touch the noncognitive by really feeling this computer keyboard as I type, or noticing the scent in the air around me. I acknowledge that there are truths that don't rely on words, and I remember the value of what I don't know. I recall that the vastness of the cognitively unknown is like the 90 percent of the iceberg – unseen beneath the water – and that only 10 percent is visible through the shortcut, tagging function of our word-tools.

I can hear the counterarguments. My mind tells me that what I'm saying about Connectivity can't be real because it seems different from the logic of the material world we live and work in. Since I can't touch, see, hear, or smell Connectivity, it can't be real.

Why does my mind view computers, business, math, and science as real, but reject the reality that I and other human beings breathe the same air, live on the same earth, and do not exist in separate vacuums?

My mind, using the limited symbols of word-tools, is not equipped to answer.

Then I retrieve the sense of my whole self and remember times in my life when "I knew" but words could not describe that knowing. I remember how fiercely my surface-self ego clings to word-tool knowing, sometimes as if my life depended on it.

With fear as its driver, my surface-self ego holds tight to a superior idealistic perfection that is certain in its knowledge. But its knowledge is no wider than a bunch of snapshot photos strewn on the banks of the moving river of life. The sense of Connectivity comes closer to carrying the living movement that word-tools cannot.

So when I concoct a story that others are thinking or feeling that Steve is dangerous, a loser, a nuisance, or undesirably bad in some way, I realize how unserious it is. Even though it happens so frequently, it's not meaningful, not in me toward them and not in them toward me.

With Connectivity in mind, I view unexpressed thoughts and feelings as not worthy of attention. Then that negative aura – which my worrisome, negative belief system conjured up – coils like a twisting bit of smoke and dissolves into the vastness of the air around it.

It's my choice, at least it's my indirect choice. As long as I don't feed them with my attention, I can view my stories, and the stories other people imagine, as puffs of smoke that disappear into nothingness. Or I can embrace them as "truths" like the iron shackles that slaves are forced to wear.

Can I open up to possibilities wider than those provided by my limited this-not-that symbols? Can I open my outlook to include my nature as A Whole of The Whole?

I can. And it feels good.

Expanding Out of Conceptual Restriction

One day after a physical therapy session, I walked to the post office to drop off some mail. There was slight pressure in the back of my mind to get home soon so I could type three new sections of material I had written. But I felt relaxed after the session, and I walked instead of driving in order to get some sun.

My usual mental word-noise was quiet as I walked. I stopped to really look at and feel the amazing detail in trees, flowers, and bushes. I felt the warmth of sun on my skin and noticed vibrant colors and many different shapes.

One bush had hundreds of tiny purple flowers with many bees drawing life from them. I stood watching the bees buzzing among purple flowers for many quiet minutes. I thought, *There must be a hundred bees on this bush!* Then I quieted the word-talk and continued walking and looking.

I saw a woman sitting in her front yard. We held each other's glances and said hi. We began to chat and ended up talking for about twenty minutes about her house and garden and about some of our experiences. I felt a close connection, and I think she did too. At one point there were tears in both my eyes and hers. We connected with our whole selves, not just with words. We didn't even ask each other's names until the end of the conversation.

As I continued walking, I noticed something lurking in the background of my thoughts: *Work. You should be working.* I noticed the constriction of that *should* and the tension in my face to go with it. It felt like a self-criticism rising up, like a disciplinarian about to try to force me to do what it wanted. It was a familiar *should* that I encounter almost every day.

After I watched this thought-threat for a minute or so, the tension in my forehead and face gradually faded away. Then I realized that walking, looking at the plants, and talking to the woman were forms of working. Isn't caring for my health by walking in the sun contributing to my work? Isn't Connectivity with the sun, trees, flowers, bushes, bees, and with the woman adding to my work? Don't these experiences all feed my energies to write because they bring feelings of gladness to be alive?

But in my word-dominated, separatist mindset, I tend to define work narrowly as "typing those three sections". Trapped in my word-tooled world of *shoulds*, I'm not able to see that the idea to type three sections is arbitrary – there was no reality-based need to complete three on this particular day, or to finish any of them. But earlier that day, because I'd put words to it, the idea of doing three sections took on the status of an absolute. I continue to struggle with this word-domination.

What if the idea of work could be expanded to embrace a wider span of life rather than being limited to the standard category of activities I get paid money for? It's so easy to forget that eating, breathing, taking care of my body's health, and so much more is part of making the process of working worthwhile. I now view work without Connectivity as not only wasteful, but destructive.

I've found my best work comes when I take care of my life energies. Just as young children need to have fun as they experience the "work" of playing, I need flow and enjoyment running through my actions too. I've discovered that when I take care of my Feel Good Now energies, my work feels like play. I need the "work" of experiencing the base of living, unfiltered by the confining preconceptions of word-tools. I need it as an adult who's still learning about the universe and Source, just as children need it as they learn about the world and its workings through play. I remind myself again that all our work-related conceptual tools originally came out of the whole of life.

My mind is saying, *Steve, you are making work into something that it's not. You are ruining the this-not-that function of the word "work"!*

Yes, I am, I say with gladness. I am widening it to include some of the interconnections that the this-not-that bucket of *work* does not include. I am reminding myself that I work in order to live, not live in order to work. Work is a tool for living, just as words are.

And so I expand away from the narrow *should* that I've carried because it chokes off the flow of my energies, and because it can't carry the web of Connectivity. When I break free of the narrow confines of rule-bound *shoulds* and sense the welcoming expansiveness of Connectivity, I enjoy what I'm doing in life rather than feeling that I have to do it. Don't you too want to let go of conceptual restriction and expand your living to embrace more enjoyment?

A Goal Without Consequence

I've selected the following goal as something to aim for regarding how I use words: connect my words to reality, to life, as directly as possible, both in thoughts to myself (self-talk) and in communicating with others.

As a selection, I regard this aim/goal as having no morality behind it, no good/bad, no right/wrong, no succeed/fail. It has no "you did it!" and no "you screwed up again!"

It's a goal without consequence.

I want to experience taking the sting of continuous assessment out of this goal by removing consequences. What would happen if I held the goal without evaluating myself, without concern about whether or not I make progress or "achieve it", without the thought that it must be brought to completion?

Well, I am trying it. And I repeatedly remind myself that even if I talk for hours without connecting to life, it doesn't make me a failure. At the same time, it doesn't make my aim any less desirable. I can hold to the benefit of connecting my words and thoughts to life, even when I don't act in accordance with that goal.

I've found that judging my progress slows me down, while allowing myself to grow into an aim makes me bloom.

If I sense I'm talking too long without connecting to life, which is a form of being lost in concepts, I usually shift some attention toward remembering the benefits of the goal. This in turn can help rekindle an interaction between what I'm saying and what is real. What is real is the whole of the person I'm talking to; my mind chattering is less real. So when I remember again the benefits of the goal, I naturally shift attention from my mind to the whole of the person in front of me. Rather than talking at them, I am now talking with them; I am listening to the other person rather than placing most of my attention on my mind-chatter.

"Indirect Not Direct" is about why I view life-supporting goals as not subject to our direct control. It fits here too. Since we don't control outcomes in the direct ways our word-tools lead us to believe, harshness about meeting goals doesn't work. Of course the best way for you to see this is not by reading this material, but by looking within yourself.

Judgment and comparison disconnect me from life. I find rigid use of goals to be just another form of disconnect, another form of being lost in concepts. Judgment, comparison, and rigid use of goals are a consequence of me holding word-tools as the dominant way to view and interact with reality.

Ahh, perhaps you are hearing the same voice I am. Mine is telling me that a goal without some muscle behind it, a goal without a threat, will not be reached. How can I be motivated without something pushing me? To make it real, something unpleasant has to happen. I have to feel bad in some way if I fail or else the goal is of no use. Is this just me or did you pick up on this message too?

I've tried motivating myself with this punishment mentality for most of my life. It creates resistance, rebellion, and immobility. As I continue to repeat this mistake, I see that my attempt to use goals to "make things happen" works only in a short term way and in the simplest of circumstances. So I aim to dethrone my punishment mentality.

I'm aiming to set aside punishment and move toward a nurturing approach that allows growth in a way that goes with nature rather than fights against it, a way that does not create resistance and immobility.

Perhaps there are ways to use goals to motivate enjoyable action. But for most of my life, I've experienced goals as powered by threat of a negative or by the tension of a promise withdrawn if I fail to achieve the outcome. By using a goal without consequence, I'm exploring the possibility of another way.

When I remove threats, I open up the field of enjoying my goal of connecting words to real life, doing it as it flows naturally and watching for opportunities to be part of that flow. There is no need to create a threat of measurement and failure to make me want to do it. The goal started in the first place because I chose it and want it. Choosing and wanting do not necessitate measuring progress; only the inadequacy of my egoic surface self requires measurement of this kind.[31]

To evaluate and judge is to put symbolic tools that don't exist except as tags above life itself which does exist. Word-tools are not "what exists", they *represent* what exists. What makes my goal worth having is that when I catch myself not connecting words to reality I can, without blame and without the word "failure", remember that allowing myself to grow into connecting my words to reality is what will bring it about. The allowance to grow, not the force of evaluation, keeps my goal connected to what is and avoids misusing word-tools as if they are more than mere representations that indicate a general direction to look in.

But, when I set firm goals backed by evaluation and judgment, my me-vs-them superiority rises up from where it was lurking in the

---

[31] This is somehow connected to the feeling I describe in "Enjoying Knowing is Different from Enjoying More Than."

background. When I look deeper I find the reason behind wanting to use goals this way is my own feeling of smallness. Stuck in my surface self, I am in need of a boost because the disconnect caused by viewing words as all powerful leaves me with a sense of inadequacy. My growing self has become buried under layers of limited word-tools as I have forgotten the Source from which those tools came.

When I measure against some socially accepted standard, it's even worse – now I have an entire society approving of me taking a superior position. Then when I catch myself evaluating the street person as undesirable because he does not earn his own way, I've got crowds of people supporting my evaluation. Perhaps many of us have some form of this faulty reasoning. *Why doesn't this street person set goals and then make sure he accomplishes them so he can be like most of us? Why doesn't he evaluate and threaten himself with failure like we do?*

I've found I can work to undo this jump to evaluate by shifting attention to a description more connected to reality: *He appears to be without a home and job, and is essentially a human being like me, someone who grows best without threat of punishment and blame.* With that description, I use words in such a way as to highlight the Connectivity from which they come rather than the separations to which they lead.

For me, goals are attained more effectively without the comparisons, threats of punishment, and superiority involved in continuous measurement. I view these negatives as a way of misusing concepts that insulates human beings from the whole of Connectivity that is life itself.

The internal organs of my body function without consequences for "failing" to meet goals. They keep going and even adapt and self-repair without comparisons, threats, or superiority. They move toward positive states naturally and with the flow of Connectivity that allows whole-self growth and whole-self being. That's a "movement toward" that I can enjoy for its own sake. And that's what it feels like to have a goal without consequence.

What Mattered Then – What Matters Now

During most of my life I put primary attention on differences that fueled comparisons and flaws. That's what mattered to me. I viewed it as positive. I thought the way to improve things and solve problems was to compare "what is" with "what should be" in order to find flaws, discover improvements, and figure out how to get more out of every situation.

But the differences so important to me were purely conceptual. The differences that drew my attention were only between this grouping and that one: *trees* are different from *flowers*, *women* from *men*, *Americans* from *foreigners*. These differences in groupings excluded the uniqueness of any one person, flower, or tree. When I was lost in the purely conceptual, uniqueness was insignificant to me, and so was the life experience from which the word-tool categories came.

With my attention only on conceptual groupings, I missed the rich uniqueness of the difference of individuals: the many-faceted wholeness of *this* actual person; the unity and fullness of the life of *this* flower, *this* tree, *this* cloud in the sky. I rarely noticed this ever present richness as I walked out of my house or drove down the streets every day. And if I did, I would quickly dismiss each as just another *person*, *flower*, *tree*, or *cloud*. My mind would immediately categorize each specific as just a member of the cluster "I already knew" through the concept/word.

My mind would chatter, *There's a cloud . . . oh yes, I know those. There's a flower under a tree . . . yeah, I've seen those hundreds of times. There's someone who looks like a street bum . . . ahh, that's the kind of person I want to avoid.*

My world was processed. It consisted only of the fabrication of word-products, filtered through conceptualization with no appreciation for the uniqueness I had lost.

To me, groupings and their word-tool products were the only things worth my attention – the actual reality of the specifics that made up these groupings were not. The power of the word-tool grouping overshadowed the uniqueness of the actual life from which the groupings came in the first place.

Of what importance is that particular person, that one flower or tree, and what does that one cloud matter? What really matters are the categories of people, flowers, trees, and clouds – those we study in science. And further, what really matters are ideas like justice, honesty, productivity, etc. Framing my life around scientific groupings and moral principles was far more important than experiencing reality firsthand.

I had missed the whole of reality because I became lost in the power of groupings, concepts, word-tools.

And of course I justified all this by using a word-tool explanation: *Conceptual thinking is what makes human beings human; it's what differentiates us from animals.* At the same time I was ignoring the reality that as a human being I fit into the category as one of those "animals".

What mattered was: earners vs moochers; Republicans vs Democrats; nonreligious vs religious – groupings carried by concepts. What mattered was methods, procedures, principles, standards, measurements, judgment, morality, logic, reason, noncontradiction, mutual exclusivity – products of word-tools that lie many layers of abstraction away from the reality of actual experience from which they were extracted.

I was unaware of my role in choosing the conceptualized patterns I focused on. I viewed the patterns I chose as *the* real patterns, and thought that those patterns were right for everyone. They were *the* objective truth, applicable to everyone whether anyone in particular agreed or not. Falling head first into the ocean of concepts, I ignored the possibility of other patterns that may lie outside the frozen, word-tooled radar screen that I viewed as reality.

Spotting what was *bad* and *needed to change* or what *could be better* made me "smart". And yet I gradually began to see that this outlook distorted my view by narrowing the reality I attended to.

As an example I would catch my mind saying, *This person Anna is bad*, implying that that's all she is. After all she can't be both bad and good; our this-not-that word-tools don't allow for both. Then I would begin to wonder why I felt the compulsion to clutch onto this classification, and I'd remind myself that Anna is so many other things that I'm not aware of. I would remember the vast arena of what I don't know, and how easy it is for me to forget that all of us are part of interconnected life processes that are the Source of all, including Anna, myself, and these word-tool classifications.

It still amazes me how positives suddenly begin to materialize when I open up to something wider than my category groupings. I find myself saying things like: *Wow! I never before noticed the bright glow in Anna's eyes and the tender quality of her face when she's not upset.* After shifting from my initial negatives to these types of positives, I sense that Anna begins to feel safe as we talk. And so do I. We all feel safer when we aren't bound up and ruled by conceptual worlds detached from reality.

Gradually I begin to notice an outflow of kindness in Anna's actions and expressions. That's something that wouldn't have happened if she (and I) had continued to feel only the negativity of my initial negative judgments. If I had continued my attention on negatives, her outflow of kindness would have been disallowed by those judgments. And as I've discovered time after time, the *bad* I think is so real in others is actually a creation of my own, not something real outside me.

Once I align with Connectivity, my conceptualization of Anna as *bad* seems like an illusion. With my constricted judgment relaxed, my view opens up to her as a unique human being who is much more like me than she first appeared.

When I approach reality with preconceptions, I miss out. My preconceived word-tool buckets are firmly closed to anything outside of their unforgiving walls. Uniqueness and the core Being of a person are not permitted by the conceptual enclosures of *beautiful girl*, *Anna is bad*, or *street bum*. The aliveness of a person, or even of an object, is lost when I rely solely on the judgmental labeling I find myself so often using.

As long as I view reality only through word-tools, I limit that reality and miss a multitude of positives that can be discovered, enjoyed, nurtured. I become a pawn of word-tools rather than someone wise enough to know when to use the tool and when it doesn't apply.

Now, like magic, as I continue to practice shifting attention, positives arise often and in all kinds of places I never suspected. I no longer feel trapped by my own compulsions to label as I become more aware of the limitations of word-tools and learn not to take them too seriously.

Much of my life has now become one enjoyable surprise after another. And now that I've shifted from a surface self to a whole self, what matters to me has changed. Now it's the magic of Being with life rather than preconceiving against it; now as I point my attention to Being as often as possible, I feel the enjoyment of connecting with life directly rather than only through the filtering of word-tool groupings.

What mattered then was feeling smart because I was one who could spot problems and improve things. What matters now is living. The wisdom of Connectivity has replaced the illusion of being smart through misuse of word-tools.

Comprehensiveness – Parts and Wholes

For as long as I can remember, I've created tension about needing to check every option before choosing. I feel compelled to get maximum benefit out of anything I am involved with. *I must look at every option, every possibility, or else I might miss the best one!*

When putting together a jigsaw puzzle, you need every piece to complete the picture it forms. That's a situation where comprehensiveness is useful. And perhaps comprehensiveness applies to some aspects of computer programming and engineering. But most of the time I misapply this to situations where it doesn't belong, and I do it in a way that makes it seem an issue of crucial importance when it's not.

It's the drive to make sure every base is covered, or the fear-driven compulsion to ensure nothing goes wrong. It rests on the idea that the crucial things in life are outside me not inside.

We are surrounded by things that were assembled by putting parts together to form wholes. I often call these manmade things *fabrications*. In a world where fabrications surround us – computers, cell phones, appliances, buildings, cars, etc. – it can be difficult to notice things we didn't assemble, things that grew into being wholes through natural processes. (For more detail, see "Fabrications vs Life and Nature".)

But I do encounter things that are not created by assembling parts, and one of those is me. Another is you, and every other human being, and every living thing.

I haven't done a jigsaw puzzle for years. Yet I get caught up in thinking I have to be comprehensive as I try repeatedly to apply it where it doesn't fit. I attempt to use a parts-based/fabricated approach with natural wholes. I wonder if comprehensiveness is stressful because it doesn't help me make decisions involving people, which are wholes that grow to "completion" in a natural way.

When I write, I can easily get caught in demands of covering all possible points and answering all potential arguments. When I buy something new, I enslave myself with the need to check out every option before I choose. *What if I check only ninety-eight out of one hundred options and miss the one that would have been best by far? What if I miss what would have been my favorite because I failed to check those other two?* I wonder how many people do this in looking for a romantic partner: *What if I commit to this person now and then later find someone better?*

I'm beginning to realize that decisions involving natural wholes are best made from a natural-whole perspective. But I'm so immersed in the world of fabricated stuff that I can't seem to break free of the fear of missing one part of the puzzle. I'm caught in a *should* that demands that I must find and place every piece to reach what my mind has defined as the all-important completion.

For me, comprehensiveness is the pressure to be perfect in a world of things that seem to be more separate than connected. What if they aren't? What if they are more connected than they are separate? What if the separation comes partly from the this-not-that of our word-tools and partly from being immersed in the stuff of fabrications that are completed by attaching together many parts?

I sense I've been blinded to the Connectivity of natural wholes that would make my comprehensiveness unnecessary. If I put more attention on growing in life, and less on putting parts together, perhaps I could break free from this self-inflicted *should*.

Sensing a natural whole is different from what I'm used to – it comes out of realization that is much wider than the narrowing processes of logical analysis and assembly. I've found that I get to a whole by acknowledging and trusting it as a whole, and by acknowledging and trusting myself as a whole. This includes trusting the type of knowledge that is not analytical, not logical, not word-tool based – it's a trusting of the not yet known that is outside my radar screen/surface self.

Acknowledging and allowing growth is key to sensing a whole. My belief that I need to "make things happen", and to force or mold a specific shape or end result, relates to our world of manufactured stuff. Compulsively checking all possible options is a form of trying to force life into an end result as if it were a jigsaw puzzle that would be incomplete if missing one piece. It's an attempt to force wholes into the word-tool world of this-not-that, and it hasn't worked for me.

To allow and trust interconnectedness in life, I've had to stop rejecting the mystery of what I don't know. I've had to stop trying to force everything I encounter through the this-not-that certainty of word-tools. I've had to stop immediately dismissing the noncognitive, and to stop fighting the feeling of "not knowing" by immediately putting everything I encounter into word format.

To open to Connectivity, I've needed to begin to believe in life, including so many things I know nothing about but that work for me every day. My disallowing and mistrusting have softened as I've been able to shift attention to the value of what I don't know, including how electricity comes into being, how the glands of my body work without instruction, and the energetic interconnectedness of all that surrounds me as discovered by the physics of quantum theory.

Putting attention on a whole as a whole, without using word-tool technology to break it into pieces, has helped me loosen the stronghold of compulsive comprehensiveness.

And it has helped me sense the whole of Source. As I allow and trust life to be the moving and growing that it is, rather than using comprehensiveness to force a preconceived end result, I live more harmoniously with reality, more as A Whole of The Whole.

To Identify Is to Follow the Crowd

I've generally viewed myself as quietly rebellious. When I was very young I remember being labeled an introvert. I was hesitant to speak at social gatherings, and I saw myself as shy.

Though shy, I often broke rules that many people typically did not – arriving late for work in a company where the boss expects you to be early, crossing the street against the light when no cars are coming, and climbing out the window of my bedroom when mom locked me in to punish me.

I thought of myself as a shy rebel, as different, and as somebody who quietly doesn't go along with the crowd.

But just now as I write, this pop-in surprised me: I *was not* a rebel, I *was not* any different from the crowd because I walked through life labeling myself just as most everyone else does. I defined myself as "quietly rebellious" as if these words described the essence of me. I held these identifications as a form of pride that said, *see, I'm different*.

During much of my life, identifications like these led to isolation and separation from others. Especially those that involved me as a know-it-all, superior intellectual.

- Every time I judged someone, I was above and they were below. I created an image that isolated/separated me. *See I am different/better/more-than.*

- During my sixteen year marriage, I went to California expecting to find a perfect job that would match my commitment to the intellect. I planned to commute from Utah, hoping my wife would agree to move to California later. For the two months I was there, I put all my time into job hunting and objective philosophy studies and did not contact old friends who lived in California. I had isolated/separated myself. *See I am different, better/more-than, and so brave to be doing this all alone in isolation.*

- During this time of life, me-vs-them was nearly always present. The *me* also included the relatively few others who studied objective philosophy, so it turned into *we*-vs-them. Viewing myself as a member of this group my mind could easily say, *See, I am different, better/more than, and also smarter.*

But just forming and carrying the thoughts "I am *abc* or *xyz*" or "we are *abc* or *xyz*" were ways of complying with what the world expects, in the most widespread, average, follow-the-crowd kind of way I can now think of.

By identifying/defining myself so specifically, I was doing what most people do. And I was giving words far more power than is warranted by their limiting this-not-that nature.

It doesn't matter that my specific labels, e.g. *quiet rebel* and *intellectual*, are different from the specific labels others put on themselves. What matters is the process itself – labeling myself and then locking into that word-enclosed identity as if it were the most important thing about me. That process is the same for anyone who does it. Only the specifics vary. The consequences of limited living are the same for all of us who trap ourselves into a word or an image-based identity.

But what else is there? How can I live without thinking of myself as someone with a specific identity?

I've gradually come to sense the "I am" without the this-not-that specification, without the limitations of a word-tool label or trait or characteristic, and without the separating/isolating thought patterns necessary to support the identification. When I sense this, the disjointedness within me and between me and others is gone. Instead I feel Connectivity.

My sense of a less defined "I am" arose partly through the Feel Good Now practice of mentally shifting away from negative tensions and judgments. Over and over again I found subtle support for this vague sense of "I am" from pointing my attention toward positives with less specification. It was as if the effects of my Feel Good Now practice were accumulating. I was gradually stepping into the value of what I don't know through doubting my initial judgments whenever I sensed the little bit of stress, the internal tension, associated with feeling less good.

This reminds me of a quote I included in the previous section "A Sense of Unfiltered Neutrality". Author Tara Brach's context may have been a bit different, but her words fit well with how it felt to move away from my own self identifications. She said, "I don't feel bad or good *about* myself; I just feel good."[32] To me, this points to a less-specific sense of self, something new and strange, a sense that felt very good as I encountered it more and more often through my many Connectivity experiences.

This new, more generalized "I am" feels like an open, relaxed sense of Being, with no trace of the tense, edgy feeling I get when I'm using word-tools with certainty. This "I am" assigns no meaning to comparison based concepts such as *different, better, more than, braver, smarter,* etc. When I sense this less specified "I am", I feel no need to bolster myself with labels that make me "differently good" in comparison to others. Within this new sense of self, there is no need to compensate for feeling inadequate, victimized, and small because "I just feel good".

---

[32] Tara Brach, *Radical Acceptance: Embracing Your Life with the Heart of a Buddha*, audiobook read by Cassandra Campbell, Chapter 3, 10:20 (Tantor Audio, 2012); in print format Chapter 1, page 9 (New York: Bantam, 2004).

Identification of myself as a *rebel*, as different from and better than, and as firmly committed to the intellect and to word-tools as the only truth – all this was following the crowd in a way that's deeper than I ever thought possible. Identifying myself in this way was a process I adopted at a very young age but didn't become aware of until a relatively old age.

The identifications that I thought made me uniquely different were really just a way of being just like everyone else. Perhaps many in this "everyone else" category also think their specific identifications make them uniquely different. But the locking into an identity is the same for all of us. Just like the rest of the crowd, I had trapped myself in the narrow this-not-that confines of the limits of language tools. I had buried the fundamental sense of "I am" underneath layers of specifics that used word-tools to create a false self, the ego/surface self.

Now, as I remove layer after layer, I sense the uncovering of my essential nature: the "I am" that is prior to all word-tools – prior to expectations, *shoulds*, comparisons, and evaluations. Even just the small glimpses I've experienced have felt incredibly liberating. Oddly enough, by giving up the specific identifications of me, I feel more fully myself than ever before. And at the same time, I feel more fully connected to others than ever before.

Part 3: A Whole of the Whole

Against Word-Tools?

When I was a child, more attention went toward just Being: feeling the sun on my face, breathing in scents of spring flowers, and relishing the sensations in my body as I lay on the grass in my yard.

But with more and more of my focus on word-based tools such as correct ideas, methods, logic, decision making, etc., less and less of my attention went toward simple Being. Except for some exposure to music and other arts, anything noncognitive was nonexistent for me.

By their nature, all word-based cognitive tools have limitations. Once I came to be aware of the limitations, I was able to reactivate attention toward Being.

But guess what? I occasionally overreact regarding the limitations of word-tools. I make the mistake of viewing word-tools as something to be "against". I sometimes view them as *bad things* that pull me down. Coming away from word-tool dominance was a process to be patient with.

As I started to become aware, I would so often catch myself being lost in concepts and then making a choice based only on logic. But then I would shift my attention to the whole of something natural, such as a tree or a flower. If met by many possible choices, I'd aim to select whichever one seemed more wholistic or the one that brought within me the most positive energy rather than the most logic based option. As first steps, this kind of shifting attention toward Source helped me break away from my word-tools-as-boss obsession. As I practiced choosing against logic, I became clearer that more wholistic choices exist, and that they seem to work better.

I had a dance teacher who used to say, "If fear is the *only* thing holding you back, do it." To me, this was not logical until I realized that the word "only" implied that there must be many positive things drawing me toward what I was considering. Otherwise why would I need to be "held back"? I viewed my dance teacher's suggestion as "Don't avoid positives just because you feel fear. If fear is the only negative, then do it." I've discovered that when I'm lost in concepts, fear often overshadows the positives and makes them almost imperceptible.

So often in my life, positives have seemed hidden by fear, just as they are hidden in my dance teacher's statement. Now I realize positives are hidden only when we allow reality to be swallowed up by word-tools and their products. When we allow nothing else, we don't see all that we've disallowed – we place 100 percent of our attention on the stuff of the world and the unquestioned busyness of our daily surface lives.

Using my dance teacher's suggestion, I also sensed that the positive reasons didn't need to be explained logically. The engagement of the positives can simply *be*, they don't have to be put into word-tool form. I began to sense that choosing without clear reasons often put me in touch, just a little, with something that was real but wasn't easily expressed in word format.

I chose against logic today. I went to the coffee shop that was farthest from my house, even though there were four other shops closer. I had no errands near the farthest shop and no other reason to drive that far. I could have easily, and with less time and car expense, gone to one of the nearer shops. But when I looked at how my inner energies seemed to respond, I felt the most positive energy for the shop that was furthest away.

I still do a lot of choosing "against" logic. As I come out of being totally lost in concepts, this choosing "against" seems like a preliminary step, like using training wheels on a bike before your body knows how to balance. When my mind starts churning around all the logical reasons to avoid the social gathering, for example, but my energies are pulling me to go, I use the churning logic as a sign that I'm stuck in word-tool domination.

So what I'm calling choosing *against* logic, would be better referred to as choosing *for* positive energies, like with Feel Good Now. Because of the positive energies that my fear is working hard to hold me back from, going to the social event is likely to bring more enjoyment than avoiding it, no matter how much logic spins around about why I say I don't want to go. I've found that most of my logic churning is tied to this type of fear so easily kept hidden by gyrations of thought.

Now I view thought and logic as belonging to a category which forms only one of many different tools available to me. And I don't let this category dominate my choosing. I might have gone with the "logical" coffee-shop choice today if I had a time constraint and an errand near that shop. Or maybe I still would have gone to the shop I felt the most positive energy toward and made it a shorter coffee session. Either way I'm much more open to allow the many potentially-hidden options into my consciousness when I'm not trapped in the *should* to be logical.

It's not that I am against word-based tools, such as logic and cognition, it's that I support using a wider scope of possibility for my choosing. I aim to put my attention toward a whole-me sense of what I want. And if the whole-me choice seems counter to what logic would say, I remind myself that logic is only one type of tool, that it is highly limited as are all word-tool products, and that for most of my life, I've been blindly immersed in it to the exclusion of all else.

Once I see it as the tool it really is, there is no need to be against it. I don't feel that I need to be against a hammer, or a ruler, or a spatula, because I clearly see each as just a tool with a specified function. I feel no threat of being dominated by them. So I say to myself, let's specify the function of the language/word-tools we use. Let us step back and see words as the tools they are with all their limitations. Let us stop viewing them as the only way to know, and as the only catalysts for doing. Let us stop misusing and getting lost in them.

It's not that I live more fully because I often make choices that seem to be against logical thinking. I live more fully because I've opened up to the whole-self functioning of my entire Being.

So am I against word-tools? No, although it may occasionally sound as if I am.

Rather, I am for whole-self functioning, free of the effects of word-tool domination, such as the logical mind as boss. For me, even though there is the whole of Source, there is no boss – I have dethroned my egoic surface self from its dictator position and I'm not replacing it with another boss called Source. The causes/effects/variables come from far too many different places, plus I haven't experienced Source as something that tells me what to do or punishes me for not doing what I should. I am A Whole of The Whole, and I aim to use all the available energies and tools to navigate that whole.

Kill It! It's Only a "Robot"

A movie called *Automata* tells of robots developed to help humans stay alive after solar storms have wiped out most of Earth's population. The robots had been programmed to always protect and honor life. And their actions fit.

Somehow, the robots learned to repair and enhance their own functioning. They learned to advance themselves. Yet their advancements were not for the purpose of ego boosting, they were purely to survive and to serve life better.

Some humans lashed out and destroyed robots out of fear, anger, and unconsciousness. Despite this, the robots always honored the lives of humans, even those humans who had destroyed other robots. The robots continued to enhance themselves, even at the risk of losing their own functioning through destructive actions of some of the humans.

The enhancements initiated by the robots seemed to threaten the humans because the robots were designed to obey orders given only by the humans. The humans did not understand how the robots were enhancing themselves, so they continued to react violently against the robots.

Not only did the robots seem more conscious and compassionate than most of the human beings, they appeared to be wiser than the humans about words being only tools.

In one conversation toward the end of the movie, the main character asked a robot, "Are you the boss?" The robot replied,

"'Boss' is a human thought structure."[33] Their interaction seemed to suggest that, for the robots, there was no such function as a *boss*.

In another interchange, one of the robots said, "Surviving is not relevant. Living is. We want to live."[34] Here the robot seemed to be putting "quality of life in the moment" above "survival at any cost". That is, if survival required destroying lives, survival isn't worth it because that kind of survival isn't really living.

Most of the humans in this movie were clearly lost in concepts. Yet the actions of the life-loving robots were clear to see. The humans were so afraid of what did not fit their thought structures that they could not see, nor honor, life-giving forces coming through the form of a robot.

Conditioned by layer upon layer of conceptual misuse, most of these humans could not acknowledge love of life when it was right in front of their eyes. They functioned only through the filtering of their frozen, word-dominated surface-self "knowledge".

Even the main character, who was beginning to notice their life-giving qualities, said to one of the robots, "You are only a machine".[35]

How could people discount a life-loving force this way? Only through concepts. Only word-tools in the mind make this possible.

Creating the shorthand tag of a conceptual group requires that details and a wider perspective akin to wisdom are ignored. The reality of uniqueness and Connectivity is dropped. When I've used

---

[33] *Automata*, directed by Gabe Ibáñez, written by Gabe Ibáñez, Igor Legarreta, and Javier S. Donate (Los Angeles: Millennium Entertainment, 2014) DVD.
[34] *Automata*.
[35] *Automata*.

words without realizing this distortion, I too have behaved with disregard for life. When lost in concepts, I too am easily blinded to reality and to life, just as the main character in the movie was when he said, "You are only a machine". From his perspective, based on his conceptual framework, he was right. But there is more to life than perspectives and conceptual frameworks – there is more to life than word-tools.

When I lapse into the blindness of totally believing my word-tools, my energies are just as cruel and dismissive as those of the humans who "killed" the life-loving robots in this movie. Am I blaming myself? No, I was simply acting unconsciously as I forgot that word-tools, beliefs, and thoughts are only real *as symbols*. They are not reality – they only symbolically represent reality.

The life-giving actions of the robots were a reality – a reality not allowed by the narrow filtering of a conceptual framework. The word *machine* was taken more seriously than the reality and honoring of life. Words were created as tools for serving life, yet in this movie, the humans lost sight of what matters most as they gave higher priority to word symbols than to life.

I am gradually weaving into my Being the realization that reality and life come first, both first in time and first in priority. As this occurs, another realization has begun taking shape. The separations around us that seem so real are actually more a product of the this-not-that nature of words than of reality as a whole. Words are only symbols created to point us in the direction of what is real. And in the same way, the separation between me and you is more symbolic than it is real.

Who cares what symbolic label we put on them? Look at what they do and how they actually contribute to life. And the "they" can be anything, whether we attach the words *machine* or *organism,* or *alive* or *dead*, or *different* or *same*. All the words are just symbolic.

What's real is whether or not there is consciousness rather than blind fear behind the doing. And this determines whether or not the actions contribute to life or lead to destruction.

Although the robots in *Automata* were made from synthetic material, they were able to transcend their systems of synthetic symbols and electronic circuitry, something that for me has seemed so difficult . . . but so worth the effort.[36]

---

[36] Note – Once while I was editing this section, I took a break to put clean sheets on my bed. The words "I hate to make the bed" crossed my mind as I began. I say this often. If I'd clung firmly to those words, I would have again hated making the bed.

But this time noticing the words evoked their insignificance. Instead of being swallowed up by them, I reminded myself that "hating to make the bed" was not some truth deep inside me. It's just an image made of words that associate with an emotion I created by taking all these symbols and images too seriously. With just a tiny effort, I shifted attention to parts of the process I may be able to enjoy. I noticed and actually enjoyed the soft texture of the sheets as I worked with them. I found pleasure in securing these nice clean sheets in a way that would make my sleep more comfortable.

Shooting and smashing the life-giving robots out of fear is not so different from hating to make the bed. Both are negative energies that flow counter to the joy of living that lies right in front of my eyes.

So I say to the robot, "I'm with you, I want to live too." And to my bed-making process I say, "I am with you, and I honor all parts of this chance to live a moment of my life in a way that flows with, not against, the joy of living."

Giving Up Absolute Importance

When I set a goal as absolutely important, I can't help but view myself as absolutely important too. My mind locks in on the goal as being more important than other aspects of life. Any successful step increases my feeling of self-importance, of superiority, not just above other people but above everything around me. Consequently, I close out distractions and anything that may interfere with progress.

Instead of Connectivity with my surroundings, I intensify feelings of separateness and superiority. *After all, I'm a hero pursuing crucial ends. My goal and me, we are superior to existence. The world is here only to serve me in accomplishing my goal.*

If this begins to sound a bit edgy, and perhaps not so heroic or good, then my surface self will use different word-tools to create a more favorable image. *I'm a catalyst for a great achievement that will benefit many people. So anything I do to achieve it is for a good cause.* The end, the absolute I'm calling "good", justifies the means.

This rigid approach supports and gives my world of words a stronger hold – viewing goals as "absolutely important" is part of my being lost in concepts.

Isn't being heroic this way seen as "the best of what people can be"? Don't our movies and literature praise an unwavering (rigid) attachment to accomplishing goals?

To set a vision and commit to making it real, to work toward creating something without ever giving up, to stand firm and step forthrightly against opposition, then finally to achieve the vision, the end you set for yourself . . . isn't it the absolute importance that keeps the hero going? Isn't it the single-minded, firm resoluteness that turns your vision/goal into a reality?

This is what we are often taught. For most of my life I held this idea as "the good". The unbending hero was something I wanted to be and wanted to find in others. Even though I was never the physically tough, macho type, I carried the same sort of rigid, hero-worship of "the good" but in an intellectual way.

Then finally, I began to sense a different path, a different choice in how I could view life, a different base for things I do. Sometime during the beginning of sensing these differences, the words "A Whole of The Whole" popped into my mind. Did I set a vision or goal to find these words? Did I stand against opposition? Did I view finding these words, or any title for a book, as absolutely important?

No. I was simply engaged in a Feel Good Now exploration of ideas that surprised me at first, and then began to fit my own sense of a deeper "me" and a deeper reality. These ideas that initially shocked me at times, gradually made more sense as I applied them in daily experience and saw how they integrate into a picture of reality that is much wider than word-symbols can provide.

There was no absolute importance surrounding pop-ins like "A Whole of The Whole". It's as if they were able to flow through because I had loosened the constriction created by clinging to a righteously rigid commitment to concepts, words, logic, etc. This loosening allowed new ideas that pointed toward a fuller life of joy, and a feeling of being grounded that replaced the need for confidence or for any status-based feelings of achievement and success.

Stepping away from domination by word symbols that seemed so absolutely important, away from evaluation and judgment, and out of the grip of separateness that word-tools encourage so well – it was like unburying my body from the ground, where only my head had been above the surface, chattering away as always about the external causes of my internal unhappiness. I was now free to move and breathe rather than be restrained by the this-not-that world in which I had buried my body and my whole self.

My head, the intellect, had been the only thing I considered important. I lost myself in concepts by putting almost all of my attention on them. My body, people who don't share my ideas, nature, and anything noncognitive – I had dismissed all of this as irrelevant and unimportant. I had used absolutes to exclude every non-word, nonconceptual part of life.

What's the alternative to the heroic, righteous pursuit of visions and goals that are absolutely important? How can I shift away from what I've always considered "the heroic best" of what human beings do?

Instead of absolutist goals, how about soft aims that adapt to changing circumstances? How about actions based on the wider alignment of Connectivity rather than the narrowing limitation of logical proofs? How about functioning that allows growth and Arm-in-Arm with Source, rather than the single-minded, unwavering approach that so often becomes destructive as it charges ahead like an unstoppable bull toward an unchangeable, because preconceived, end result?

Does this mean I am giving up on values of heroism? No. I can continue pursuing, without single-mindedly excluding the wholeness of life that makes any pursuing worth doing in the first place. I can even stand firm against opposition, as long as I also remain open to what's outside the tiny radar screen of my own belief system. I can resolutely keep going, as long as I'm willing to change my path if that's what reality calls for, and as long as I use all these word-thingies as posts in the sand rather than immovable posts in cement.

Actions unshackled from absolute importance are open to natural growth of my inner seed as I expand attention to the entire environment from which I am nurtured.

This unshackling happens in two ways for me. First, it's letting go of clutching so tightly to the known while I acknowledge the vastness of what I don't know. I stop clinging to my word-tooled surface self as if it were the only path to truth, and as if it were of life-and-death importance. I admit to not being able to control it all and open up to the power of what I don't know.

Second, I surrender to my mind's nature as a jabbering know-it-all. This means I allow it to be what it is, but not more than what it can be. I don't take it too seriously.

When I am able to release my mind and its word-tools from the too stringent demand of being the source of truth, my mind is happier. Seeing the mind only as a tool takes the pressure off the poor thing because it had been trying so hard and for so long to be something it just couldn't be. And perhaps because it could never be what was demanded, it became a ruthless dictator to cover up its inadequacy.

Instead of viewing my mind as boss, instead of using word-tool products as absolutes, I expand my living to include Source, which is where all the word-tools come from in the first place. Before words there was Source, which includes, admits-to, and allows the vastness of the non-word, nonconceptual, non-mind. When I admit-to and allow this vastness, I stop trying to force life into my limited preconceptions.

For me, it's a challenge to give up absolute importance. And it's happened only partially. It's been a gradual and indirect giving up, not something I could do through willpower, not like an on/off switch.

The softness of this surrendering flows over into life in general. Yes, I can influence what happens. But I don't have absolute control – it just doesn't work when I try to force a result by giving it the status of "absolutely important".

The surrender works like water. Water is flexible, soft, and yet forthright. It goes where it will, but gently, without pushing before something is ready.

I've tried to use absolutes to force things to happen, to be the way I want them to be. But, absolutes and force don't work – not long term, and not for the whole.

In his book *Tao: The Watercourse Way*, Alan Watts quotes Lao-tzu as saying, "The most gentle thing in the world overrides the most hard."[37] Same with people, same with myself, same with the interconnected environment from which I grow as A Whole of The Whole.

---

[37] Alan Watts, *Tao: The Watercourse Way*, Chapter 3: Tao, page 47 (New York: Pantheon Books, 1975).

Panoramic Sensing

One day while driving down the street I consciously noticed all the many buildings, cars, sidewalks, roads, signs, fences, and so many other sights. It occurred to me that my attention is easily drawn to all of these fabrications, things made by bringing together material or parts. Then I realized that being surrounded by fabrications fits my habitual way of viewing the world as more separated and less connected.

I have a habit of mentally cutting things up into pieces and viewing them as being formed by an outside force. Things created by people, what I call fabrications, are formed by sticking together a bunch of separate pieces. But the wholes created in nature are not. For me it's a shift in perspective to view things as wholes.

The separate parts are easier to deal with; at least that's what I've been conditioned to think. Word-tools, by artificially severing wholes that are real, distort reality in order to create quick-to-use communication shortcuts. As noted in other sections, not taking the word-tool shortcut would be to physically take the person to the sight of what I want to tell about. We would point and look together rather than trying to describe by using a bunch of word-tools.

I often remind myself that word-tools freeze the motion of life and pull out only tiny slivers of what is in constant motion. For example when I label her as *beautiful*, or him as *strong*, or her as *smart*, I am in essence breaking the whole of that person into pieces.

That's why Connectivity has been so helpful as I practice applying the realization that words distort reality. It helps point my mind back to wholes as it reminds me, again and again, of the reality of the interconnections that word-tools cannot carry.

Tara Brach wrote, "Where attention goes, energy flows."[38] As my attention gets so easily pulled toward separation, I strengthen and maintain an illusion that "all things are single, separate, isolated". Connectivity is gone and seemingly nonexistent, as the energy of separateness flows through me and out toward all I encounter.

I remind myself that I do encounter things that are not created by assembling parts, and one of those is me. Another is you, and every other human being, and every living thing.

Despite this reminder, I sometimes find it difficult to keep in mind the many non-partitive wholes that surround me. That's how another Connectivity practice arose for me, the practice of widening the visual span of what I looked at. Instead of always looking at one building, car, or tree, I would widen the picture by including many of these things all at once.

I start by consciously putting attention on one visual element. Then I widen my attention to include more to the right and more to the left. As I expand the attention even wider so that my view spans almost one hundred eighty degrees, it often brings out a feeling of awe and a sense of nonseparation among the sweep of "separates".

This widening of my gaze, stage by stage, to sweep across an entire landscape, brings on a feeling of calm. Creating these all-inclusive views of wider visual scenes, *without putting names or meanings onto them*, and *without analyzing them into pieces*, brings a sense of gentle relaxation. It feels both soothing and energizing.

It is as if I am exercising a new sense: the nonconceptual sense of Connectivity that concepts and words cannot hold. It's sort of

---

[38] Tara Brach, *True Refuge: Finding Peace and Freedom in Your Own Awakened Heart,* page 151 (New York: Bantam Books, Reprint edition 2016).

like feeling into the continuity of my surroundings rather than just reasoning into it.

Walking through the city on my way home, I sometimes bounce around with my attention as if to sweep across more than just the visual. I scan different sensations and discover the cool air on my nose as I breathe it in; my feet on the sidewalk as I realize there is earth underneath; the warmth of sun on my head; the sounds of sirens, cars, trucks, and breezes; along with the sights of clouds, trees, and houses.

This practice has worked to expand my perspective as I cross over many interconnected wholes using many different senses. It's like an exercise in broadening my outlook that helps offset the continuous splatter of narrowing separates that word-tools and fabrications bombard me with. Allowing my attention to carry these kinds of panoramas of Connectivity brings out a sense that *I am with* the whole of reality.

Almost every time I create a panoramic view of this type, I feel a sense of gratitude and Connectivity. When I'm driving, walking, or sitting, I practice creating these wider views, and I get just a bit of a sense of touching Source.[39]

---

[39] Note: Finding my own ways to sense Connectivity helped me shift away from an exclusively conceptual knowing to a whole-Being type of knowing. I view these findings as discoveries of self-science that any of us may explore as we place more attention on our own inner experience rather than exclusively on word-based reports of scientific "experience" from outside sources.

Science from outside sources appears so proven and factual because it's made up of tightly woven word-tooled structures. But as their abstract complexity increases, these scientific structures drift further and further from reality. What appears proven and factual so often leaves out the Connectivity that word-tools cannot carry. And the layer upon layer of conceptual grouping at every level omits the uniqueness of what's real at the base of your own experience and mine.

This practice of panoramic sensing reminds me I have access to a direct kind of knowing that doesn't require word-tools.

A Different Kind of Knowing

Years ago, and still at times, I have a compulsion to check something perceptually.

- Did I lock the door? I want to see it with my eyes, so I go back and check.

- The stove, did I turn it off? Same thing, go back to see the dial in the *off* position.

Gradually, I began to trust my automated self a little more. I'd pull out of my driveway and drive thirty feet down the road. I'd think, *Did I lock the door to my house?* It would be so easy to go back to perceptually check because I was only thirty feet away. Instead, I'd remind myself of how automatic my habit of locking the door was. I would figuratively pat myself on the shoulder and mentally say, *It's okay, Steve, you can trust your subconscious.*

This is not to say that I didn't at times forget things. During this same period of learning to trust myself, I left the stovetop gas burner on at least two or three times. When I got home, I found a low flame or the house smelling of gas. First, my surface self threatened me with fearful criticism. But as I shifted attention away from the critical threats, I simply thought, Hmm, I'll remember to be more aware of the stove before I leave the house next time.

Years before, I would have followed my first self-criticism with a stream of intimidating self-torment: Steve, you better watch it! The house could burn down! The insurance wouldn't cover it since it would be your fault! How could you forget this again?! Something is seriously wrong, and you really need to correct this!

I remind myself that our culture, especially as expressed in the news, highlights worst pictures, disasters, and flaw finding. Almost everywhere I turn in the media, I can find what's wrong in the world and what bad thing might happen. Mainstream media rarely shows what's right.

And our word-tools fit well with this leaning toward what's wrong, or could be wrong, inviting separateness, conflict, and our we-vs-them mentalities. My internal threats, along with the worst pictures I sometimes feel surrounded by, are supported by word-tool limitations. Word-tools are like assistants that help keep these negatives flourishing. When we aren't aware of their limitations, they can only narrow our views. Word-tools are not suited to standing back and seeing a wide perspective. They can't take in and hold the type of awareness that a more wholistic outlook can bring.

During this period of gradually coming to trust something more than word-tooled functioning, it was as if I were taking first steps toward a different kind of knowing. I was seeing hints of the idea that my awareness didn't need to be confined to cognition. I didn't need to remember a concrete image of me locking the door, I didn't need to constantly doubt and go back to perceptually check things. I could begin to sense and trust that I did it, even if occasionally I still forgot to turn off the gas burner. Just as I trust my whole self to circulate blood and make my glands work, I can trust my whole self to lock the door and turn off the stove.

Sure, we call the automatic functioning of the body autonomic, and we've traced this functioning to brain functions that are different from those that underlie choices like checking the lock and the stove. But when my mind goes to these bits of scientific knowledge, I regard it as getting sidetracked back toward being lost in concepts. The science provides interesting surface details. But if I forget that science is limited by its word-tools, I can easily get pulled away from the wider awareness that is always waiting to be uncovered when I can open up to more than what word-tools provide.

So for me it has been a challenge to trust. But I could see that doubting and perceptually checking were stressful, and that they were bound to our highly limited word-tools in the form of what some call "the voice in the head". I began to experience more and more that trusting my whole self carried less tension. The trust developed as I stopped believing the threats of my doubtful, worrisome mind, and experienced the calm and reduced tension that came out of that.

Sometimes I felt a global discomfort and I would go back to check the stove. Other times when I felt discomfort, I looked inside more carefully and saw it was fear driven; I could recognize my usual worst picture and cautionary, logic-based intimidations.

I am now wary of deciding and taking action based on my logic-based, worrying self. I sense a growing comfort in relying on my global whole self. If I feel a global comfort that doesn't seem to have my logic-only rigidness, I follow that sense and go back to check the stove or the lock. If all I can find is a push from logic-only rigidness that "you should check to make sure", I reject that cautionary warning as part of my word-based conditioning, as if it were just the noise of a menacing mind. I remind myself again that my internal body functions don't need constant checking. And neither does my whole-self functioning.

And guess what? The stove and the lock on my door have been fine. All that worry and caution was nothing but wasted energy. I've found that I can trust the workings of my wider whole self, and no longer need to feel threatened and trapped by my logic-dominated, afraid-of-the-world self.

For me, this was a different kind of knowing than what I'd been used to. And it carried with it a new way of viewing the world. Through watching my mind, I was opening up to a wider-ranged, less-constrained form of being in the world. It seemed foreign to my way of making absolutely sure things are right.

And surprisingly, this stepping away from dependence on perceptual/cognitive certainty brought a more widely secure feeling, an assurance that seemed almost like confidence, but not the comparison-based kind I'm used to where I walk around feeling "I know a lot, so I'm sure of myself". It felt infused throughout, as if it emanated widely, including me but without a focal point on me. It felt grounded without any need to worry about loss or safety – trust instead of fear, and flow instead of doubting and worrying.

Does this sound risky? I find it far more risky to remain in a fear-based, rule-bound state that relies only on word-tool logic as the basis for action. Total dependence on any tool, seems much less secure. That type of constriction is not living, it's only avoidance of dying.

Just as with flaw finding, where I can find flaws anywhere and everywhere, if my primary driver is to avoid dying or danger or loss, my mind will find reason for avoidance anywhere and everywhere. That's how the mind works when dominated by the this-not-that nature of word-tools.

So I am sensing hints of a different kind of knowing. A knowing that is wider than a word-tool that works as a shortcut by including only one type of "it" while excluding everything else in reality.

This different kind of knowing has been with me always, but buried under many layers of word domination. It's a knowing I've ignored and denied until recently. Yet it operates every day and every minute in the functions of my body and in the natural world that surrounds me. As I sense this wider knowing, I also sense that the trust I am building fits more than just my whole self. It fits the whole of reality, the energies of life itself, the life that came before words and functions without needing them.

Evaluation – A Misuse of Word-Tools

Once I became aware I was almost continually evaluating people or life situations as good or bad, I began to notice a sharp edge underneath. I started sensing a feeling of crusty roughness inside whenever that type of judgment crossed my mind. It's an edginess that feels like I'm emitting a general irritation out toward life itself.

It also feels as though I've separated myself, as if I'm detached from what's in front of me, or as if the evaluation puts a filtering screen between me and reality.

To evaluate is to put oneself above something, usually by bringing in some type of comparison, and then concluding that one thing is better than another. This works fine if I'm purchasing something simple at the store and choosing based on what I view as best for me in my particular situation. But this makes up a very small proportion of the evaluations that flow through my thoughts – most are about people or situations.

I've come to view evaluation as misusing word-tools, just as I've come to see putting myself above anything as invalid. Reality is the base of everything, including the words, thoughts, and ideas I use to compare and measure. I now see it as a mistake to take a seat above reality and judge interconnected wholes such as people and situations. Words, and the highly limited thought patterns made up of them, simply don't warrant that.

The miniscule portion of reality that words carry, along with their limited this-not-that functioning, makes them inadequate for the kind of judging my mind does most of the time. Words indicate general directions to look in, and they aren't even close to being able to carry "the whole truth". I like what Eckhart Tolle says: "Words are only pointers."[40]

As this-not-that shortcuts, words can take us only a short distance, and only on the surface. And that short distance depends on using them with awareness of their limitations as only tools. When I attempt to use them for more than they can be, I take away from life rather than add to it. When I apply evaluations and judgments, I am distorting what's in front of me, and I know this through the tension they create inside. It is often almost unnoticeable, but when I'm alert to it, I find tension whenever I judge.

Evaluation sets up an opposition between me and what I'm looking at. But there is no opposition in source reality — opposition arises only through our interpretations, only when we introduce word-tools. A whole does not oppose itself. But our this-not-that tools create artificial opposition buckets. They function as tools of exclusion that allow nothing but "this kind". They lead to separation rather than highlighting the Connectivity of reality that constantly surrounds us.

Source is the whole, and it is outside of bad and good, which is to say it is beyond evaluation using our limited word-tools. It just *is*. I just *am*. You just *are*. Even though it is outside evaluation, Being itself is good in a sense because *it is*.

As an outflow of Source, every Being is ultimately good, as good as life itself. Its core is good, even if that core has been buried under layer upon layer of word-tool opposition and destructiveness.

I can hear my mind counter-arguing: *Steve, if anyone is detached*

[40] Eckhart Tolle, a lecture I attended titled "An Evening with Eckhart Tolle", June 17, 2016", quote is also included in the announcement for the lecture accessed December 2, 2017 at https://www.soundstrue.com/store/eckhart-tolle-denver

from reality, it's you for offering such a crazy idea. How can evil be good?

I'm not saying that being a killer or destroying life is good. If I see destructive actions, I consider what I can do to contribute to a change. But change does not require me to introduce the same kind of evaluative killer energy that fueled the destructive actions in the first place.

Righteously calling out that "The killer is evil!" is one of the causes of destruction. I sense killer energy inside me when I hear myself saying: *It's right and good to destroy evil killers; I'm not like them because I am destroying destruction – I need to kill them because they killed first and I must prevent them from killing others!* These are statements I hear from my mind, and I'm in the process of considering how I can contribute to changing them.

So how did I come to claim that evaluation is a misuse of concepts, of word-tools? How could I admit to what many, perhaps most, would call an insane point of view?

I began to get a sense of it by repeatedly breaking through my own negative labeling of people around me. Over and over again, I kept finding goodness at the core of people who I had initially judged as *bad* in some way. When I looked beyond the surface of what I created with word-tools, I found glowing treasures hiding beneath, and this led to feeling a deep sense of interconnectedness that I now find everywhere.

As I experience Connectivity, I find that every Being is ultimately good.

But when I'm stuck in my egoic surface self, I don't see this ultimate goodness. All I can see is the realm of separateness created by trusting word-tools as if they were more than life itself. So when I find I am in this stuck place, I remind myself to trust life, not the words flowing through my mind.

When I'm constricted inside and not open enough to drop my labels, I believe them as true and react negatively to people around me. My own constricted reactions then prevent both of us from finding the goodness at the core of each other. That's because the negative energy I introduce by stuffing a person into a word-tool bucket makes us both *bad*. Neither one is open enough to allow our hidden treasures to show.

No person can fit inside of a word-tool bucket – every this-not-that is far too restrictive. Word-tools barely touch the surface of a whole person or a whole situation.

Evaluation and judgment are cognitive creations, and it is out of place to use them to judge that from which they came. A hammer, a scissors, a computer – along with any gadgets, devices, or tools we create – are inapplicable to evaluating the sources from which they came. Yet we've been conditioned to misuse word-tools this way.

Life experience is the starting point for all symbols. Symbols can only represent, but life is *what is*, life is what's being represented by the symbols, and as such life always takes precedence. When we make the mistake of attempting to evaluate a person or situation, we are acting under the illusion that word-tools have no limits, as if the symbols are more than the reality they are meant to stand for.

When we engage with life, we find we want to share what we find. We want to communicate it. But to fully communicate it to another person, that person would need to experience that engagement for themself.

When I use words as if they are without limits, I don't accomplish communication, I detract from it. I create something that looks like communication but isn't, because the tools I'm using just can't do it if I'm unaware of their limits.

As we pull concepts from life experience, most of what's real remains behind. The limitations of a this-not-that allows a word-tool to carry only a tip of the iceberg of the reality it came out of. (See "Uniqueness and Connectivity" for more on the reality that is left behind.)

I cannot rightfully put myself above reality by presuming to evaluate or judge it using word-tools that were derived from It. Yet that's what I'm doing when I place good/bad evaluations on human beings. When I apply word-tools to judge the value of life or its Beings, I am misusing those tools.

I feel it in the bodily tension, I sense it in its wider implications, and I can see the negative results. When I presume to evaluate what is real, I misuse the word-based/synthetic standards that can only be secondary to life. When I forget their limitations, I give them a power wider than they are able to handle.

Our good/bad, right/wrong, succeed/fail evaluations don't serve life. They are a form of blaming life for not measuring up. *I think this person should be honest; I think life should be fair; I think there should be no more killing* – all these are forms of telling reality what it should be. It's a misuse of words because what I think reality should be is groundless compared to what reality actually is.

I have a business background, which leads me to wonder, what about employers? Don't they have to evaluate? Suppose I do nothing to contribute to an employer who pays me. Should the employer continue to pay me? Since word-tools are inadequate for judging, since I am a complex, interconnected whole with hidden treasures at my core, am I not saying it is a misuse of word-tools for the employer to judge my work and tell me I'll need to look for another job?

Of course not. But "firing the lazy bum" is far different from "it's not working out, and we can no longer pay you for what you do here".

Words are certainly appropriate for describing results of actions, but not for evaluating the value or core of the person who does those actions. The this-not-that, limited function of word-tools is appropriate when the employer says: "We agreed on these results; what can we do to get there?"

We choose our relationships, and we can use the neutrality of selectivity without judgment when we do it. Or we can accompany our choices with the blame baggage of evaluation and judgment. We can use word-tools in accordance with their limitations, or we can misuse them.

If the cabinet doesn't fit in the space, if I don't give the cashier enough money, if I didn't hit my brakes soon enough as I crash into the car in front of me – all of these "not enoughs" simply are. They are happenings.

Evaluating these "what is" happenings as poor workmanship, trying to cheat, or acting negligently are simply ways to create victims and aggressors from happenings that are in reality neutral. It is me who overlays the evaluation through my misuse of word-tools.

I often remind myself that change can only happen if I don't demean what I want to change, and only if I don't demean myself, others, or reality. If I want something to be different, there's no need to position myself as superior. I find that setting myself apart and above can only lead to more of the same or worse.

When I take the position of evaluator, I disconnect from the reality of life. I take myself out of reality as if I could float above it. I lose myself in the symbolic realm of word-tools, detached from the grounding I could get by connecting to Source.

Pop-Ins

I was too constricted to let life flow before I became aware of the limits of word-tools and of the thought stream that played them.

But then something different began to happen: I repeatedly noticed that most of my thinking was off base, false, or useless. Then and now, of all the thoughts flowing through my daily mental streaming, I rarely if ever find one that fits the whole of reality.

What does fit reality is a sense of Connectivity. And the sense of Connectivity arose only after I challenged my judgmental beliefs about people and situations. Finding that one thought after another did not fit reality, was like shining a light on my mind's ability to create illusion. And this led to an opening which allowed the first of what I call *pop-ins*. Here are some of the first pop-ins that came through.

- Judge your experience; not people, events, circumstances, or situations

- Wow! I don't believe in right/wrong or good/bad anymore!

- The value of what I don't know

- Indirect not direct

- A goal without consequence

- Enjoying knowing is different from enjoying knowing more than

- Grateful Being

- Using words in such a way as to highlight the connectivity from which they come rather than the separations to which they lead

- A Whole of The Whole

Each of these pop-ins came to me without effort, planning, or intention. As each popped into my mind, I wrote it down. Then every time I looked at it again, I liked it! I felt as if I were an outsider admiring someone else's words. Each one surprised me, because it seemed to come out of nowhere.

During the writing of this book, another image popped into mind. Each day, each week, I had a vague sense of feeling *Arm-in-Arm* as I put the words on paper. I still experience this feeling often even though there isn't a specified something or someone that I'm arm-in-arm with.

Pop-ins relate somehow to the sense of being Arm-in-Arm. And neither of them depends on figuring things out or proving them in a logical way.

I experience this "walking Arm-in-Arm" as cooperation or like a partnership where there is no boss. It's feels like a harmonious movement that's in tune, like me being aligned with what's around me. It's a sort of moving in tandem that feels like functioning as a whole. It's like fellowship, unity, and oneness.

What am I Arm-in-Arm with? Where are the pop-ins popping in from? When I push myself to put a word to it, my answer is Source. Perhaps I am at times Arm-in-Arm with Source. And when I am, I'm also moving as A Whole of The Whole.

When I allow this kind of natural movement without willpower, pressure, or force – aligning with, not resistant to, the whole of my environment – I sense creativity from a "oneness" that is new to me and continues to grow. I wonder how many others have this type of experience. I hope many of you do because each time something pops-in, I experience the joy of surprise and of gratitude for being alive.

Bad Deep Down

I know a man who is gentle, kind, intelligent, and genuinely compassionate. He once told me that at times he senses something bad deep down inside himself. I was surprised to find that as we talked, it seemed as though he felt this unspecified badness was more real than the good.

Today in the coffee shop, another friend voiced a similar idea of badness being more real than the good. She even said that her deep-down badness voices itself when she gets quiet for meditation, bringing forth statements such as: *I could be more kind* or *I'm a jealous person* or *I care too much about money and surface stuff*. We both wondered why the deep-down bad could seem more real than the good.

If the voices of our badness arise when we quietly relax into sensing who we really are, isn't that evidence that the bad is more real?

For me, this deep-down badness comes in the form of doubting my unique expression. I doubt my work and am tempted to give in to predominant viewpoints in the world: the importance of status, appropriateness, business success, selling, and popularity. All of this is doubt is held up by the mistake of believing that comparison, judgment, and superiority are generally valid for living daily life.

Instead of looking inside myself and tapping my own uniqueness, I look outside for how to do things and for what to be. I compare my work to what is commonly viewed as successful. My mind tells me to give up my uniqueness because it can't coexist in the world of status and popularity. It tells me to be safe and do what other successful people are doing. It says: "Don't create the new through your uniqueness. Follow a predetermined, already successful pattern." (Note that *pattern* can also be word-tooled as formula, template, or method.)

All that is just another way to describe my state of being lost in concepts.

The answer may seem obvious at this point, but why does the sense of a deep-down badness seem so prevalent? I wonder if it's because so many of us follow the crowd rather than our own uniqueness. Perhaps it's because we haven't found and fully committed to tapping into the deep-down goodness of life so we can find and shine our unique light out onto the world.

Maybe following the status-based, need-more, flaw-finding world of comparison and judgment keeps me aligned with the bad that happens in my world. And maybe that's what makes deep-down bad seem more real than the good in me, and more real than the good in all of us.

I find the following from Eckhart Tolle's *The Power of Now* to be relevant. A questioner said they didn't like the words *sin*, *unconsciousness*, or *insanity* because these words made them feel something was wrong with them, it made them feel judged. Eckhart's answer surprised me:

> Of course there is something wrong with you – and you are not being judged.
>
> I don't mean to offend you personally, but do you not belong to the human race that killed over one hundred million members of its own species in the twentieth century alone?

Eckhart goes on to explain:

> It is not a question of guilt. But as long as you are run by the egoic mind, you are part of the collective insanity. [41]

[41] Eckhart Tolle, *The Power of Now,* Chapter Six: The Inner Body, pages 109-110 (Novato, CA: New World Library and Namaste Publishing, 1999).

By looking within, I've discovered that my egoic mind functions by judging and comparing in order to create an illusion of superiority which is actually just a compensation for feeling inadequate because, being lost in concepts, I have lost touch with the goodness of my deep-down self and with the goodness of every form of life.

I'm not guilty, and neither are you, because we've been conditioned to function this way, to create a surface self and forget about our whole self. And yet, if I follow my egoic surface self rather than my whole self; if I turn away from my Unique Expressor because I value safety over creativity; if I follow the world's status-based, need-more, flaw-finding modes of comparison and judgment, don't I then add fuel to the fear-based confusion that leads to bad things happening in the world?

If I follow the dictum *I must do what they do to fit in and succeed* then I must also continue the illusion of separation and the we-vs-them energies of negativity.

All of this (supported by the misuse of word-tools) keeps energies more aligned with we-vs-them, and less aligned the vibrational possibilities of realizing the reality of Connectivity.

But when I stay fully in touch with my uniqueness by allowing the whole of me rather than losing myself in the this-not-that me, I experience Arm-in-Arm Connectivity that shines light on the illusion of separation and on the damaging nature of my enemy-mode mentalities. Those are times when I am not contributing to the destructive, unconscious insanity.

A few weeks before writing this, after talking to a friend who is well read in philosophy, I wrote the following in my notebook.

There is such a pull to compare mine with the outside, and

sometimes to enter and walk someone else's world. But if I walk in someone else's world, my unique expression will go unheard.

What's fun and amazing is to enter another's world while continuing to walk in mine. And my world is so enriched by the experience of entering another's world!

In my excitement about what this friend had read, I was tempted to stop my writing and read, read, read all the many exciting books he told me about. I experienced being pulled to walk another's world.

I experience the thought *I'm bad deep down* when I've lost touch with my whole self, and forgotten what I really am. Words encourage this loss by masquerading as holders of what's real, while at the same time excluding the uniqueness and Connectivity that is reality. So we think we are bad deep down when the reality is that we are good.

Perhaps fully committing to our uniqueness helps to expose the masquerade of our deep-down bad so that it no longer seems so real. Perhaps the thoughts of being *bad deep down* dissolve when we walk Arm-in-Arm with Connectivity, and as we enter and even honor the worlds of others but continue to walk our own, allowing our Whole-of-The-Whole uniqueness to shine through.

Being As the Payoff

While reading Eckhart Tolle's *The Power of Now*, I found the following: "Say 'yes' to life – and see how life suddenly starts working *for* you rather than against you."[42]

Life working *for* me has changed. It's less wrapped around specified results in the world. Now that I'm less lost in concepts, I don't as much view the results as primary. Life working *for* me doesn't feel like clinging to a goal, such as getting rich, or having romance, or house, or car, or even finishing this book.

Now I experience the primary payoff in the form of peace and gratitude and in the form of a cheery playfulness and affection toward life. I experience it in the form of simply Being.

Before I experienced Connectivity and Grateful Being, there had to always be some kind of payoff from the outside world. It was the cause and effect of "do something" then "get something" – money , attention, friendship, romance, adventure, good sensations – that was all I had known as payoff; it was what life was all about.

As a very lost-in-concepts guy, payoff also included the satisfaction of logical consistency. I needed to know why and how things would happen beforehand. It was as if all the reasons had to be lined up neatly like a row of dominos ready to be activated perfectly. It included the feeling that things must be as they should be. Things had to make sense to feed a pretty-picture endpoint as a payoff.

The way life is working for me now is deeper and fuller. There is a sense of inner peace and flow and of simply being here, feeling my

---

[42] Eckhart Tolle, *The Power of Now,* Chapter Two, Consciousness: The Way Out of Pain, page 35 (Novato, CA: New World Library and Namaste Publishing, 1999).

sit bones on this chair, on this floor, in this building, on this street, in this city, on this earth – this expansive sense of Connectivity feeds a feeling of gratitude for the simple fact of being alive.

I still often feel trapped in my word-tool world of surface self/ego and separateness. But I remind myself that life is not an all-or-nothing phenomenon. It's not that I've finally made it, because I'm more aware of the limits of my conditioned mind. Sometimes it feels like I've slid backwards even further. My mind tells me that increased awareness isn't working the way I had hoped. That's my mind seeking the surface payoff of cognitively measurable progress.

Then I experience again a moment of standing at the kitchen sink washing a mug or a spoon, looking out the window at the trees as they move with the breeze, feeling the warm water from the faucet as it flows over my hands. That's when I sense just my Being in those moments as the ultimate payoff. It's not specifically the trees I see or the warm water I feel. It's a payoff that has no object, as if the payoff is in the experiencing itself, as if the awareness itself feeds me in a way I had not before been conscious of.

This is a kind of living that word-tools can't help with. It must be sensed, realized, experienced. It can't be reasoned out or figured out using tools limited to a this-not-that labeling function – tools that are unable to flow with Connectivity as they try to freeze life and put it into rigid buckets.

Taking this further, this new outlook toward life feels like a merging of cause and effect. The cause becomes the effect. The doing itself becomes the payoff.

It's not that I no longer want secondary payoffs, such as money, intimate relationship, house, or car. It's that action toward any of these aims is transformed into Being as the primary. Being becomes the only end that's necessary, the only reward of ultimate importance. The experience of Being offsets the need for something outside me that has to fit the expectations of a pretty picture payoff.

When I don't hold as primary my preconceived agenda of a surface payoff, gratitude for the moment can move into the forefront and Being itself becomes the payoff.

A New Kind of Right

When the shocking thought *Wow! I don't believe in right/wrong good/bad anymore!* popped in, it wasn't from any thought of rejecting morality. I never would have dreamed of throwing out morality.

It was seeded by noticing blame and how blameful thoughts impact me. I think it started there because blame is closer to first-level concepts than morality is. First-level concepts are those at the home base of experience. They are closer to the real life happenings of an actual person, closer to what you and I see and feel directly. I can see, feel, and experience what blame does to me and to others. Blame resides right next to life experience. Whereas concepts involving the right/wrong of morality are more distant from this firsthand base of reality.[43]

Before coming to view right/wrong and good/bad as mostly detrimental, I was firmly committed to using moral concepts to judge. I believed it was the way to make myself and the world better. Honesty, independence, fairness, rationality – I believed actively measuring against these moral concepts was constructive. "Am I being honest? Am I acting too dependently?" And I judged other people by measuring against these rights and wrongs and then frequently concluded they were bad or undesirable.

---

[43] Here I remind myself that concepts/words are products of a process of grouping-together that leaves out most of what is real in order to create a short cut for communicating. The grouping that forms morality is many levels away from first-level experience. As an example of conceptual levels, *furniture* is a concept that is one level up from first. I can experience a *chair*, I can sit on it. I can do the same with a *table*. I can experience it firsthand by using it to support my dinner plate. But I can't sit on a *furniture* and I can't support my dinner on a *furniture*.

That's because a *furniture*, like morality, doesn't exist. But a *chair* and a *table* do exist at the first level of life, just as a specific person, animal, or plant do. Morality is many levels away from life, which is part of what allowed it to be used so destructively for so long. Replacing morality with a new kind of right, one aimed at the reality of Connectivity, will help us shift to more constructive ways to live.

That's why it was such a shock to me when the thought of not believing in right/wrong and good/bad popped in.

Experiencing blame doesn't feel good. In shifting my attention away from self-blame to something that felt a little better, I experienced firsthand an upturn in my energy and actions. Through practicing Feel Good Now, I saw the uselessness of blame in my living.

Here I want to repeat these words from Karen Horney's writings because they connect to the question of whether or not self-blame is desirable:

> There is a wide divergence of opinion about the desirability or necessity of a disciplinary inner control system for the sake of insuring moral conduct.[44]

Inside me, there was never a "wide divergence of opinion". An inner control system was an unquestionably good necessity. And yet, I have never liked feeling controlled by inner voices of discipline and blame. Have you?

But how can we be moral without blame and punishment? How can we be good without the discipline of feeling bad about oneself?

Again, I see Dr. Horney's further thoughts on this as worth repeating here:

> There is no doubt that such disciplinary methods can succeed in suppressing undesirable factors, but there is also no doubt that they are injurious to our growth. We do not need them because we see a better possibility of dealing with destructive forces in ourselves: that of actually *outgrowing* them.[45]

---

[44] Karen Horney, *Neurosis and Human Growth,* Introduction: A Morality of Evolution, page 14 (New York: W.W. Norton & Company, 1991).

[45] Horney, page 15. Dr. Horney also uses the words *inner straight jacket* in referring to these self disciplinary methods.

Instead of blame, I can learn to allow growth in myself and in others. It's not easy for me to avoid criticizing what I'm doing or what others do. But I have at times experienced what it feels like to relate to a person through the lenses of neutrality rather than judging/blaming.

As I sense the Connectivity of a nonjudgmental way of being in the world, I also sense my judgment impulse gradually diminishing. As I have felt more and more Connectivity, I've begun to see that word-tools are too limited for such wide reaching pronouncements as "how could you do such a stupid, bad thing?" or "you should have known better", whether directed at myself or at another person.

Even though I've discarded right/wrong and good/bad, I still feel I want to act in *good* not *bad* ways. I want to take actions that nurture my growth, and the growth of others. I've come to sense a more general, different kind of right/wrong and good/bad operating.

This more general kind of *right* is not riddled with the specified rules/guidelines from parents, religions, governments, societies, cultures, etc. Those rights/wrongs goods/bads mostly limit our growth and lead to feelings of rebellion.

Once I became aware of the tyranny of the *should*, and of experiencing it within myself, I realized that *shoulds* were a form of measuring against a standard and that they function as a blaming tool that we don't need. Nothing good ever came from these inner disciplinary tools, only a great deal of hurtful mind noise. My idealized self was always getting after my real self for "behaving badly".

This *shoulding* and blaming created a split inside. The self that started as a whole when I was a baby with no words became two selves as words became more prevalent in my life: (1) an "all in the head" right/wrong critic and (2) the genuine Being who simply wanted to grow and experience life without constraint. Now that I've experienced functioning as a whole again, I see that I feel so much better as a genuine Being without the unnecessary constraints of an evaluating conscience. Awareness of the limits of word-tools helped me experience this.

Right/wrong and good/bad is dominant in a split self, but it's irrelevant to an integrated whole self. Traditional morality has no place in a growing self that functions as a whole.

Life comes before the squiggly black lines and sound vibrations we create to symbolize it. Life takes precedence over word-tools, and over the moralities which are formed from these symbols.

So what is this new kind of "right"?

Connectivity – acceptance of me and all that is, as a growth-oriented interconnected process of Being and creativity.

It's right to see the countless dot-to-dot connections as I stand on this floor, in this house, on this street, among these people, etc.

It's right to look in the eyes of someone I've initially labeled negatively, and perhaps touch their face with my hand, and then dismiss the label as irrelevant to their actual Being, which is deeper than any label.

It's right to acknowledge how much my body "knows" automatically without any help from word-tools. A type of knowing that harmonizes with countless interconnections. A type of knowing I cannot fully grasp with my limited cognitive tools. Though I don't understand it, I see its results, just as I see the results of the electricity I do not understand when I turn on the light switch.

It's right to connect as often as possible with all that sustains my life: Earth, sun, air, people, animals, plants, and even the energy from nonliving objects. It brings a sense of peace in the moment when I honor whatever object I see, touch, hear, or experience in any way.

My awareness of the rightness of Connectivity grew as an Arm-in-Arm process of interacting with what was around me. Arm-in-Arm with what? With Source, with the whole of life that preceded words and doesn't need them to function. Shifting away from being lost in concepts was a process of recognizing, acknowledging, and honoring Source for what it is – the reality that concepts can never fully describe, and the reality from which they came.

Source is the starting place for all human processes including the particular type of symbol system we call language. Language is only one of perhaps many types of symbolic representation, and of many types of communication tool. I ask myself: What other tools might I find if I look outside my word-dominated radar screen and acknowledge the value of what I don't know?

Word-tools are limited because they cannot carry the vast interrelationships of the whole of reality. Once I recognize that limitation, I realize the potential for more than what our symbol system can represent, and I'm able to bring Connectivity into daily living.

I view Eckhart Tolle's words as fitting: "Right action is action that is appropriate to the whole."[46]

To me, this simple statement summarizes a Connectivity which is a new kind of right for me.

---

[46] Eckhart Tolle, *A New Earth, Awakening to Your Life's Purpose*, Chapter Eight: The Discovery of Inner Space, page 238 (New York: Plume, 2005).

Creating a Mental "It"

What does it mean to be identified, to have a distinct identity? For as long as I could remember, I didn't really know. The word *identity* was unclearly identified in my mind.

Then when I studied objective philosophy, I began to view *identification* as knowing an object or a person clearly enough to be able to express that knowing in concepts/words. It was about identifying exactly what this or that is through concepts. Identity was purely conceptual, as were all parts of my life back then – to identify something meant to put words to it. Once I've put words on an object or a person, they've been identified.

Recently, I've begun viewing being identified as like playing a role, for example, the roles of mother, husband, business owner, tennis player, etc. Many of us identify with these functions and find it difficult to view ourselves in any other way. We become trapped in a definition of "what I am". It's easy to fall deep inside the word bucket of our roles and to be totally immersed. When we make the mistake of defining our essence as a role, such as mother or president of the company, we set the stage for loss and disappointment when those functions end.

Today I noticed I was feeling subdued and less bright than usual. So I made notes to describe what I felt in more detail. The thought to make notes came after I read the following from Eckhart Tolle's book *The Power of Now*: "Unconscious, the way that I use the word here, means to be identified with some mental or emotional pattern. It implies a complete absence of the watcher."[47]

---

[47] Eckhart Tolle, *The Power of Now,* Chapter Two, Consciousness: The Way Out of Pain, page 40 (Novato, CA: New World Library and Namaste Publishing, 1999).

After reading that passage, I asked myself: What does it feel like to be identified with the mental/emotional pattern I feel today? I wrote:

> Life seems dark. The playful, joyful vibrancy I often feel seems to be gone; possibly never to come back.

> "It" seems like everything – there is nothing else except this "it". Life feels like an all-encompassing darkness, with an always/never heaviness – it will always be, it will never go away.

After writing this, I wondered:

> Maybe being identified is to create an imaginary "it" . . . a freeze-framed "it" . . . a disconnected, narrowed "it" that traps me inside of a label and inside of my tiny radar screen/ surface self.

I noticed that the "it" feels as though it's closed to alternatives – there is no way out. The always/never heaviness carries no openness and is not teachable. "It" seems to know with certainty what is real.

Once I've created this "it", once I've put words to my feeling, it's as if I have invented a "truth" and fixed my mind on it. I've embraced a frozen, forever state where I become trapped in my small, certain, and closed surface self. I'm trapped in my own identification and there seems to be no way out, because when I'm in it, I'm closed to the value of what I don't know.

I've turned a feeling experience into "what I am" and "what life is".

Embracing word-tools as boss, and as the only way to know life, supports this type of trap. The words I use to describe my experience create impermeable walls of certainty around subdued moods like the one I experienced today. They take a feeling that was in motion and stop it in its tracks. What may have moved on is now stuck with me. That's what a word does – it freeze-frames the motion of reality and puts it into an immovable this-not-that bucket.

This happens again and again when I use word-tool labels to identify myself or my surroundings. A dark mood of doubt and fear, or of feeling victimized or superior, becomes an unstoppably solid image of me and of life, at least during the moments I identify with "it".

When I'm identified with something in this way, the life that I am at core, the whole self that breathes so fully and grows so freely when allowed, becomes buried again under layers of the "this is how it is", this-not-that nature of word-tools.

When I'm identified this way, there is no watcher. It's as if I have put away or buried the awareness of my watcher. I am unconscious to anything except my world of frozen word buckets.

But I'm glad that these identifications pass by pretty quickly when I'm aware enough to notice them and to see them for what they are. Just yesterday I caught myself stuck in evaluation, criticizing myself for "not measuring up", which is a form of identification. I immediately felt bad. Then I reminded myself "don't go there, it's an invalid area; judging and comparing are wisps in the wind I can easily let go of when I remember they are limited byproducts of word-tools."

As I bring myself back to the Being that carries a peaceful, joyful, love of life, and to the richness of this moment of living, the identifications gradually lose their grip and dissolve.

Words are not the strong thing in life, Being is. The consciousness of Being brings back my watcher – it is my watcher.

Reason Is Faith

This seems totally crazy from many perspectives. Why am I having this thought that reason is faith, and that faith is reason? I think it comes out of awareness of the value of what I don't know.

Given that I know some things, isn't it reasonable to acknowledge what I do not know? Isn't it reasonable to realize that the radar screen holding what I do know is small? Isn't it reasonable to admit that what we label as *knowledge* often changes because it's made up of concepts that freeze a sliver of *what was* and can't keep up with *what is*?

Isn't it a mistake to value what I know and at the same time ignore where my "I know" came from in the first place: the vast arena of what I don't know?

Why not value both what I know *and* what I do not know? And might it make sense to emphasize what I don't know, since that's the source of what I do?

Up to this point I've asked questions from an "isn't it reasonable?" perspective. What if we now ask a few questions from a sort of "trust life" point of view, akin to having faith in what is?

Am I not functioning from some sort of faith-like sense starting with the first day of life? As I begin with zero cognitive knowledge, don't I rely on some sort of allowance of the value of what I don't know in order to learn anything?

When I watch a new baby, I see a sense of open wonderment. Having no word buckets, a baby's readiness to receive from whatever is out there flows with a curiosity that has no limits.

With no rigid walls to narrow its openness, the baby is free to be both vulnerable and without fear.

But as an adult coming from objective philosophy, I thought it was foolish and stupid to believe in the unseen, unevidenced, or unmeasurable. Anything outside my frozen reality seemed like blind faith, and I wanted no part of it.

Then I began to notice evidence for this unseen arena, such as the atmospheric electricity monitors at the golf course described in "The Value of What I Don't Know". Such electricity monitors were totally outside what I knew at the time.

Once I began experiencing Connectivity, I felt an all-embracing sense that most people are like me, and that they care deeply about life. I found that they had their own ways of caring, ways that had been unknown to me when I saw them only through my judgmental conceptual filters. I began to feel a kind of kinship that had been in hiding while I was immersed in my world of logic and word-tools. After years of being so fearful about people being enemies, I was now feeling kindness and affection toward them, and I could sense the same coming from them.

Having these feelings was a shift in experience I never dreamed possible as an objective thinker. Stepping away from "me" as a person devoted only to reason had seemed unimaginable. Yet it was happening. My use of the word-tool "reason", and locking myself into the view of excluding anything nonobjective, was beginning to diminish.

More and more, I notice how much I rely on what I don't know. As I've noted in at least one other section, I don't know how electricity works, but I know how to turn on a switch to use it. And I don't know how most organs and systems in my body work. They work somehow, but I don't make them do what they do – it happens without me using word-tools or logical thought. I constantly rely on what I don't know, and sometimes on what nobody knows, not even experts.

I rely on these and so many other happenings in the world without cognitive evidence. When I walk outside the house, I rely on a sense of Being that does not require understanding by means of reason, logic, or any word-tool product.

Much of my life, perhaps most of it, is dependent on stuff I know nothing about through word-tools. Yet because I talk so much and write so much and see truth as coming only through the filters of cognition, I often forget that there are possibilities for different kinds of knowing that I haven't considered. So much of my life lies outside my field of concepts/words, but I rarely if ever acknowledge it.

Am I a fool if I believe that I don't know everything? If I acknowledge that realities exist that I don't have cognitive evidence for? If I realize that there are arenas of knowledge I can't put into words, because words are too limited and ill equipped for handling the whole of what is real? If I am a fool, then I'm a grateful happy one.

When I come out of my stupor of being lost in concepts, I realize that what I know through thought, emotion, or any word-tool products came out of the arena of the unknown. I realize that definitions, everything in books, and all that is taught in schools originated from life experience. And I acknowledge that it is all made up of symbolic representations. It is not "the truth". It is not equivalent to reality itself. I realize that our modern way of living came out of the whole that existed before it. I call that whole *Source* because it includes the arena of the unknown from which the known comes.

Why is it reasonable to exclude and ignore unfamiliar types of knowing, noncognitive types, just because we can't describe them using word-tools, just because we haven't yet conceived of them? Yet before, when I was an "objective thinker", anything that could not be expressed by word-tools was not allowed by reason.

Why do people call it onl *faith* to acknowledge the possibility of realities we don't yet have evidence for, when every baby must acknowledge the unknown through a sense of faith-like openness, or else it would not be able to learn anything? A sort of wordless trust in what's outside starts each of us off toward knowing.

If a baby used concepts as I do – judging, belittling, complaining, comparing, and labeling as if it owned the truth – if it closed-out more than it allowed-in, just as every word-tool does, then that baby would never develop as a human being. Happily, babies are open to something more than the mere logic of the cognitively known.

I was one who viewed the unknown and the unfamiliar as unproven, impossible, and irrational. Now with an expanded view of what's possible, and now that I've been able to see the synthetic nature of the narrow corridor of unwarranted certainty, I wonder how I made it through my first fifty years.

I've come to view the reason vs faith distinction as not useful to my life. I live each day with the feeling of trust that things will work out, even if I don't understand how. At the same time, I use not only reason and logic, but also feeling and intuition. I now sense other types of energy-based knowing even when I don't fully realize I am using them.

I am no longer invested in limiting the ways I am able to touch life. I have sensed what's it's like to allow life to be fully what it is. That is, to experience the wordless whole without choking off the flow of it with my this-not-that word-tools. To reason without being lost in concepts is to trust the arena of what I don't know, it's to have a sense of faith in what is, and to allow it without resistance. Realizing that reason could never exist without starting from a sense of faith as a baby does, has opened up my world to a vibrancy of living I never knew was possible.

Uniqueness and Connectivity

Word-tools are of course useful despite all I've been saying about their limitations. Even though they are this-not-that buckets that omit uniqueness, word-tools can help point my attention.

As I point my attention to a specific place over and over again, I can ask "Does this work for life?" I can bring Connectivity to the forefront as much as I'm able and then ask myself whether my energy flow is positive or negative. If it involves a word-tool that has a contributory effect, I keep using that tool to point my attention. For me in this way, word-tools start me off in a potentially beneficial direction.

But the direction I'm pointing may be destructive. For example, if the word-tool bucket is judgment related and I'm using it to blame myself or others, then it's destructive. Or if my prime focus is money, status, or control, then it's not in alignment with life, because I proceed by operating in a vacuum of separation rather than the reality of Connectivity.

When I remember the reality that the word-tools cannot carry, I use word-tools constructively, in alignment with life-giving creativity. When I forget, or when I follow societal norms that don't acknowledge that words are only limited tools, I more often use words destructively.

The reality missing from our word-tools is uniqueness and Connectivity.

When we create a concept/word, such as *dog*, we leave out particulars such as small or big, white or brown, fluffy or smooth. The uniqueness of each dog is left out in order to put all the different dogs into a single grouping. In order to make the category grouping we call *dog*, we have to leave out the specialness of each. That's how we create the shortcut *dog* to indicate that kind of four-legged thing. We then use the shortcut in communication instead of taking a person to the specific dog we are talking about, where the person could experience firsthand this particular dog with all its uniqueness.

Connectivity is also left out, at least in the way most of us use words. I find that most of us are in far too much of a hurry to use words in a way that would fill in the whole picture of what is real. Being the shortcuts that they are, words are uniquely suited to being in a hurry. Perhaps they even encourage it.

Whenever we use a word, countless interconnections – influences and contexts that make up the full reality of what we are trying to point attention to – are omitted. The symbol *dog* is like a tag for representing a particular Being that comes from two other dogs, and each of them from two others. Dogs breathe air, eat certain food, and need sun and water – just as all human beings do. They react in certain ways depending on what people around them do, and on countless other factors. Historically, dogs may have come from wolves. I could go on listing these interconnections until the end of my life.

But in using the word *dog*, or most other words, we rarely carry interconnections. The words don't bring a whole picture to our minds. (That's the whole point – our minds are limited, which is why we've created word-tools to fit those limits.) We use the word *dog* without the whole of the Being this dog brings with it. We leave out most of what is real in order to create a quick-to-use tag.

We try to replace what is real with a symbol representing what is there. The depth and fullness of what is real is lost to the surface essentials of what is there, and only those essentials needed to form the concept are retained. The word *there* is meant to fit the snapshot nature of the tiny sliver we pull out when we stop the flow of reality in order to create the concept.

By leaving out uniqueness and Connectivity, we think we've boiled down what is real to its essentials. But the essence of a Being is much closer to what's left out than to what is carried by word-tools.

Do I really sense that the essence of "me" is covered by concepts such as shape, functions, mental capacity, or some definition such as "man is a rational animal"?

And what about specific characteristics about me? Do I sense that my uniqueness is carried by this: "Steve is a man of a certain height, weight, coloring, with a certain cultural background, job and relationship history, education, and health"? Yes, these are unique characteristics that are aspects of reality that word-tool leave out. But how can these surface aspects carry the essence of what is fully real about the depth of the whole Being that is "me"?

A word is only a tool. But I so often use it as if it carries the whole reality of "what is". When I use it this way, I am unconscious because I have detached the use of my tool from its ability to work constructively. In myself, I find a lot of arrogance in this detachment. And I continue to uncover more angles on how convenient it is to misuse these tools to bolster the pseudo image of superiority I find passing through me so often.

I realize I am repeating but here is a slightly different summarization. Life is continual motion that involves countless interconnections. Words are symbols that pull out a mere moment of the motion, only a sliver, only a snapshot. They're tools we can use to indicate "what is there" in the simplest of ways. But they do not even come close to representing the fullness of the whole of

Being "what is real". How could a dog, a flower, or a human be fully known through a system of symbols that are synthetically extracted through the boiling down process of conceptualization?

They can't. To even begin to realize the essence of a Being, I must begin by experiencing it firsthand and face-to-face and with all my senses and energies present. Bringing only my box of cognitive tools to a conversation can't even come close.

Our cognitive minds can't grasp reality as a whole. This is one reason we created our word-tool symbol system – it's an attempt to break up that whole into pieces that are small enough for a cognitive grasp. But these stop-action symbols are only imaginative attempts at being with the whole. And they can aid in pointing us in the general direction of this "being with" only when we acknowledge their limitations and realize that they don't exist except in our minds, and, of course, as sounds and squiggly symbols on paper. Yes they are real as sounds and squiggly symbols, but they are not the reality of what they were created to represent.

Word-tools allow us to generally indicate one thing (*dogs*) versus another (*cats* or *tables*). As general indicators, they provide us with a limited something that is better than nothing. They make it so we don't have to constantly drag each other around and point at things.

But in using words, we easily forget the value of firsthand looking and pointing and of fully experiencing the unique thing we have in mind. Forgetting that each concept/word came from the realm of looking, pointing, and experiencing, we misuse our language symbols.

How do we misuse them? We distort the reality from which they are drawn by using them as if they can fully represent that reality. They distort by leaving out uniqueness and Connectivity, which includes the continuous motion that makes reality real.

Is it possible to use them without distortion? Yes, but to do it, I must learn to view them differently than I'm used to. I can't continue to walk through life like a zombie believing and acting on the conditioning of my mind-dominated culture. So I practice.

With an eye toward always looking beyond them, I practice using word-tools as only general indicators, not as tellers of absolute truth. That way, I am more apt to honor them as the highly limited tools they are, and to honor the whole of life as the interconnected reality that it is. But, when I use synthetic systems of thought, such as morality, which are products of word-tools, I've totally lost touch with their limits.

Morality involves countless interconnections that cannot be carried by word-tools. They cannot carry a context wide enough to cover what is either good or a pathway for growth about a specific human being.

Word-tools are suited for simple, generalized communications, such as "Please pass the salt". Or for simple descriptive communications: "As I stood two feet away from that man, John, I saw him squeeze the trigger of the gun he held. The bullet came out of the gun and hit that other man, George, in the midsection of his body. Then George fell to the ground."

Or words are suited for concept-to-concept activities that are many layers of abstraction away from what's real. Computer tools are one example of concept-to-concept work, and we've certainly seen the benefits of this. There is no moralizing in this concept-to-concept work. Here, we use words in a way that fits their limitations.

However, if we forget to connect the results of our computer work to the base beneath the many layers of abstraction, if we forget Source, often if not always the computer tools end up being used to destroy life. And then we all lose. When this happens, the tools have taken precedence over the life they were meant to serve. We've become lost in our tools.

What happens when, being lost in concepts, we combine an *I'm right you're wrong* (*morality*) with amazing technology that results from our concept-to-concept work? The wars of the twentieth century with humans killing more than 150 million other humans demonstrate that what first appears as amazing becomes shockingly frightful when it is detached from Source.

So we do the best we can with our limited word-tools. And as I use them, I continually warn myself of their limitations and of their status as only a tool.

The crossing over of many particulars (creating a grouping) makes words powerful in a way that's very seductive for me. I felt that power grow as I learned to integrate conceptual structures, such as logic and science, and all kinds of methods and techniques. But this power is an illusion that actually cripples me as I get lost in it. I lose my way if I use this word-tool power without recognition of Connectivity – that is, without tying the word-tool to Source, the life experience from which it came in the first place.

Imagine being a primitive man who had experienced only foot travel. At that time, moving from one place to another had never been done except by putting one foot in front of the other. Each footstep was grounded in the earth that it pressed down on. As such, I am more apt to be connected to Source.

Then suppose I discover that I can ride on top of an animal, such as a horse. I climb up high onto a horse's back. I start to feel a kind of dominance, arising from the height and speed I had never before known. I feel I am larger now in some way as I separate myself from the earth I previously embraced with each step. Now for the first time, I'm above all that's below me, including the earth I had previously been intimately connected with. I'm above earth, and I'm above humans and smaller animals that are still limited to their own relatively meager foot travel.

Word-tools, as I've learned to use them, create this same height and speed, with the feeling of dominance over those still limited to the foot travel of looking, pointing, and experiencing the reality of life directly. The joke is on me as "the intellectual" who thinks he can gain more from the detached, ego-feeding forms of thought than from direct connection to what is real.

I for one have gotten lost in this false power of viewing life through symbols. I was happy to ignore uniqueness and Connectivity as I rode my high horse of disconnected logic and reasoning. And as I was so busy prancing around feeling superior, I forgot the extent to which I lost touch with the full reality of life experience. I had lost the joy of living; I had given it up for a high-horse feeling of superiority over reality. I still do that sometimes when I forget Connectivity and Source, but now less often.

That high horse feeling is also what makes it easy to view other humans as enemies, those who have ideas that are different from mine. It makes it easy to think the world would be better off without "that kind of people". Note *that kind* comes out of the grouping of a concept. I view misuse of concepts as the fuel for most, if not all, of the killing throughout human history.

On this high horse of word-tools so many of us feel superior, each believing that we own the truth. The fallacy of believing we own the truth becomes *our* reality, and if I continue with the fallacy rather than question it, *our* reality becomes *the* reality. And anyone who doesn't agree with *the* reality must be our enemy.

As Philip Shepherd wrote "The horse didn't just enable people to dominate; it taught them to want to".[48]

Once on my horse, I can trample the ground beneath me and anything that gets in my way. If I believe this power and identify myself with it, I end up equating *my* reality with *the* reality, and can't help but use word-tools destructively. That's when I trample the ground of Source and of life as I continue to ignore uniqueness and Connectivity.

If on the other hand, I use words as tools with their limitations in the forefront of my mind, and with awareness of the uniqueness they discard and the Connectivity they cannot carry, then I can use word-tools as amazingly life affirming.

Let me bring back uniqueness and Connectivity to my life; let me feel the fullness of the whole of life experience that awaits, and the Source that stands by to be with me Arm-in-Arm toward creatively contributing to life.

Let me use words in such a way as to highlight the Connectivity from which they come, rather than the separations to which they lead.

---

[48] Phillip Shepherd, *New Self, New World: Recovering Our Senses in the Twenty-First Century*, page 351 (Berkley: North Atlantic Books, 2010). (I am grateful to Philip Shepherd for the chapter in this book called "Horse and Rider". The images he provided fit how I experience my own destructive word-tool superiority.)

My Body "Talks" – Can I Hear It Without Words?

Almost every morning, I spend quiet time gently touching and putting attention on my belly as well as other parts of my body, such as calves, feet, neck, and chest. I first discovered this type of practice[49] in a book called *Unwinding the Belly* by Allison Post and Stephen Cavaliere.[50]

With the help of that book, I discovered a form of sensing and depth of feeling I hadn't known possible while completely immersed in my word-tooled, mind-dominated world. I've ignored my poor body for so long, always making it last priority to the pressures of my surface world. When I did attend to it by going to the gym, the attention was to force it into shape through pushing. Relaxing into gently touching, and simply just being with it, had been out of the question. There were always more important things to do.

But when I take time to gently be with my body, without any goal or result in mind, I find a plethora of feelings I had never known before. First there are the sensations in the skin of my fingers as they touch my belly. Then there are the sensations of the skin on the surface of my belly.

And there's more than the sensations of skin to skin, I can also feel the shapes underneath the skin with my fingers. It's not like feeling a square then a circle – it's not that distinct. But I feel rounding, tube-like shapes, and sometimes textures that feel like tiny pebbles. And it's different in different areas of my belly.

---

[49] My use of the words "type of practice" is an example of me as overly focused on instruction from outside myself. It leans toward lost in concepts and the this-not-that of word-tools. Changing these words from "type of practice" to "ways of Being" would better fit using words in such a way as to highlight the Connectivity from which they come, rather than the separations to which they lead.

[50] Allison Post and Stephen Cavaliere, *Unwinding the Belly: Healing with Gentle Touch* (Berkley, California: North Atlantic Books, 2003).

Then when I can open up to an even deeper experience, I become aware of the internal sensations within those shapes and internal tissues themselves.

So all at once, there are sensations on the skin of fingers, on the skin of the belly, and within the tissues and organs underneath the skin. To me, it's like an abundant outpouring of the energy of being alive. But if my mind is busy chattering with worry, blame, planning, judging, comparing, then I miss it all.

During most of my life I did miss it all because my attention was always on thoughts in my head. Whenever I did touch my skin it was as a means to an end, it was only an automatic task-oriented state of mind. I didn't experience anything except the concept of finishing a chore such as: *get that spot of food off your face,* or *get rid of this itch,* or *make this shower fast so I can get to my next task.*

So for me taking quiet time to gently touch my body, and to notice my breathing while doing it, has been great training in the practice of sensing Source. We could call it training in the practice of realizing the noncognitive, the non-word–tooled. It's as if I'm uncovering consciousness of an unfiltered whole, the whole of my body, the whole of reality.

Today as I was doing it, I stopped and wrote the following to describe the experience.

> I feel responsiveness beneath, almost like the tissue appreciates what I'm doing. It's not a conceptual response, no word-tools there. A sensory experience without words. I use words while I'm doing it. I ask "what does it feel like?" But it's not a conceptual answer I want, it's simply the feeling of being fully alive with myself.

When I catch myself with word-based answers like *lump* or *tender spot* or *tension*, I am often able to gently nudge my attention to the sensations themselves without activating a web of associations such as "what could this lump be?" or "why is this spot tender or tense today?" That's more of being lost in concepts, lost in the faulty significance of the symbolic, and it pulls attention away from the straight-from-life sensations. Pushing those sensations through worrisome concepts sabotages my ability to hear my body, to engage these noncognitive experiences without the middle man of word-tools.

When words such as *that hurts* or *that feels good* come to mind, I can often relax and let them flow past as simple happenings. I can avoid building more word-product on top of them as I gently nudge my attention back to direct experience.

It's how the tissues and shapes respond sensorially that I want to uncover, and it's as if I'm gradually removing layers of word-tool judgment, evaluation, comparison, and fear which make up my habitual ways of processing. It's a shifting away from mind-based, limited word-tooled information, and toward a pure sense of Being with my body.

With this practice, I've seen I don't need to go through conceptual "what" and "how" groupings. I can access reality directly rather than only through synthetic tools that omit uniqueness and cannot carry Connectivity. And I find a kind of peaceful pleasure flowing through when I'm in touch with my body without words.

It's a feeling of being open to the "yet to be known", as I trust in the value of what I don't know. It's openness to the response of the tissues, whatever that response turns out to be, as I gently move my hands and experience sensations without jumping to conclusions. This practice creates a connection – me in Connectivity with the unfiltered "what is" of my body.

It's my whole self I'm using and tapping into, not just the word-tooled self. It brings in the dimension of the noncognitive "me" which I call source self, as contrasted with functioning from only my word-dominated surface self.

Actually, since the chattering mind so often starts and restarts, I probably really feel the sensations I'm describing about half the time, perhaps less. But even a small proportion has had a huge effect for me. Compared to my near continuous stream of word-tooled stories, just these few moments of silence and deep sensation have made a world of difference to my feelings of positive energy and gratitude for life.

The Pull to Narrow My Awareness

Each morning I choose one of many nearby coffee shops to start my writing for the day. Lately, I've based my choice on the level of positive energy I feel rather than on an analytical process of logical thought.

One of the shops has what I've long regarded as my favorite coffee. I went there every day without deviation for many years. But one morning, I noticed my energy pointing me toward a different coffee shop, rather than the one with my favorite coffee.

Then I imagined someone asking why I would choose something other than my favorite. My mind instantly pumped out a stream of cognitive reasons, as if I needed to justify my choice to this imaginary questioner.

> On recent visits to the shop serving my favorite coffee, the pastries seemed dry and the taste of the coffee seemed to have an edge I didn't enjoy, with flavors a little on the fruity side. Although high in quality, the edge and the fruity notes are not what I like most in coffee. Also, the shop with my favorite coffee has small tables, which offer less space for working.

> One more factor, the shop with my favorite coffee has music that strikes me as an extremely formal type of Classical. I like Classical, but this music seems rigid and feels less relaxing.

> Other shops have larger tables, pastries that are more pleasing, and a different feeling in the space and clientele.

These details may seem boring. But observing them brought me to realize that I often undo a whole-self, energy-based choice by hiding it beneath layers of needless word-tools.

What this tells me is that forcing an energy-based choice through the filters of word-tools is not only wasteful but damaging. My wholistic choice carried the sense of me today, in relation to all that was around me. It was a choice made in Connectivity. But that Connectivity gets broken when I try to force it through the this-not-that filters of word-tools.

In his book *Blink*, Malcolm Gladwell describes what has been called verbal overshadowing and includes the following as an example. If we see the face of a stranger and then are asked to pick that person out of a police lineup, most of us can do it. But, if we are first asked to describe details about the face in writing, we "do a lot worse at picking that face out of a lineup".[51] Trying to force the memory through word-tools is more than unhelpful. Our nonverbal knowing, and our energy-based choosing, works best when we don't interfere with it.

When we cloud our nonverbal knowing by forcing it through word-filters, we sever the flow of its wholeness, and thus disable the functioning of our whole selves.

The detailed justification of my coffee shop choice disrupts the flow of choosing and taking action. It does this because words are narrowing devices. By leaving out uniqueness, they exclude much of the reality carried by a wholistic choice. And their inability to carry Connectivity distorts my choices by supporting the illusion that I'm separate from what's around me.

Wholistic choosing encompasses a wider range of reality. As I get more comfortable with this energy-based kind of choosing, I sense that pushing a *why* onto it ultimately forces a reduction of what's real. The severe narrowing that occurs when we form the shortcut

---

[51] Malcolm Gladwell, *Blink: The Power of Thinking Without Thinking,* page 119 (New York: Little, Brown and Company, 2005).

of a concept diminishes the fullness inherent in my positive energy, whole-self-based choice.

This pushing for cognitive justification not only suggests lack of trust in my whole self, it also includes mistrusting my surroundings and doubting my Connectivity with life.

So, I appreciated this imaginary question, because it helped me realize how often my lost-in-concepts way of functioning takes the potency out of a whole-picture, energy-based choice.

It helped me to realize that words don't translate reality. Rather, word-tools significantly reduce and narrow the field in order to be the indicators and pointers that they are; they are this-not-that shortcuts. When I forget these limitations, word-tools become misleading. I repeat that in my experience a word doesn't translate reality, it is simply a tag on a string attached to a whole that has so much more to it than its word-tooled name.

This all makes me wonder if "energy" is the language of reality, and I wonder if energy carries everything, including what a word-tool does not.

When I forget the huge gap between the pointing-to of word-tools and the Being of the whole of reality, it creates an unhealthy tension. As it pulls me into the realm of the symbolic, it pulls me away from trusting reality.

As I allow awareness of my whole self to just Be, and learn to trust action from that Being without justifying myself in word-tool terms, I find I can simply enjoy what is around me.

How many times do you make a decision based on a positive energy awareness, and then find your surface self *shoulding* you into justifying it in cognitive form? How often do you run into another person who, out of habit, asks you to justify a choice logically? I venture to guess that most of the time these justifications are not necessary, because it makes no difference to anything the other person might do. He or she is simply asking *why* out of habit, out of being lost in concepts, and often as a way to fuel judgment, superiority, and advice giving.

I wonder how often we feel threatened when we see someone who seems to be making choices in a way that is different from what we are used to; that is, from awareness rather than from word-tooled analysis. Lately I've noticed myself pulling back from asking *why* about a choice. And it feels like the peace of accepting what is, without the need to run it into a corner by forcing a justification.

On the other hand, I love the word *why* when I'm trying to better understand what someone is trying to point to in reality. But usually my quest to understand works best if I ask them to describe their experience as fully as possible, to give a concrete example, or to tell me more. This has worked better for me than being lazy by using the shortcut of asking *why*.

Now I view pressure to justify as a warning. I realize the needless tension caused by trying to force an energy-based sense through the narrowing confines of word-tools. I stay attuned to this warning because I don't want to shift away from more widely aware places of Being, I want to shift toward them.

I practice tuning into this warning almost every day. When I feel a pull to justify, I recall the vastness of what I don't know, that which is outside my radar screen/frozen reality. I remind myself that words are only tools suited for simple communications and that reality and life are the source of these very limited synthetic symbols.

I benefit greatly from word-tools but not if I view them as the primary means of knowing reality. My life flows better as I allow more direct tools of knowing such as: positive and negative energies; my body which knows how to run itself without cognitive instruction; "now" moments rather than thoughts of past and future; and a sense of Connectivity with everything that is real.

So I say to myself, *May I come to accept my awareness without demanding it be justified*, which means without narrowing and reducing it with word-tools. The fact that I am writing this book, and that you are reading it, shows we are walking down that road, away from the shackles of word-tool domination and toward a wider sense of knowing, a sense that is not narrowly constrained by words because now we've learned to use them as the limited tools they are.

You're Not Allowed to Touch Source

Not so long ago, I believed word-tools were the only way to view the world, the only means of holding truth. Often when I encountered an experience that was nonconceptual, I evaluated it away by using words such as *bad* or *not for me* or *I don't like*. I was reinterpreting my experience by filtering it through word-tools, and consequently narrowed my world by excluding what didn't fit preconceived categories. I pushed away my own experiences because they didn't fit into the small boxes word-tools could provide. And yet, some of these experiences still remained with me.

Once as a young boy, I lay on the grass outside my house looking at the sun through closed eyelids. I'd never done that before, and it felt like a new discovery. I was amazed by the bright red and orange colors. I was surprised I could see so much light through my eyelids. I liked the experience so much I lay there still for a long time on the grass, just looking and enjoying.

Later when I remembered this experience with the sun, I would reinterpret it as just the workings of biology. Or I would evaluate it as a silly kid's experience because I remember I had felt a little cross-eyed as I laid there on the grass looking through to the sun. So even though it had felt good as a young boy, it was easy as an adult to dismiss it as meaningless child's play.

But the experience stayed with me. I thought of it many times throughout the years. It was as if that experience had remained always by my side. As noted in other sections, when something stays with me this way, when I remember it repeatedly across many years, I call it a *marker*.

During the months of finishing this book, I've begun looking through my eyelids more. Sometimes with the sun and sometimes without it. It's become a way to put attention on my body and it helps quiet the constant flow of words in the form of judgments, worries, plans, etc. I think of it as an unusual way of connecting to Source.

But more than that, it feels like a form of going deep within myself while at the same time going deep into the wholeness of reality. It's like the depth of me coming together with the depth and vastness of Connectivity. I wonder what peculiar ways of sensing Source other people have.

As a young man in graduate school, I had a closet-sized office with no window where I studied. On most days, I would read and write there for hours. At times I would stop and sit for what seemed like long periods, doing nothing and staring toward the wall in front of me. It felt relaxing and a bit soothing. At that time I labeled it in a derogatory way as "zoning out". But now I know that these were moments of quiet stillness.

Now I am able to look back at these experiences as moments of peace, not cluttered by the noisy thought-chatter of word-tool logic. They were moments of quiet with no thought, no worry, no doubt, and no mental torment. Even though I was accomplishing nothing by the standards of my word-tool dominated world, they were meaningful in some way that I can't define.

But back then, viewing myself as needing to be productive and intelligent, I did not allow myself to embrace these simple moments of Being. Back then, these moments seemed too silly to be taken seriously.

So why did the moments stay with me for so many years? It puzzled me until I became more aware that there are types of living that are beyond words. There are ways of Being that words can't fully describe.

I realized that words are so very limited as tools. They lift out only slivers of reality. I began to see more clearly that they do not constitute reality, that they are only shortcuts and symbolic indicators of what is real. Only then did it become more apparent that they don't carry the wholeness of life, and that there was a reason these marker experiences stayed with me through so many years. Words are simply not applicable to some of the best moments of living.

I also remind myself that word-tools aren't applicable to the value of what I don't know. I can't freeze and put in a bucket something that hasn't yet been specified. Yet I find it reasonable and even logical to acknowledge this vast realm of the unknown. I see that words can't address it, and at the same time I see the enormous value of acknowledging it. Word-tools are incapable in the realm of the unknown, and yet being open to learn anything depends on honoring it.

When I viewed word-tools as the only path to knowledge, I rigidly denied the unknown. I refused to acknowledge that everything known was once unknown. I now view this as denying my own experience, and denying myself, because I couldn't use my word-tools on those experiences. I was like a carpenter who says, "Since I can't use my hammer on this, I'll deny that it ever happened, I'll deny its reality". As a carpenter whose only tool is a hammer, I could deny cars, watches, and computers as unreal. Anything my favorite tool did not create didn't really happen and doesn't really exist.

Other experiences which I call Grateful Being[52] also can't adequately be addressed by word-tools. Moments of silent eye contact – when I felt more loved than any other time in my life, and when tears and a sense of beauty arose and intensified during the silence of meeting others through an embrace of the eyes – those moments of living are also times I sensed the touch of Source coming

---

[52] See the section entitled *Grateful Being* later in this book.

through, the touch of something deeper than cognition. These also can't be addressed in cognitive terms – they must be experienced to be understood.

I've now come to realize that shutting out what I had called silly types of experience was shutting out myself and shutting out Source. I hadn't been open to allowing Source as a possibility because it is outside the range of where word-tools reach, and I regarded word-tools as everything. Even the idea that word-tools have a source was not allowed.

As I began to shift attention away from negatives, I allowed myself to hear the realization that *before words, there was life*. I was finally able to take seriously the reality that before cognition there was wordless nature, including animals, plants, earth, sun, and air.

Now it's clear to me that the life-giving energies of reality came first, before thought and before words. And these energies are the ultimate origin of the concepts we create – *word-tools do have a source!*

Allowing these realizations circled back around to make word-tool limitations more apparent. In interactions with people each day, I began to notice how words imagine away the uniqueness of each Being, and thus lose vast amounts of reality. First I would hear the labels that come across my mind when I see or meet a person: *lazy, irresponsible, arrogant, wealthy, beauty queen, obese, macho, grumpy.* Then I remind myself of the miniscule amount of information these labels carry, and how they distort my experiencing of this person. Then as I set aside the narrow closure of the words, and shift my attention to the more expansive reality of the whole human being, the Being that goes far beyond word-tools, beyond these labels which I mistakenly embrace as carriers of truth.

I became more aware of words as merely communication shortcuts that serve as useful indicators only if we acknowledge their limitations when we use them. To ignore their limitations, and to ignore the Source from which they were derived, is to misuse them.

While excluding what was possible and real because it didn't fit the word-tooled realm, I was also rejecting my own life experience, allowing word-tools to filter out vast areas of living. Noncognitive living was not allowed or was dismissed as a deception. In order to view my own wordless experiences as worthy of consideration, I had to come to a place where I opened the door to more than just word-tools.

I'm so glad to have opened up to noncognitive ways of knowing and living, ways I had previously reinterpreted or judged out of existence through misuse of word-tools. Eventually, I also realized that narrowed ways of viewing reality were the roots of my self-doubt and self-torment.

As I finally acknowledged the value of these noncognitive ways of living and knowing, it brought a kind of freedom that is indescribable. It feels like the peaceful joy of being released from a jail sentence I thought would never end, a constriction that sapped the joy of life.

The pseudo world of word-tools as the only road to truth no longer has a hold on me. Now what holds me is a sense of flowing forward Arm-in-Arm, an allowed growing I don't have to strain for. Now I treasure those "silly" moments of "wasting time" and "zoning out" because when I experience them, I sense an expansive, more abundant, and generous reality: a reality of Connectivity. What was previously not allowed now fills my life as I realize that words are just one of many types of limited tools we can choose to use or to misuse.

A Beautiful Mind

Today a friend told me she received flowers from her new boyfriend. She was happy and excited. She beamed like a sun as she spoke about it: "It's the first time I've ever received flowers, and I didn't even know what to do with them!"

I enjoyed the image of her receiving the red roses, but I especially enjoyed her beautiful energy in the moments she described it. It seemed to be a joy that flowed with no possibility of negativity.

Then her brightness dissipated a bit as she told me her birthday was a few weeks away. It was as if worry came to both our minds immediately, "What might come next with this new boyfriend?" We both thought of the possibility of being let down if there were no flowers from him on her birthday. Then my friend mentioned that during times she didn't have a boyfriend, her mom would send her a stuffed teddy bear and a flower on Valentine's Day. We both hoped the next Valentine's Day would be different.

As if it were in the air, both our minds were drawn to fears of upcoming disappointment. For just a few moments, the possibility of "being let down by life" seemed to overshadow the joy of receiving flowers for the first time.

It's so easy to latch onto images of a hoped-for future accompanied by associated fears of those images being crushed. For me, this happens when I forget to bring awareness to the immediate moment, thus allowing my mind to churn around a wished-for and feared-about future. The fear of being "let down by life" can easily drag me down to a place of despair.

One of my own places of despair ties to being alone on holidays and weekends. For years I've been haunted by images of me feeling as if I have no friends or family, proven by my being alone during times when most people spend time with others. It's the pattern of: they have, but I don't.

Previously, I was too logical, rational, and invulnerable to let these images come to light. They were buried deep, and created tension in my body, but I didn't let that anguish surface. I was too "intellectually tough" to admit to images of me being a loser in this way.

As these images lurked in the background, I would feel a darkness pulling me down. It came on weekends and holidays when I had no social activities planned. Eventually, I called this the "lonely guy" image. Once I named it, I realized that I had felt dragged down by "lonely guy" for as long as I can remember – feeling small, excluded, and rejected by people and by life.

Others had parties or dates on weekends but "poor me" didn't. Others had family or friends to be with on holidays but "pitiful me" didn't. This was a form of comparison (others had, but I didn't) that felt like a devil that wouldn't go away. If this devil wasn't haunting me through tension in my body, it was tormenting me with thoughts. Usually it did both – and usually I didn't notice the torment because my attention was fully consumed by the mind chatter as if it were reality rather than thoughts about reality.

During times of life when I was married, I rarely felt "lonely guy". But when I lived alone, he was almost always there, with his threatening images of me as lowly, pathetic, unwanted, and unlovable – the feeling that I didn't belong in the world the way others did.

Sometime after my sixteen-year marriage ended in divorce, when "despicable me" had been alone for many years, I saw a movie called *A Beautiful Mind*. John, the main character who was a university professor and mathematician, saw images of three people who were not actually real. But they appeared to be as real as everything else in the movie, as real as my "lonely guy". My "lonely guy" seemed to be the truth about me, and John's images seemed to be the truth about his life.

John ended up in a mental hospital. (I'm happy to say that hasn't happened to me.) His psychiatrist diagnosed him as schizophrenic and prescribed shock therapy and medication to control John's delusional symptoms.

After being released from the hospital, John began to think he could use his mind to figure out how to live without being haunted by the images. At one point he stopped his medications. He thought he could solve this mental illness through thinking, just as he solved math problems through thinking. At this point in the movie, John seemed to see the world almost exclusively through the word-tools of logic, reason, and science.

Later in the movie, still believing his three imagined people were real, John nearly injured both his wife and his baby son. John's wife was faced with a decision to sign commitment papers that would force John back to the mental hospital. Just after we learn that she doesn't sign the papers, there was a tender scene where John's wife said the following.

> *You want to know what's real? This.* [she tenderly touches his face and holds her hand there on his head] *This.* [she picks up his hand and puts it on her own face] *This.* [she moves his hand from her face to her heart] *This is real. Maybe the part that knows the waking from the dream, maybe it isn't here* [her hand is still on his head]. *Maybe it's here* [she moves it from his head down to his heart]. *I need to believe that something extraordinary is possible.* [she and John embrace][53]

---

[53] *A Beautiful Mind*, directed by Ron Howard, written by Akiva Goldsman and Sylvia Nasar (Universal City, CA: Universal Pictures, 2002) DVD 2006.

This scene means so much to me because John's wife seems to be pointing away from the head-dominated surface self and toward the heart, toward the noncognitive, and in my view, toward an awareness of whole self. In my experience, this is where the extraordinary is possible.

"Lonely guy" is a creation of that head-dominated surface self, for me, and I think for many others. I'm out of touch with my whole self when I imagine being alone for a holiday or a weekend and compare that to images of what "could be", that is, me with family and friends. "I could have what others have on holidays/weekends, but I don't." There's the "they have, but I don't" comparison. And it feels as though life has let me down again because my wishes for that feeling of family and friendship have not been made real.

John suffered while his head-dominated surface self believed his imagined people to be real. Once he was convinced they were not, once he viewed them as merely creations of his mind, he was able to see them without taking them seriously. He eventually told two of his imagined people that he would no longer talk to them – with a feeling of tenderness and gratitude for what they had shared together, he essentially said goodbye.

Later in the movie a colleague of John's named Martin asks if the delusionary people were gone. John says:

> Nope, they're not gone. And maybe they never will be. But I've gotten used to ignoring them . . . and I think as a result they've kind of given up on me. You think that's what it's like with all our dreams and nightmares, Martin? You've got to keep feeding them for them to stay alive?[54]

With my "messy roommate" experience, I became aware enough not to feed my crazy thoughts by taking them seriously, not to

---

[54] *A Beautiful Mind.*

view them as reality. In the movie, John stopped believing the reality of his three imaginary people, even though they continued to coax, threaten, and guilt him into engaging with them. My thoughts continue to do exactly that – coax, threaten, and guilt me into engaging with them. But since realizing they are not the truth-tellers I once believed them to be, the tugging from my crazy thoughts has become less intense and less frequent.

In the last scene of the movie, John and his wife are walking through a large foyer, having just left an auditorium where John had been awarded the Nobel Prize. John saw his three imaginary people in the distance, far across the large foyer. His wife asked what was wrong. John's reply was "hmm . . . nothin' . . . nothin' at all",[55] and they continued walking toward the exit arm-in-arm.

Something amazing relating to this last scene happened to me and my "lonely guy" image on Christmas Day of the year 2015. I spent the entire day alone, without friends or family. It was an ideal occasion for "lonely guy" to pull me down by taking over my thoughts and feelings.

A couple of times during the day, I felt "lonely guy" tug at me to interact with him. It was just a whisper of the sense of dread I had experienced so many times on days like this. But I didn't feel the dread! As "lonely guy" lurked in the distance, I felt as I would imagine John felt in this last scene of the movie.

It was as if I could see my "lonely guy" image in the form of John's three imagined people, and I responded by saying "hmm . . . nothin' . . . nothin' at all" and then walked on through my Christmas Day.

For the first time, I was able to sense the "lonely guy" image pulling at me but I did not accept the invitation. I saw the image but did

---

[55] *A Beautiful Mind.*

not allow it to take me over. Somehow, its lifelong power to drag me down had softened. On Christmas Day of 2015, I saw "lonely guy" as a creation of my mind and I no longer took it seriously. For me, this was something extraordinary. It wasn't just possible, it happened.

Since then, I have appreciated "a beautiful mind" as a mind able to disengage from the false images of expectation, comparison, judgment, and from any sign of "poor little me". It's a mind that is no longer completely ruled by the distorting images created by its word-tools.

I wonder if being able to experience this disengagement from "lonely guy" was helped along by my realization that concepts and words are only limited tools, and not the truth-tellers I had taken them to be.

I wonder if I could have experienced this extraordinary happening without realizing the vastness of what I don't know that I don't know, and the pervasiveness of Connectivity.

I wonder if it could have happened without uncovering, to some extent, my whole self from beneath the many layers of word-tool negativity that haunted me for so long.

Unique Expressor

My mind loves to constantly label. There's a *tall* person, a *muscleman*, a *beautiful* woman, a *mean-looking* guy, a *fat* person, etc. When I take these labels seriously, I feel tension – the tension of categorization, of viewing the person through the narrow lens of an inflexible bucket.

But when I dismiss the labels as narrow distortions that constrict the way I interact with people, I feel more at peace. When I observe without labeling, I feel myself orienting to a person with my whole self, not just my word-tooled self.

So I view putting attention on traits or characteristics as destructive and limiting to my functioning. The main issue is not that it's a wrong against the other person, it's that it constricts my own outlook and the way I respond to people. The limitations of word-tools are real. When I delude myself into believing them as carriers of "the truth", I am less effective and less happy in the world.

What then is "me" without traits and characteristics? It's easy to see uniqueness in terms of traits and characteristics. But how am I unique in a deep-down, nonsuperficial way? How am I unique if I exclude the traits and characteristics that seem to make me unique?

Being a man, of a certain age, gray hair, medium height, married and divorced twice, who worked in insurance and education industries, and studied objective philosophies – all these are surface happenings that I no longer view as serious or defining. Smart or stupid; wealthy or poor; kind or mean; determined or lackadaisical – I've come to view all of this as surface stuff that comes and goes.

So if the non-surface essence of me excludes all of that, what am I left with? Are we all exactly the same at the core? If we go far beneath the surface, is there no uniqueness?

All I can say is I don't experience it this way – I sense uniqueness deep down in my essence and in the essences of others, without the need to use word-based traits and characteristics. Even though I see human beings as the same in our capacity to be aware, and in our nature as Beings of Source, I sense a uniqueness that is deeper than what we see on the surface, a uniqueness that does not require the category labels we put on ourselves.

How is this deep-down uniqueness different from surface traits and characteristics?

I sense it as the "wanting" of my seed, as the deep-down source of my growth. It's the natural growth that is not under my direct control and deeper than surface identities I create.

I can't force or shape my growth toward a specific end result. But I can foster/nurture my growth toward an end (of sorts) that is not cognitively known to me now, but will become known if I allow it.

If I bring back uniqueness and Connectivity, thus coming away from word-tool domination, then the end result will be beneficial, whatever it becomes specifically.

If I remain dominated by word-tools, thus continuing to cutoff uniqueness and Connectivity, then the end result will be damaging, whatever it becomes specifically.

Once while sitting in a coffee shop, I looked around at the uniqueness of all the people who were there. I wrote this:

> Isn't every person here an exciting expression of a combination of synthetic essentials and the Being/life force which underlies and makes each one possible?

Experiencing Connectivity has brought me to view the source of uniqueness as the same for all. But the growth result is different. It shines out in novel ways and through novel expressions, all of which can be found only through allowing, not through assuming the superior position that "I can make it happen". When I've tried to push or mold my growth result, it isn't unique. Rather, it comes out as a preconception, a template I copied from somewhere in the surface world in order to force a result.

The uniqueness flows out from the whole of "me" in Connectivity. And it flows out in countless forms of colorful expression.

This doesn't make any sense from the perspective of my mind's viewpoint of "me" as separate. It can be understood only through acknowledging the reality that: If there is only me, there is no me. So me as the deep-down Unique Expressor is me in Connectivity, it's me as A Whole of The Whole.

I view the Unique Expressor as being prior to words, as a happening that can't be described by word-tools. Yet I sense each seed, each deep-down expressor as creating novelty as it arises to the surface in its growth. It's an unpredictable novelty that we see when the seed blooms in the unique way that only it can.

As illustrative of this sense, I'm picturing in my mind newborn babies I have recently seen. Looking into their eyes connects to a depth of knowing that is without words. Yet if I spend time to look closely, I see the uniqueness shining through in novel ways – one baby as different from another, and yet at the same time, they both share the same light as their source.

My Unique Expressor at core reflects my growth, driven by the deep-down and wordless "wanting" of my seed. Then, the way my Unique Expressor nurtures my environment (my garden) is also the way I embrace Connectivity.

I've heard the idea that what I need to know will come to me when I need to know it. That I don't have to obsess about knowing how I will do something before I arrive at the specific situation. That I will have the whole to which I can respond when I arrive face-to-face with the situation – and it is only then, and only if I'm connected to Source, that I'll know what is needed from me.

It's the same with the end result of anyone's unique growth. Each Unique Expressor, each "me" in Connectivity, will know the specifics of its end result when he or she arrives and not before. Why? Because there are far too many factors to try to grasp, factors that our limited cognitive tools aren't equipped to handle. I will know what "me" in Connectivity will become only as I go, not before. If I try to force a conception ahead of time, I stifle the natural growth of what would have happened.

I am not a Unique Expressor who controls his destiny. If there is any influence that is direct, it lies in where I point my attention joined with acknowledging that word-tool overlays are veils that hide the truth. It's an acknowledgment that has helped me stop taking word-tools so seriously and has freed up conscious energies that I can then point toward the Connectivity and the awaiting embrace of partnership with Source. And it's through all this and because of it that my Unique Expressor is nurtured best and can blossom best.

Openings Create More Openings

I discovered *directing my attention* was a focal point for creating my world and for the quality of my experiences.

One proof of this was flaw finding. Discovering I could find flaws everywhere and anywhere dissolved the meaning and believability of my flaw finding. It provided an opening that then showed me that I choose where I point my attention. And this led to another opening showing me that if I could find negatives everywhere, I could also find positives in those same places.

It was like opening a door in a newly discovered way. Engaging the power of directing my attention changed how I view and feel about the world. It was a door that had always been there. But I had been opening it only to what made me feel bad. And I didn't even notice I was doing it. Feeling bad had become such a norm that as far as I could tell, I felt good. And this "good" seemed good because it looked as though most other people were feeling the same. I was not able to see that I actually felt bad until I opened that first door in a new way.

And then, it was as if there were many windows behind that door that were just waiting to be opened. They were not in view before. But once I opened up to the effect of directing my attention, it was as if new windows popped out of the walls, inviting me to further action not available before.

It was breaking through thinking I owned the truth. It was a crack through which I could see the vastness of what I don't know. The crack helped thaw my frozen self just a little, and this loosening helped me see outside my radar screen. I could now sense that what I don't know has great value. I discovered that it is logical to look beyond logic.

Practicing Feel Good Now by shifting when I felt tense/bad/negative, first with small negatives and then gradually with more challenging ones, I discovered more about previously unseen openings, and I saw that each opening begets others that I had been closed to before.

And with the shocking surprise of my pop-in – "Wow ! I don't believe in right/wrong good/bad anymore!" – other windows opened up as I found endless curiosity and positive energy through interacting with people and situations I had previously judged (shut out) as wrong, bad, flawed, etc.

Although avoiding superiority is still a great challenge for me, I've opened many other windows by coming away from the devil of comparison and realizing that my sense of separation and emphasis on individuality is not real. It made it more obvious that Connectivity is pervasive and that the whole of Source provides the origin from which word-tools are derived.

Appreciating the limits of word-tools – their this-not-that nature, their makeup as shortcuts indicating only the tip of an iceberg, and their consequential omission of uniqueness and inability to carry Connectivity – brought even more windows into view.

Opening that first door, by pointing my attention differently, opened windows that had seemed invisible before, and expanded what was possible in my world. Allowing for the unknown, and being comfortable with not knowing, helped give vibrancy to moment-to-moment living. Each point of awareness expanded my views, outlooks, and perspectives – and my Being.

The more I use thoughts/emotions as the limited tools they are, rather than as objective known-for-sure absolutes, the more I find my world opening up to the whole of life. And I find it difficult to contain my excitement about it!

Along with this, the notion that "I make things happen" has changed. I sense a flow that doesn't fit conceptual force or any other type of force. This also involves a different kind of knowing and a sense of Being that doesn't depend on word-tools.

As a Unique Expressor that allows rather than tries to force, I feel the flow of being Arm-in-Arm with an indescribable whole. I smile at myself as I call it indescribable and then immediately try to describe it with the word *source*. I first chose the word *source* to indicate the whole of life experience from which we derive our words. But as I opened window after window, my sense of Source expanded to include the noncognitive.

More and more windows continue to pop into visibility. What an amazing process! Perhaps "openings creating more openings" is akin to what some call transformation. This was for me a transformation away from misusing words as if they carry the truth to using them only as pointers toward the real living that always awaits my firsthand experience.

Enjoying Knowing Is Different from *Enjoying Knowing More Than*

About a year before writing this book, I noticed something that seemed new. It was sheer delight and pure enjoyment about *knowing*. It was not about knowing more than I did before. And it wasn't about knowing more than someone else. It was enjoyment *without the comparison of more than*.

Before this, much of my enjoyment seemed to come from knowing or having *more*. I put so much attention on learning something new so I could finally *improve* myself, or get a *better* job, or get a *bigger* house or *better* car. Enjoyment was focused on more than and better than.

But this new feeling of delightful enjoyment about knowing was different. It had no comparison, no more than, no better than, no improvement.

I felt this kind of enjoyment when these pop-ins came: *Judge your experience, not people, events, circumstances, or situations; A Whole of The Whole;* and the title for this section, *Enjoying knowing is different from enjoying knowing more than*. I felt delight with each one when it first came, and I feel it again each time I see or think of it.

It was simple joy that arose from combining words in a way that points to life experience. And these pop-ins are examples of another pop-in that brings delight every time I encounter it: *Using words in such a way as to highlight the Connectivity from which they come rather than the separations to which they lead.*

These pop-ins began to come after I opened my viewpoints in a way that allowed more life to come in. And this feeling of pure delight in simply knowing, without any payoff or comparing, came many months after.

This joy in words may seem strange, especially coming from this book as I emphasize how limited words are and how much I have misused them to feel superior and to intimidate and degrade people.

In this case however, words came together in a different way. They connected with life experience with no involvement of how I felt about myself. It was much simpler and direct. It was sheer excitement about what the words lead to and where they came from. They lead to Connectivity rather than judgment and separation. And they came from non-word processes, a motion or energy more like Source and less like in-the-head figuring out.

I think of it as being like the way a runner enjoys feeling the body move, with no thinking, reasoning, or worrying present. Or the delight of a puppy dog jumping into the snow for the first time. Or the pure joy of creation felt by an artist when a piece of music or a painting comes out, without thoughts about others' enjoyment or of anything that may come next.

That's what is carried by the difference between sheer enjoyment, and enjoyment because of what's interpreted as personal progress – pure enjoyment of this moment is without any comparison and without any feeling of "I'm great". It's a moment of just this, just here, just now. It's uncontaminated by any better than, more than, or best/winner type of comparison.

One better-than, more-than example that recently passed through my mind is: "I'm so much better at listening to my sister than I used to be". This comparison comes from my surface self/ego.

But I've also experienced "listening to my sister" without the comparison: "I enjoyed the feeling of open quietness as I listened to my sister today". There was no pat on the back here and no need for one. It was only the sheer delight of enjoying a moment of living. It was a whole-self kind of joy.

For me, it's easy to cross over into feeling that I deserve a pat on the back or some sort of credit for making progress. But I find that any better-than/more-than comparison creates a background that pushes me to meet criteria I ought to reach or surpass. It creates a new *should*, another dictate to strive, strain, stress, and blame for. If I don't listen to my sister as well next time, I've reversed direction and am now doing worse. When my enjoyment is based on progress, measurement takes the forefront and joy is replaced by pressure to perform.

This type of *should* fits my flaw-finding habit where everything I see needs improvement and everyone I see should strive and create the stress necessary to reach new and ever-rising levels of doing.

The constant need for more – producing more, doing more, getting more, seeing more, buying/owning more, eating more – is for me a malfunction that partners well with my efficiency monster and next-next-next diseases in creating stress.

I find that more than also fits with constant neediness. *Before I was small, now I feel bigger and better. Before I was inadequate, now I'm much more than I was.* Feeling small and not enough always leads me to needing more: *even though I just got what I was striving for, since I was inadequate before, I must still be inadequate compared to what I could be or should be.* With my attention on this more-than comparative type of outlook, I endlessly maintain feelings of inadequacy and smallness.

Comparison is so ingrained, and it always makes me feel small. It's a constant rollercoaster of feeling inadequate, then pressured to do more, then inadequate again, then pressured to do more.

So many of us live our lives feeling small, then big, small, then big. Feeling down, then on top of the world, down, then on top. I too, ride these rollercoasters, but I've become tired of this type of ride.

I've noticed that ideas I apply to myself, I also apply to others. When I've had a morning filled with thoughts of self-criticism, my day proceeds with ready and eager criticisms of others. Others too can always use improvement; they can always do better than whatever it is they are doing. The ideas I torture myself with, I also push out as potential torture for others. It's as if I don't want to be alone in riding my rollercoaster of comparison, progress, and *shoulds*.

While writing this, I realized that this experience of pure enjoyment without measurement carries a pattern that applies to many other specifics. It turns out to be a general pointer that can also be expressed in these forms:

- Enjoying doing is different from enjoying doing more than.
- Enjoying having is different from enjoying having more than.
- Enjoying anything just because *it is* is different from enjoying it because it boosts my self-image in some way.

The pattern is the same. The enjoyment in each fits the "now" moment of living rather than comparisons to the past, to an ideal, or to any other image. These frozen snapshots of "the past", "an ideal", and "an image" are unreal stressors I create with my mind, supported by the this-not-that nature of word-tools. I prefer to enjoy the flow of living now, without interference of the freeze-framing of conceptual measuring.

Even though I still ride the rollercoaster of comparison, the awareness of catching myself feels so much better than not realizing at all. Viewing myself as on a ride is better than being totally unconscious of it and mistaking the ride for life itself. Life itself is not this kind of rollercoaster unless I make it into that by embracing the more-than obsession.

Enjoying the "now" moments of knowing, doing, and having, rather than being stuck on the perpetual more-than rollercoaster, has created a new kind of aliveness in me. It's the kind of aliveness that enjoys just Being and is different from the focus on more than that I embraced for so long.[56]

---

[56] Note: I view Eckhart Tolle's book *The Power of Now* as fitting here, and I highly recommend it.

Admitting Frees Me from Appearing

I've found moments of peace by letting go of the pressure to "appear". By this I mean the pressure to be some image defined by my surroundings.

- The pressure to be what *they* would *approve* of.
- The pressure to be what *they* think I *should* be.
- The pressure to be *this* in order to get *that* job.
- The pressure to wear *that* jacket, or have *that* car, in order to get *that* girl.
- The pressure to bring *this* gift in order to fit what people *expect*.
- The pressure to *show* that I care.

All of these specify something about how I should appear to others. When I am lost in my head, these messages seem all important.

For me, "showing" and "appearing" crowd out the possibility of Being. Life is better when I can simply Be myself, rather than trying to match or fit a predefined image. To fit the image seems false, like pretending. If I "make the appearance" that people expect, it's as if I'm being phony in some way. It's a pressure I've always disliked feeling.

My mind wants to dress up "making an appearance" to make it seem good for all: *I'm taking others' feelings into account when I go along with what they expect. I'm showing them I care.* Or I could even dress it up into a form of Connectivity. I could say: *I am considering the whole of my interconnected surroundings.* All this – dressing up, making an appearance, going along, showing, considering all – is for me, a form of making excuses, made up of conceptual products whose transmission is made possible only by word-tools.

To care is better than showing that I care. To enjoy the prospect of going to a party or family gathering is better than feeling obligated or going in order to spare everyone's feelings but my own. To be me as a whole self is better than being what they will approve of or what I "should" be.

Word-tools are models for appearing. They carry only a miniscule sliver of what is real, yet they masquerade as worthy representatives of what they can only name. They are the kind of tool that makes it easy for me to appear. In dropping uniqueness, word-tool groupings gloss over the unrepeatable specialness of what is real.

By grouping across differences, they invite me to drop my own unique inner growth whatever that may turn out to be, and replace it with repeatable patterns from outside. *Be like them – they know and have already done what you are doing. So observe and do it like them.* Rather than tapping into my surroundings as support for my growth, I find it easy to copy, mimic, and please what is around me. In short, word-tools make it easy for me to fake it.

All these appearances are means for getting things from outside as if no inside existed. That's what makes it all surface. My outside molds itself according to what their outsides need or expect. Appearances chasing appearances with no admittance of the source self that lies deep below. Source self goes unrecognized, both as me and as the core of others.

If I remember the limits of word-tools, I am more apt to ask about uniqueness, to gain awareness of the whole reality of this flower or this person or of myself. When I keep the limits of the conceptual in the forefront of my attention, I'm not satisfied with a glossed over, this-not-that shortcut because I know it can't replace my own firsthand experience. I want to get in touch with the whole, not just the surface. To deal with wholes such as life forms or complex situations, I need uniqueness and Connectivity.

Wondering about uniqueness and Connectivity opens me to more than appearances. It counteracts the power of my word-based surface world to narrow my sight to the sliver of a symbol. Wondering in this way leaves me open enough to admit that there is an origin to those symbols, that there is something that comes before all the images of what people expect and what we should be. I sense something much deeper than the pressure to meet the demands of surface appearances that seem to constantly surround me.

The root is Source. The root is life without words. It's the awareness, the Being, the consciousness that underlies my surface appearances and everything else I experience.

This Being, with Source acknowledged, doesn't pressure me to do *this* in order to get *that*. Source doesn't push for glory, because it doesn't need to appear – it simply is. Source shines without any hint of lack, inadequacy, or fear of not having or being enough. And that shine leads to a natural flow that fits the wholeness of my Being, rather than just the surface of it.

The roles we play: father, mother, friend, spouse, employee, smart, helpful, kind, reasonable, and logical – none of these appearances could exist without Source. Without Source these are just paint on the surface. Without Source there is no surface.

But if I admit[57] to these surface phenomena as roles, and as the limited tools they are, then I begin to release myself from the clench

---

[57] Note: The word *admit* has two meanings that seem to point to the same center. One is "to confess to be true" or to acknowledge. A second is to "let in, allow entry, receive, welcome". Both seem to suggest an openness. With *admit*, there is no need to conceal, camouflage, or gloss over.

of feeling they are all important. Then gradually my fear of the world of appearances is diminished. If I set aside the conceptual filtering that wipes out the unrepeatable specialness that was glossed over when the concept was formed, I have a chance of sensing the vastness of uniqueness and Connectivity.

When I admit, I am more apt to ask and allow questions about uniqueness and Connectivity. Because when I admit, as opposed to just appear, I am open to the whole of reality not just to the sliver I so often use to boost the surface self that remains weak because it lacks connection to its Source. When I admit to the *I am* of a whole self, the pressure to fit narrow, predefined societal images tends to fade away. The pressure to appear is replaced by the freedom of admitting.

And then my paint, the outer coating of myself, admits to its nature and its origin. Then my surface self as only a tool stays true to the fundamental of my whole self. The surface world of appearances is offset and largely replaced by the whole of reality, and I am no longer ruled by only the cognitively filtered part.

Admitting myself as A Whole of The Whole, my surface doings change – they become grounded, vibrant, constructive, and filled with love for what is.

This morning, I listened to a recording of Eckhart Tolle and Oprah Winfrey as they discussed chapter seven of Eckhart's book *A New Earth*.[58] A questioner asked about reacting to troublesome situations. Eckhart talked about three levels involved in how we respond.

- One is whatever it is that disturbs us
- Two is our reaction to that thing including physical, emotional, and thought-based reactions
- Three, which is usually overlooked, is our awareness of both these two levels

I understand the third level to be awareness itself which makes the first two levels possible. For me, this third is the level of Being, the level of connection to Source.

An hour later at a coffee shop, I randomly pulled a book from my bag called *Longing to Know* by Esther Lightcap Meek. I opened the book to page 46 and discovered a description of three stages of looking at Magic Eye® three-dimensional pictures.

- First was looking at the picture
- Second was "struggling to look through it at something as yet unknown"
- Third was looking through the picture at the three-dimensional image

The three-dimensional image offers the surface picture which is readily available with a quick glance. But deeper within it lies the three-dimensional image which differs from the surface.

---

[58] Oprah Winfrey and Eckhart Tolle, *A New Earth, Awakening to Your Life's Purpose: A Worldwide Web Event,* Chapter 7 (accessed October 16, 2017) https://www.youtube.com/watch?v=QwWgpEJxDI0 26:45

A word-tool is like the surface picture. It pulls a snapshot out of the movement of life in an attempt to create symbols we use to indicate something real. A word is a surface-glance phenomenon.

However, words can't hold what is necessary to "look through". As shortcuts for communication, excluding uniqueness and Connectivity, they can only indicate what direction to head if you want to experience the whole, the buried truth that is not apparent when one is lost in the world of concepts. Words are like arrows that point toward the full reality of what is, they are only highly limited symbolic indicators.

As I was making notes on this in the coffee shop, a man came in and sat at a table across the aisle such that we were facing each other. I noticed him and looked at his face, and my mind tossed out a reaction that he seemed tense and closed to conversation.

At this point I had experienced the first two bullets in each set above but not the third. Except I missed the second bullet of Meek's since I immediately jumped to believing the man was tense and closed without having put any effort toward "struggling to look through". At this point, I viewed my mind's judgment of "tense and closed" as an astute observation.

And regarding the third bullets, I hadn't yet opened to an awareness of the first two levels, and I had not yet "looked through" to anything deeper than my initial surface reaction.

Regarding the three-dimensional pictures, Meek continues with the following:

> We don't leave the particulars of the picture's surface behind; we rely on them to focus beyond them. The particulars now deserve to be called clues or *subsidiaries*. We are aware of them, but only as we move ourselves through them and by

means of them to grasp a farther focus.[59]

What Meek writes here tells me that if I leave particulars behind, I dismiss parts of life I need in order to move further into life.

In my experiences with shifting from negatives to positives, I've found the shift doesn't work if I reject and criticize my own initial negatives, such as my judgment of the man in the coffee shop as tense and closed. If I blame myself for jumping to those judgments, I've only switched one negative judgment for another. Instead of judging the man negatively, I'm now judging myself negatively. The energy remains negative.

If I reject and criticize my initial negatives, it's as if I'm trying to leave them behind. But I need them in order to move beyond them. So if I criticize them, it's as if I reject particulars that are necessary for me to see the deeper meaning beneath the surface.

It doesn't work to "leave the negatives behind" by rejecting them, because those negatives are part of what aids me in shifting away from them and toward a fuller more positive awareness which also includes them. I need all of reality to understand and deal with the whole of reality.

I need the negatives and yet I don't feed them with unnecessary attention. The negatives serve as indicators and as part of the process of moving through (and beyond) them. Also, and perhaps most importantly, rejecting my negative judgments through criticism or tension creates resistance to reality, the reality that these negatives were first to flow through my mind.

---

[59] Esther Lightcap Meek, *Longing to Know: A Philosophy of Knowledge for Ordinary People,* page 47 (Grand Rapids, MI: Brazos Press, 2003).

At the same time as I'm remaining alert to rejection and resistance, I remind myself that the negatives are not made into truth by flowing through my mind. Rather, what I see is that most of what flows through my mind is untrue and useless. I don't use word-tools to call the negatives *bad*, and at the same time I don't accept the negative judgments as truths.

If I'm aware that the man in the coffee shop being "tense and closed" is *my* negative judgment not a known reality, then the awareness itself becomes a positive *which includes the negative* as a step in the direction toward seeing through to a deeper unknown, i.e. toward the entire three-dimensional image. This awareness of the difference between my negative judgment and the full reality of this man sitting in front of me encompasses the first two levels of Eckhart's threesome.

So perhaps acceptance of both negatives and positives is inherent to a wider awareness.

If I'm aware that "tense and closed" are (1) a source of negative energy I want to shift away from, and (2) indicators for my need to widen awareness, then I use the whole of the experience as part of "grasping a farther focus".

That was looking at Eckhart and Meek from the perspective of shifting from negative to positive energy. This may seem repetitive but now let's look from the perspective of identification, which includes a sense of the certainty of knowing. For me, word-tools appear to support this type of certainty but actually don't.

With Eckhart's third level, I bring into awareness the difference between what seemingly disturbs me and my reaction, including physical, emotional, and thought-based. This third-level awareness serves to undo my identifications. First by shining light on identifying my reaction (tense and closed) as equal to or true about what seemingly disturbs me (the man). And second, by shining light on identifying my reaction as equal to or true about me, i.e., *I am a guy who carelessly tosses out negative judgments*. In both cases, the third level awareness shines a light that exposes the false nature of each identification.

When I'm lost in concepts I forget that words are tools, that they are only shortcuts, and that they don't carry most of what makes up the full reality of what they only indicate. I forget that the label a word gives us is like a tag on a string connected to the real thing. The tag doesn't equal the real thing. The tag only carries a name for the thing. That's what *every* word is, it's only a tag.

That's why judging, comparing, blaming, etc. are not valid ways to use words. Once their limitations are understood, carrying the negative energy of derogation is more easily seen as a blatant misuse of word-tools. Their limited functioning as tags for real things simply don't support their use for bringing down anything real. Yet this misuse is prevalent, as is our conditioning to carry on with this misuse.

So from the perspective of identification, words work for simple things such as "Would you please pass the salt?" And they work in creating material comforts, such as all the stuff we live with, including cars, computers, houses, etc. But the limits of words simply don't allow them to be constructively used to evaluate complex wholes, such as human beings or life situations.

In forgetting the limitations of word-tools, I miss the awareness, the third level Eckhart Tolle referred to. I misuse word-tools in thinking of any man as tense and closed and I misuse them again if I criticize myself for putting those words on him. Both are judgmental identifications without even a possibility of carrying an awareness of the wider reality behind the whole Beings of him and me. Tying together a series of "tags on strings" doesn't expand the labels enough to carry the whole of what they are labeling.

If I reject or resist any of these negatives, I miss looking through the picture because I leave behind the particulars by means of which I could grasp a farther focus. Another perspective on this is that the particulars left behind include the uniqueness and Connectivity that word-tools don't carry.

If we leave the particulars of the picture's surface behind, we can't rely on them to help us focus beyond them. We close off the possibility of looking through the surface picture, and we miss the opportunity that awaits us to grasp a farther focus and to connect with the deeper reality of Source.

So I have come to view negative judgments, along with any "what is" of reality no matter how "bad" it seems, as part of the process of seeing a wider picture. I can choose to regard all of it as a step in the process of moving myself through my initial conclusions to grasp a farther focus. Only then can I see and connect with Source that initially seems to be hidden from view.

But guess what? It's not as hidden as I so often think. About a half hour after that same man came into the coffee shop, he looked my way and commented on the book I was reading, *Longing to Know*. We began to talk, and I discovered that he had written a book and had been a psychologist. I very much enjoyed our talk and we exchanged contact information. I'm glad I had not been too tense and closed to allow myself to see something deeper than the surface picture of my own judgments. If I had believed I was using word-tools properly, convinced of the truth of my labeling, I would have missed an enjoyable interaction with this man.

Once again, as so many times before, my initial judgment did not fit reality. Realizing judgment as misuse of word-tools led to a wider awareness that allowed me to sense something deeper in this man. What seems to be so hidden from view, as in Magic Eye® three-dimensional pictures, is readily available all around me.

I can see it when I am open enough to allow for the unknown, and when I don't cling to cognitive certainties which I've discovered again and again to be damaging and useless.

Arm-in-Arm

A couple of years before finishing this book, I stopped working to earn money so that I could write without distraction. I sold my house to give me the living expenses to support this work. I don't think I could have taken this risk without sensing what I call Arm-in-Arm.

I first began to sense Arm-in-Arm about three years ago. I would sit down in the morning to read, and almost immediately start writing without knowing ahead of time what I was going to write. The writing just poured out of me. Within a few months of that, the words Arm-in-Arm popped-in. These words fit well with the seemingly new type of sensing I was beginning to be aware of.

I had written for many years in business, personal studies, and at university. But the pouring out that spurred this book was far more fluid than anything I had experienced before.

This sense I call Arm-in-Arm feels like a partnership with neither partner in charge. There is no boss in this partnership. It's a sense of creation that I like very much, adventurous and fun. It's also a delicate learning process for me because I cannot directly make happen the creativity that arises. I cannot push/force it. The fluidity in my writing seemed to begin only as I was able to allow, rather than control.

It doesn't flow if I try to be a boss or direct the process. But at the same time I'm not powerless, I have some sort of influence that I don't yet understand. It strikes me as a delicate, soft, gentle, nurturing relationship with all that surrounds me – internally with my mind stream and especially the energy of my inner body, and externally with the social and physical environment.

As an example, when the words "A Whole of The Whole" popped in, it was as if they came from nowhere. I didn't plan or try in any way to bring them out. They just popped in while I was walking toward a table in a coffee shop. When I sat down, I wrote the words in my notebook.

At first I thought the words didn't make any sense, but I liked them. During the next few weeks, whenever I read the words "A Whole of The Whole" I still liked them.

Later, I realized that these words fit what I'd been gradually sensing as I experienced Connectivity with people. I thought: it's not that I'm a part and you're a part; it's not that we are all parts that make up a whole. It's different from that.

To say that I'm a part of a whole conveys separateness. It is to mistake wholes that grow out of a complex unified sort of Connectivity with the manufacturing we do when we "glue" pieces together – it confuses natural wholes with manmade fabrications.

I find "separateness" to be a confusion coming out of failure to recognize the limitations of word-tools. I now view separateness as more of an illusion and see Connectivity as more aligned with reality. Sure, it's obvious each of us is separate. But now I view this separation as an exaggeration of skin, highlighted by the limits of word-tools. As this-not-that devices, they cannot carry the Connectivity that science has now verified regarding energy flow through and across entities.

But when I'm lost in concepts, that's what I feel: the separateness of being a part, as if I existed in a vacuum. I also feel the me-vs-them that our this-not-that word-tools fit so well. When lost in concepts, I don't feel the Arm-in-Arm of coming together and walking together.

My mind argues with all this. It protests by saying: *Come on, Steve, it's obvious that separateness is real. There are separate things all around us. I look out my window and see a separate person, a tree, a flower, a building. What are you talking about?*

Then when I let go of my closed, constricted frozen form of knowing, I remember that the person, tree, flower, building are all interrelated in countless ways. They all are supported by the Earth and the energy and light of the sun. They all use water. People rely on plants and animals for food. Countless people contribute to producing this food and all the fabricated things that surround me.

When I allow these interrelationships to enter my consciousness, it is as if there is a swirling of the so-called separates that doesn't support the notion of any one of them being independent. Their interrelations bring them much more together, and it becomes much less reality based to view them as apart.

The Connectivity of walking Arm-in-Arm is everywhere when I don't close it out by believing my word-tool conditioning as "the truth".

It's the limitation of word-tools – the this-not-that severing and shrinking of the whole of reality – that makes "difference" appear as reality-based separation. The creation of a grouping that omits uniqueness, along with inability to embrace Connectivity – this is what leads to emphasis of boundaries. And those boundaries turn out to be less reality based than the interconnectedness through uniqueness that is more prevalent, but less immediately apparent. The boundaries we take to be so real are illusions created by lack of awareness of the limitations of our communication tool.

Yes, there are surface differences between that person and me. But the deepest aspects of being human are the same for all. Now that it's more widely known and accepted that energy is emitted by all – the person, the tree, the flower, the building, and everything else – we more clearly see the essential sameness and Connectivity all around us. I now more frequently sense being immersed in Connectivity rather than in the illusory separateness created by the inadequacy of word-tools.

Once again, words/concepts are not the type of tool that can carry either this essential sameness or the Connectivity all around us. Word-tools are limited to the functions of forming groupings and differentiating those groupings. And it's so easy to jump to the conclusion that difference in groupings equals separate. But it just isn't so.

It's difficult because we are so accustomed to fabrications in our world – things put together by assembling separate parts. Alan Watts writes, "We must make a distinction between an organism which is differentiated and a machine which is partitive".[60] Our extraction of concepts from the whole of reality and our use of words to convey these conceptual differences doesn't mean there are actually parts that are real as separate entities. Words are not reality – they are only symbols we create to put name tags on reality.

Again, I review in my mind what a word is: a this-not-that tool; a frozen/fixed packet pulled from an ever-changing energy flow; a tiny sliver of information; a synthetic symbol we use as a shortcut to skip the effort of actually experiencing firsthand the full reality of what we are trying to meet.

Then I recall the value of what I don't know, and I remember that I don't even know what I don't know, and that I've seen things I never before conceived come into my tiny radar-screen range of surface knowledge.

---

[60] Alan Watts, *Tao: The Watercourse Way*, Chapter 3: Tao, pages 50-51 (New York: Pantheon Books, 1975).

Now I can ask: *What types of knowing, what types of communication, might be possible that no one has yet conceived of? Could there be alternatives to our word-tool system? What non-language types of communication tools might be possible?*

My mind rebels by saying: *If you can't put it into words, how will you explain it and how will I understand it?*

I answer my mind by asking: *What about physical touch? Isn't that a non-word way of communicating? What about music and art? What about when a dog, or other animal, interacts wordlessly with human beings?*

When I say there can't be communication without words, I'm like a fish unable to see outside the world of my word-tool water that seems to be all there is because I am immersed in it.

Finally I also notice how superior I feel standing above reality, placing people, situations, events, etc. into the confinement of my word-tool judgment buckets. Do I want to stay on my high horse of superiority and continue to exclude every possibility that does not fit my particular word-based system? Do I want to keep believing the fallacy that I own the truth?

For some reason, this reminds me of a quote frequently attributed to Mark Twain: "It ain't what you don't know that gets you into trouble. It's what you know for sure that just ain't so."[61]

Arm-in-Arm doesn't go with superiority. Arm-in-Arm can feel like confidence, but it's a humble confidence without any edge of self-importance or of having an upper hand. It's a confidence

---

[61] Although frequently attributed to Mark Twain and included in the movie *The Big Short*, many assert that Mark Twain did not originate this. Though familiar to many, there seems to be no definitive author for this quote.

that doesn't know for sure, because it arises from the whole and is outside the splintered type of knowing that is cognition based, outside the this-not-that world of word-tools. It is more like a calm, peaceful sense of feeling grounded in an all encompassing way. All-encompassing is something word-tools can't do.

It's understandable that we fall into the error of misusing our word-tools, that we forget that life came before words, that we view separation as real while remaining unaware of Connectivity.

It's understandable that we have a very difficult time giving up control, even though we find over and over again that *making things happen* doesn't work. My mind comes in and says, *Maybe next time it will work.* But once I sensed walking Arm-in-Arm with life, which I believe so many others have also realized, it also becomes understandable to feel a partnership that is beyond words.

Words indicate tiny aspects of what is. But "what is" is one interconnected whole that cannot be separated into pieces except through imagination.

If we acknowledge these limitations, we can use words constructively and with wisdom as the tools they actually are. We can use them for simple, practical tasks, and for building "stuff" we fabricate, such as cars, planes, buildings, computers, etc.

If we misuse them and allow our surface self/ego to dominate, we become destructive. Then words become tools of battle we call judgments. They set our minds to seeing enemies that aren't real, enemies we created through misuse of these tools that exclude all of life but their one grouping. When I'm lost in my enemy-mode, Arm-in-Arm doesn't exist and separateness seems indisputable.

So I remind myself of two things: (1) I want to use words carefully, and (2) I don't want to take them too seriously. These two things are a delicate coming together, not unlike the sense of walking Arm-in-Arm with life. The two may appear contradictory – *how can I use words carefully and at the same time not take them seriously*?

I use them carefully to undo the misuse I've been conditioned to embrace – the misuse that leads to destructiveness. And I don't take them seriously because I no longer believe that my stream of thinking represents the truth; I don't believe the separateness and enemy-mode thoughts, because I'm aware they are so easily supported by the this-not-that nature of word-tools. The symbols themselves invite distortion until we realize their limitations and that they came from but cannot represent the whole of reality.

A human being is an interrelated whole. Reality is *the* interrelated whole. These wholes simply are what they are.

As an example of my own conditioning regarding the title of this book, my word dominated surface self asks: *How can a whole be "of" The Whole? If a whole is everything how can there be more than one?*

My reply is: *I don't know, not cognitively, not in a way that words can describe.* My whole-self reply is: *An answer in cognitive terms is not important and is perhaps impossible, and if I remember that words are only pointers to reality, not the reality itself, I'll be able to accept this.* My whole self has found that "A Whole" and "The Whole" can walk Arm-in-Arm when I am able to allow and sense the delicate interrelationships involved.

So how can I use words to write this book? Am I being inconsistent? Perhaps.

Or perhaps I'm using a different kind of consistency, one that fits a wider view of "what is" by including the reality of interrelatedness. I say again:

> *Use words in such a way as to highlight the Connectivity*
> *from which they come rather than the separations*
> *to which they lead.*

That is one of my favorite pop-ins. It came out of a sense, a feel for moving forward, that I do not fully understand: the sense of being Arm-in-Arm. And for me it's okay that I don't understand, because I've experienced a different kind of knowing, one that shows me that Arm-in-Arm is different from being lost in concepts, that Arm-in-Arm works for life not against it.

There Is No Controller

Words are not truth-tellers. They are limited tools that do one thing. They provide an easy-to-carry symbol system that offsets the effort of taking someone to the location and pointing to the reality I want to share.

In order to shortcut the process of experiencing reality fully, words omit the uniqueness and do not carry the Connectivity that spans out in all directions from every reality.

Yes words are convenient. But as this-not-that tools, words/ concepts also make it easy for me to view myself and my surroundings as oppositional. When I use them without regard for their limitations, I distort the whole of Source that underlies the experiential base from which the words are extracted.

I have so often viewed people as enemies partly because I forget that words as communication tools are so highly limited. I see this same misapplication, the enemy-mode misuse of words, when I notice the way many people interact with each other. I repeatedly find that we demand too much of our word-tools, expecting them to do more than is possible given what they are.

When I make word-tools into bosses, including the thoughts/ emotions formed by using them, I create the kind of separation that leads to enemy functioning within and outside myself.

What's real is that my word-tools are not the boss-like truth-tellers I take them to be. They are not controllers in the way my superiority and judgment-based surface self uses them.

My will is not the controller of what happens in my life. And I haven't sensed the will of something outside of me, or outside of cognition, as the controller. When I'm functioning as a whole self, I am one with these outsiders and there is no controller.

Instead, what happens in my life is multidimensional. My relation to the whole of my surroundings, to Connectivity, is what comes together to form happenings in my life. My touching Source, in conjunction with acknowledging the limited tool-like role my words play, joins with every other influence to form what happens. I experience myself as an influencer whose influence is more effective when integrated with all of life, in partnership with Source.

Sensing this does not come about directly through cognition. I find it by opening up to something wider, by reminding myself that there is more to life than word-tools. I experience a delicate sense of being at one with life's movement, which includes me but is not only me. It's a sensitive Arm-in-Arm type of whole-self Being.

When I allow for the whole of Being, there is no controller. It isn't control that's behind what happens, it's Being. And Being is interconnective. Life is not a single-cause happening – if it's causal at all, it's multi-causal, the kind of causal that can't be measured or enclosed by our highly limited cognitive system of symbols.

My body, in Connectivity with the air, breathes me. My stomach, in Connectivity with my choice of food, nourishes me. My word-tooled mind, when I'm aware these tools are only symbolic shortcuts, can be used as one of many life resources that point me toward Connectivity. And I much prefer this sense of Connectivity with life's resources to the rigid dictator of truth that my mind becomes when it takes the form of a boss in order to feed separateness, superiority, and my egoic surface self.

So if I can't control my life by using my word-tooled mind, what can I do? What can I use to guide my actions?

I go where my interconnected energy takes me. I follow *me in Connectivity with all*. I remind myself that *if there is only me, there is no me*. And I remind myself of what Eckhart Tolle wrote: "Right action is action that is appropriate to the whole".[62]

Does this mean flow with whatever pushes and pulls me? Does it mean I must arbitrarily do anything that comes my way or anything someone else wants me to do? No, it doesn't mean that, though my this-not-that word-tooled mind would make me think so.

I still choose. But the choosing comes from a nonjudgmental place of selectivity, without believing I exist in a vacuum, and as I follow my interconnected energy.

I can enter the outside pull of another's world gladly, and relish the many treasures I may enjoy there. And I can do it without then switching from my road by walking down their road rather than my own. I can continue as a Unique Expressor and at the same time gain from others' uniqueness.

I am not a controller making things happen as I operate in a vacuum. And there is no one and nothing else controlling me in that way. I am A Whole of The Whole.

---

[62] Eckhart Tolle, *A New Earth, Awakening to Your Life's Purpose*, Chapter Eight: The Discovery of Inner Space, page 238 (New York: Plume, 2005).

Grateful Being

Many years before writing this book, I had an experience with a woman I love dearly. As we sat on a couch facing each other, my eyes looking directly into hers, it felt as if we were overflowing with a fullness of life I had never before experienced. With her hand tenderly touching my face, it seemed as if our souls were embracing.

In those moments, with no words exchanged, I felt more loved than at any other time in my life.

This was a *marker* for me, something I thought about often. I referred to it as "the time I felt most loved". Years later the words Grateful Being popped in to describe this experience. After this sense of feeling loved deeply, and before the words Grateful Being popped in, some other things happened that fit.

I was watching a documentary movie called *War Dance* when a related image came to me. It was also of one person touching the face of another, but this time it was only in my imagination and in a very different circumstance.

The movie centered around three children who had experienced cruel violence at the hands of rebels during years of war in Northern Uganda. The children were in a camp with thousands of refugees.

A rebel had been captured and was being held by camp officials. One of the three children asked to speak to the rebel about her brother. The scene showed the rebel and the young girl sitting on a bench. The girl asked him if her brother, who had been a bicycle taxi driver, might still be alive. The rebel told her that they had been given orders to kill bicycle taxi drivers and that her brother was probably not alive.

The girl then asked the man why rebels did the kinds of things they did. He replied "I didn't want to do those things but I was given orders, so I had no choice".[63]

Watching this scene, a sudden realization hit me – I saw that the rebel had used words/concepts to drive himself to kill. I saw that ideas were being placed above people and above life itself. Ideas (orders) were viewed as absolutes. There was no reality other than the thoughts, transmitted as words in the form of orders. I saw that choice no longer existed when words were taken seriously as carriers of absolute truth.

Killing had been viewed as unquestionable. In this contest between life and word-tools, life lost. I find this often happening inside myself, making a bunch of thought-symbols more important than human life.

Then an image came to me. All at once I pictured this rebel walking up to a victim he had been ordered to kill. I saw the rebel pause, look into the victim's eyes, and gently place his hand on the person's face. I wondered: *What would the rebel feel then, and what would he have done?*

It came to me that eye contact, accompanied by the gentle touch of a hand on the face, can in most cases break the hold of the words. It can short-circuit the orders the rebel had received to kill this human being. It can reestablish a human connection that resides down deep but so easily gets buried under layers of ideas, beliefs, and *shoulds* in the form of word-tools. I see this human-to-human connection as reestablishing Connectivity, and as something that would bring the would-be killer back to reality. This type of human connection exposes the limited nature of word-tools by

[63] *War Dance*, directed by Andrea Nix and Sean Fine, written by Andrea Nix Fine and Sean Fine (Atlanta: Velocity, 2007) DVD 2008. This film can also be found on the internet at https://www.youtube.com/watch?v=UATS5K9IZT0 (accessed October 20, 2017).

bringing back an open, non-word type of knowing, the same kind of openness that a baby has before learning words.

Another Grateful Being experience occurred with a friend a couple of years later. We were talking, perhaps about the *War Dance* movie. We stopped at one point to look at each other in silence.

After a few minutes of sustained, silent eye contact, tears began to stream down my face. Right before my eyes, and through our eye connection, I felt this friend becoming more and more beautiful as each second passed. In those few minutes, this friend became a dear human being who I felt much more affectionately close to than ever before.

About two weeks later, the leader of a mindfulness course I was taking asked us twelve students to pair up and look into each other's eyes without speaking. I was paired with someone I barely knew, and again I cried, and again it was as if she had grown more and more beautiful before my eyes. I haven't seen her since the course, yet I will always remember her.

There was nothing romantic or sexual for me in either of these experiences, and yet there was a strong sense of intimacy. It was as if through our eye contact, and through our prolonged silence, we were connecting to something sacred about being alive, it was as if we were connecting to Source.

It seemed as though some kind of energy had come up through the ground and flowed through my eyes, then through the other person's eyes, and then down through her feet and back into the ground. It was as if Source had flowed through each of us during these moments.

About a month later I was telling a stranger about these experiences and about the *War Dance* movie, and tears came again as I looked into his eyes. Our conversation had started because he had been preparing a speech about school shootings, which had reminded me of the movie.

For me these experiences are markers for a kind of human connection that is much deeper than any thought or emotion. They were experiences of deep Being between two people without the involvement of conceptualization or any other word-tool products.

The words Grateful Being are both simpler and more all encompassing than the judgment-based evaluative words I so often use. Grateful Being communicates a wider sense of the process of living, without the this-not-that snapshot feel that word-tools convey so well. Grateful Being feels to me like love flowing out, without any hint of possessiveness or neediness, and without any attachment that could turn into the betrayal of a love rejected.

My surface self/ego says, *This Grateful Being stuff is too vague, it's not real, and my logical self has never seen it.*

My response is: *What's more real? Allowing a bunch of word symbols in the form of principles or morality to drive you to kill other human beings? Or acknowledging and honoring your own experience even though you can't put words or logic to it?*

Grateful Being is a Connectivity experience with the widespread embrace of a *we*. It isn't a me-not-you experience. It's without a sense of separation, yet with a sense of uniqueness. It is deeper than, and comes before, the object-based word-dominated reality where comparison, evaluation, and measurement take center stage.

Many people first connect with Source through nature or a religious experience. For me, it was through people. It was through Grateful Being.

Perhaps I first sensed Source through people because I had carried so much flaw finding, so much negative judgment and superiority toward these living beings I had viewed as objects for so long. To me, it had been an absolute and unquestionable truth that we live as separate individuals as if in a vacuum.

Grateful Being has been like a sacred gem, a feeling of great appreciation for life and gratitude to life. It describes a connecting with people, and with Source, that I cherish highly.

Noncognitive

I came to sense the noncognitive only after my word-tooled self opened up just a little. As my rigidity gradually lessened, simple experiences of Connectivity began to seem relevant. I would remember them over and over again. Many of these moments fit what I call *markers*. Here are two of the first of these moments.

I had moved away from my home in Utah to California for a few months in order to find a job. In my usual this-not-that way, I spent all my time job hunting and studying objective philosophy, and nothing else. Except for occasional shopping trips, I was isolated. Once, at the checkout stand of a hardware store I found myself looking directly at the checker's eyes for just a second. It was a moment of quiet connection. With no mind-chatter, it was one human being stopping to touch another through the eyes. This combination of still silence and eye contact stayed with me as my first marker.

The second early marker happened during the time period when my wife of more than sixteen years and I were completing our divorce. Driving to work one morning, I felt deep sadness. Before this, when I encountered people feeling loss, I had minimized it by categorizing them as weak, stupid, and stuck in victim mode. But this time it was me, not other people suffering, and it was intense. I remember feeling the surprise of *Wow! This is what people feel when they have lost something they cared about, something dear to them that they were holding tight to.*

It's strange that within the deep sadness, there was a bit of excitement as I discovered how it felt to be intensely sad without whisking it out of the way with a bunch of words. I felt compassion for myself and for those I had previously categorized so harshly. Suddenly my categorizing people as weak, stupid, and want-to-be victims seemed totally inapplicable to the sadness and loss I was experiencing. Unexpectedly, I felt Connectivity.

These two marker moments came into being only through a sense of allowing something I had not before let into my life. Without using word-tools to discount the eye contact with the store clerk, or to cover up or defend against the feeling of loss from the divorce, I found myself simply feeling, simply experiencing these moments directly. These markers were unexpected life happenings that were outside the confines of the cognitive, conceptual world I had thought encompassed everything.

Since those first markers, I've had many experiences through which I sensed just a taste, just brief whiffs of the vastness of the noncognitive.

The value of what I don't know helped as I began to loosen my clench on word-tools buckets as the prime means for viewing life. And as I write this, I am still gradually letting go of the "I know for sure (and you don't)" feeling. Now, the judgment-filled, fast-paced, status/image-conscious, word-tool dominated world seems less and less reality based.

As I peel away the layers of "I know for sure", I also sense the vastness of not even having a clue about so much of what happens. And it's okay. It feels even better than okay because somehow the not knowing feels more supported by reality. For me, it's a new kind of confidence. A confidence without the need for comparison that I refer to as a sense of being *grounded*.

I had always defended my rejection of everything noncognitive by identifying myself with the logic and reason of science, business, and the specialized world of productivity. I had valued and admired these as the sources of our ability to live. Now I see the noncognitive, and the value of what I don't know, as sources of life and of everything I know about it. Now I see it as logical and reasonable to acknowledge and honor what is outside of logic, reason, and science.

I wonder if I would have listened to me saying this to myself ten years ago. I doubt it because then I thought that for anything to be real, it had to make sense in a conceptual way. As closed as I was, immersed in my this-not-that word buckets, I probably wasn't open enough to allow anything noncognitive. I certainly would not have listened to someone talk about Connectivity or being Arm-in-Arm.

Since then, I've also realized that the nature of any word-tool is to exclude. Each this-not-that bucket excludes anything that is not it, anything that doesn't fit its exclusive category. The category *dog* not only excludes the uniqueness of each single dog, it also excludes everything in the universe that is not a dog. I've recently realized that when I was gung-ho about word-tools, I was also gung-ho about exclusion. When I was misusing word-tools without awareness of their limitations, I was also excluding most of what makes up the reality they were meant to point me toward so that I could go and check it out firsthand.

So even though I use words here to describe my experiences of opening up, it isn't primarily my new words that brought me to Connectivity. Although my new beliefs were useful as cognitive reminders, it was something deeper that primarily changed how I experience life.

It was a type of sensing I had buried underneath word-tools throughout most of my life. My journey to recover that sensing required opening up to the noncognitive. So although as pointers my new beliefs helped me direct attention differently, *touching Source* did not come about through a change in beliefs. It was realized experientially, not just through shifting my cognitive belief system. And it was only after loosening my hold on word-tools as truth-tellers, that I was able to allow my superiority to dissipate a little so that allowance for the noncognitive could begin to grow.

Lately I've wondered how many people hold strong beliefs only through word-tools. I've wondered how many hold a word-tooled concept of God, higher power, or Source as equivalent to the deep knowing that these concepts point us toward in reality. Perhaps there are many who constructed complex word-based descriptions of their beliefs but never felt the deeper realization that underlies the symbols.

I was certainly one of these people. I filled my life with reliance on complex word-based ideas. I carried my objective philosophical beliefs only through the filters of conceptualization, never feeling the "life" I claimed they carried. I was detached, a surface self with almost no connection to the whole of reality. For me, everything had to be word-based and that compulsion created an existence made sterile by the limitations of these tools.

Perhaps also there are many who claim allegiance to environmentalism, or human rights, or justice – but it's only through the limiting filters of word-tools that they carry it. Like me, they don't realize that they have cut the string that attached the symbol to the reality. And they are left holding a pile of tags and strings with the reality left far behind. No wonder we feel so much emptiness and a desire for more that never ceases to press on us.

Previously I was not pro-environment. But as I uncovered Connectivity inside and how it encompassed the outside, I also came to feel enjoyment of the earth as something to be cared for, almost like a soulmate. In a natural way that seemed to unfold gradually, I began to turn the water off when I brushed my teeth and washed my hands. And I began to waste less paper and to reuse plastic bags and containers. This change was not primarily driven by belief or new instructions. At that time I still did not hold pro-environment ideas in word form. I found the feelings first, I found the realization of a different dimension of reality in my living before the word-based beliefs. This was noncognitive, and for me, it shined additional light on my slavery to cognition.

I was able to allow more into my life by viewing words as only limited tools. What flowed in was something non-word, something noncognitive that allowed me to feel it as wholly "mine" because it was my firsthand experience rather than just a belief filtered through and reduced by thoughts made up of the detached tags of word-tools. It was a kind of indescribable willingness for more that allowed my acceptance of what cognition cannot carry, the noncognitive sensing of Connectivity, pop-ins and Arm-in-Arm, the noncognitive sensing of the reality that underlies the surface symbols.

Where Did It Come From?

I walked past a house with a front yard that had a variety of colorful flowers, bushes, and trees. I liked it! My eyes were happy to take in the vibrancy of color, textures, and shapes. I felt as though the sight were feeding me in some way.

Then it popped into mind that although a human being planted seeds, or purchased already grown plants, and artfully placed and cared for them, the ultimate source of all of it was prior to human beings, and of course, prior to concepts/word-tools.

Then something totally different came to mind. I thought of how I was born into a hospital and lived in a fully formed home, without having any sense of the countless natural materials, efforts, and people that made possible these buildings and everything in them.

All these things were just here when I got here. So why should I be aware of the countless sources that led to the floors, walls, doors, medical equipment, stove, fridge, plumbing, etc.? Why should I be aware of the source for all this, the natural, energetic whole that came before all of it? Years before writing this book, I would have said: "I'm not interested in where all this came from – I'm not interested in sources, only results and what I want is more of them."

Why shouldn't I just keep biting the hands that feed me? The hand of life, the hand of nature, the hand of the energies of Source?

When people I meet ask what I do, I tell them I'm writing. Most follow up by asking what I'm writing about. I tell them it's about being lost in a world of words, lost in concepts, and that words are only tools but I so often use them as weapons when I judge or criticize. Many of these people seem curious when they hear this.

Then when I talk about words coming out of life, when I tell them that conceptual groupings are pulled out of life experience, the curious wondering sometimes seems supplemented by confusion and blank stares.

And why shouldn't talking about where words come from be sort of weird? Ten years before this book, I wouldn't have even listened to someone like me. As quickly as possible, I would have rejected anyone questioning the validity and truth-telling power of words. I may have thought, *You fool, you are using words to talk to me! How can you question them this way?*

Old Steve would have labeled New Steve as crazy, because ten years ago Old Steve believed that word-tools were the ultimate source for everything that makes up our lives including logic, reason, methods, philosophies, business, cars, houses, or in a word, survival. If you had challenged Old Steve, he might have said "Okay, maybe I'm off in claiming that word-tools are the ultimate source for everything. But physical reality and science are the ultimate source, and concepts/words are the key to knowing all that".

Again, it's like being a fish in water hearing someone trying to explain that water, and word-tools, aren't everything. Ten years before this book, I was that fish. The conceptual world was nearly 100 percent of my reality, the *only* means of knowing *what is*. Then I gradually became aware that I was enclosed in something I'd never noticed before, and that other realms may be part of the whole of reality.

I wonder how many people are like me ten years ago, completely engulfed in a word-tool dominated, conceptualized world. How many see the world only filtered through concepts?

It helps when I remind myself that there was a time when there were no words and no concepts, or nearly none compared to what we have now. There were times when human beings, life, and nature functioned without cell phones, computers, without machines of any kind. Yet perhaps most of us have rarely imagined a world remotely like that, just as most of us have rarely imagined a world without language/word-tools.

It helps me to think back to times when more human beings were attuned to Connectivity with the natural environment – with earth, animals, and plants. There were times when people honored, with grateful attention, the natural world including the sun, rain, and air. I bet many people from those times noticed their breathing without taking mindfulness or yoga courses. I bet many noticed their bodies, and the energies within, without going to massage therapists, the gym, chiropractors, or spiritual teachers.

Now we "honor" by going to the store to buy all the tools, plants, and décor to create a beautiful front yard. We give complete credit to the people who earned the money to buy that stuff, and maybe if we went a little further, to those who work at the stores we buy the stuff from.

It doesn't even enter our minds that the Earth, sun, and all of the rest of nature is the ultimate source of all of that shopping. At least it didn't enter my mind ten years ago. And now I feel as though I'm a brand-new baby in the realm of uncovering awareness and gratitude for the Earth, sun, and the whole of natural life. Despite being just a baby in this realm, every day I feel grateful to noncognitive reality, to the value of what I don't know, to what can't be filtered through the shortcut symbols we call words.

How can we come to see that words came after life? That words are only tools with a limited range of applicability? How can we come to view concepts and words as only tools that are not unlike other kinds of tools, such as shovels and lawn mowers, hammers and screwdrivers, pots and pans, and knives and silverware?

Many of us live our lives almost completely devoted to computer and business activities which are many layers away from earth, sun, rain, and air. We hardly notice the natural world that ultimately feeds us, we hardly notice that uniqueness and Connectivity are missing from our word-tooled functioning. At least this was true for me. I hardly noticed.

We are engulfed in fabrications that are manmade. I've found myself immersed in the artificial surroundings of buildings, cars, "stuff", and word-tools that set structures for getting to work on time, judging people as good and bad, reasons to be angry at my spouse or kids, and how to manufacture more fabrications so I can earn more money so I can buy more fabrications.

And all these fabrications seem as real as the Earth, sun, rain, plants, and animals. We are cradled in a medium of word-tools, of synthetic essentials, and insulated from the reality they all originate from, the sources that came first.

So how did I get out, just a little, of my immersion in word-tools? How did I come to sense that there was more? I too went to an office every day and sat in front of a computer. How was I able to step back from that and get a glimpse of a wider view?

Connectivity within me, with my whole body, and with the surrounding natural environment including people – for me, these were and are main roads toward realizing nonconceptual ways of Being and knowing. I call this *touching Source*.

And recently, as I approach completion of this book, I've put attention on the feeling of walking Arm-in-Arm with the ultimate

origin of it all. It's a feeling of being a partner, not a controller –
even with my body sensations, even with my thoughts. I can take
action, I can influence. But I don't have full control over outcomes.

Connecting to Source is indirect. It's not like I plug myself into
an electrical socket and get a jolt of power so I can make more
fabrications. It's not a flip of a switch, it's not a single cause that I
enact to get a result I want.

Instead, this *touching Source* is coming to sense what I can do
that brings alignment with what's around me. I now put much
more attention on the natural world of plants, animals, and
human beings. I focus as much attention[64] as possible on my body,
including hands, arms, feet, calves, thighs, hips, torso, muscles, skin
– the realities of sensation I paid no attention to for so many years.
And I put attention on the tingling of energy I can feel inside my
body, and on the countless connections that holds the whole of it
all in a grand embrace.

I repeatedly remind myself that I can't just flip a switch to get what
I want. That I will be completely lost again if I put primary focus on
outcomes like making money or becoming famous or well known.
The attention that contributes most to me and others is *indirect and
grateful*, not *willfully direct and always wanting more*.

So ten years before this book, I would have given 100 percent
credit to the person who created that front yard I liked so much. I
would have praised only the individual person who did the creative
assembling. I would not have felt gratitude for the ultimate
sources that gave that person all that was needed to create the
beautiful setting. Inside me, there wouldn't have been any

---

[64] By *attention* here I mean simple awareness, without my word-tool stories of worry, disaster
possibilities, and incessant wondering why a particular sensation is there now but wasn't there a
minute ago.

admiration, or appreciation for the natural world that came first, or for the countless interconnections that made it possible.

But now that I stay in touch with Source just a little, I can feel the reality of an outpouring of gratitude for my surroundings including people who initially strike me as unpleasant or negative. Now I'm aware of the limitations of language, and of how word-tools are so often inapplicable in the ways I use them. I'm now aware that flaw finding, lack finding, judgment, criticism, etc., are all forms of misusing these tools we have become immersed in.

This awareness of where it all came from, including me and including you, allows me to sense myself and others as A Whole of The Whole. I appreciate all the sources that provide for my growth, and the feeling of being in partnership with, not dominated by and not dominant over. And because of all that, it feels good to be alive.

Does Life Respond?

Is the energy of Source like the energy of people? Does Life Source respond to me in a similar way to how other people respond?

If I'm in a relationship with another person – sister, parent, friend, spouse, coworker, boss – and if I approach that person only when I need or want something from them, what happens? What happens if I never feel and show gratitude for a person I have a relationship with?

Continuing this description, suppose I rarely give any positive energy to this person and I find it easy to take credit for anything we do jointly, i.e., for things that would never have happened without this other person.

What happens when a relationship between two people is just a one-way energy flow? The result would usually be some form of destructiveness; anger and resentment builds and that causes suffering. It often explodes and/or the relationship ends.

When Sally feels that Jim only takes takes takes, but never gives, she may use word-tools like "I'm being used and manipulated" or "I get nothing, he gets everything".

I've carried these ideas around too, but now I view Sally's statements as a misuse of word-tools. I see through its cover-up to the distortion the story creates. And yet, the stories are understandable. They may be the best we can do given our social conditioning in using word-tools. But now I see that the conditioning and the nature of the tools themselves promote a we-vs-them, victim sense of life.

What I've realized is that these distortions fit my previous relationship with Life Source – I was almost exclusively a taker and manipulator. Life gave, I took. Here are some details about my previous relationship to what surrounded me and to Life Source.

- I initiated contact with the world around me only rarely and only when I wanted or needed something.

- I had no concept of gratitude for my surroundings; that is, for what I took from animals, plants, the Earth, sun, air, or anything else from nature. I thought it was all mine to take and use without crediting the source. What allowed me to adopt this approach? The narrowed eyes of word-tools. By reducing nature to separate categories that were detached from me, using the exclusionary this-not-that of word-tools to shut them out from the privileged class of "human", it became easy to use natural surroundings dismissively.

- Sure, I had heard about giving back, but I viewed it as "mumbo jumbo" because I saw myself as an independent person who rightfully works for and earns what he has.

- And sure, I recognized contributions from friends and associates in a surface way. But this kind of acknowledgment remained shallow without a sense of gratitude for nature and Earth as the ultimate sources. I used Source but never fully acknowledged it. I had no concept of the reality that recognition of anything ultimately traces back to life itself. Since then, I've sensed that to acknowledge people cannot be done fully and genuinely without accompanying it with gratitude for the whole of life.

We are taught to go through the motions and I did that. Tit-for-tat trades with people, thank-you's, and making sure to give proper credit to other people. Sure, I was well trained to do a lot of that. But there is a difference between doing something from word-tool instructions and doing something because your whole self, your deep-down seed of growth, brings that doing through you.

This whole-self kind of doing comes not from training but from fully Being. It's not going through the motions, not done as a means to an end. This type of whole-self doing is new to me because for most of my life, I experienced the trades, thank-you's, and credits with expectation of payback. There was little or no sense of sincerity, genuineness, or deep-down Being. It was all surface interaction.

And none of my instructional training in doing doing doing – i.e. going through the motions in order to reach an end goal – acknowledged Life Source. I carried no conception of gratitude for anything more than what the instructions told me in order to accomplish the goal. There was no appreciation for the origin of it all: the noncognitive. The trades, thank-you's, and credits I put into play were unreal because they were only instruction-based without a tie to what came before as the source of it all.

Gradually through the past few years, I've found a genuine, sincere gratitude toward Life Source. It's a sense that resides deep down, at the energy level, without words. I wouldn't be writing this book without it. I wouldn't have received the pop-ins or the feeling of Arm-in-Arm.

Through Connectivity, I've experienced Grateful Being. This is not gratitude for a gift of trade or a tit-for-tat interaction. It's a simple, pure outpouring of genuine feeling of love for what is. The reason it's difficult to get across in words is that it cannot be carried with word-tools. It is a kind of Being, a feeling for living, that comes before words. You can see it in the eyes of a baby. And now that sense of Being has come back so that you can see it in my eyes too.

Now, I feel sincere gratitude toward Life Source for each day I live.

I don't mean to mislead. I don't feel this all the time, perhaps not even half the time. But when I do feel it, I sense a different form of knowing, one that is not made up of word-tools or of thought/ emotion. On the other hand, when I'm immersed in viewing the world through my conceptual filters, I feel tense and victimized rather than grateful. I'm stuck in the this-not-that separateness of opposition to what is.

I've heard people, and myself, say to life or to God: *Please give me friends, house, car, companion, job, etc. Why can't I ever get these things I've wanted so much and tried so hard to get?*

My answer to myself now is that I tried so hard but without Connectivity to the Life Source that partners with me. My answer is that I'm not an independent earner, I simply do not exist in a vacuum. Everything I credit myself as earning can occur only because I breathe air, benefit from the sun's energy, and get support from the Earth. I exist as A Whole of The Whole supported every day by the natural world and by Source, the vast noncognitive realm from which the world and all cognition come. And when I don't acknowledge and embrace this, when I ignore the Connectivity that encircles every breath and action I take, I feel bad and don't get what will enrich my life because I'm not open to receiving it.

Since feeling my newly uncovered gratitude toward Source and toward life and this world, I've become aware of two different kinds of asking: (1) asking for stuff, or (2) asking instead, *What could I do to contribute?* Since every breath I take, along with the sun and the air and the earth I stand on, was given[65] to me freely by Life Source, doesn't it make sense to sincerely want to contribute to Life Source, i.e., to the whole web of Connectivity? Doesn't it make sense to want to partner with Life Source in its giving and creativity?

---

[65] Once I notice what seems so easy for me to miss, I realize I get so much from "what was here when I got here". See "Where Did It Come From?"

Putting out sincere offerings to help and contribute, without demands, without claims to justice, without a feeling that "I deserve it" or "I'm entitled to it", and without my frantic focus on lack or on my preoccupation with next-next-next, brings energies that support wonderfully different things happening in my relationship with Life Source.

Being Like a Tree

At times it feels as if everything in the world is trying to tell me what I should do, think, and be. The surface world bombards me with how to's, and they press from all sides. "Do it this way, not that" seems to come from everywhere, woven together with my own internalized conditioning of good and bad *shoulds* and self-evaluations.

There seems to be a continuous impulse to put a word to what I am. Both me and the world rush in to describe my identity in the form of "I *am* this-not-that". These identifications are then used as bounce-off points for how I should be better. The description of "I am" provides a baseline for the pressure to improve that identity, all expressed using the limited, synthetic symbols of word-tools.

My mind, along with outside advisors all around, tell(s) me what my identity is, and then, what my self-improved identity should be. (This is all backed by pressure from the conditioned compulsions of Efficiency Monster and Next-Next-Next.)

One morning as I lay relaxing on the floor, putting attention on my breathing, I glanced out of a nearby window at a tree and the sky above it. I realized that the tree feels none of this surface-world tension to do, think, and be. The tree has no chattering mind, and there is no pressure and no resistance caused by uninvited outside advice.

For the tree, there is only the Being of a direct embrace of Connectivity with all that's around it. It has no need to filter its experience through concepts. All of its "attention" is placed on and woven together with its surroundings, of which it is a whole. Its energy flows with, not against, what is around it.

Yet for me, so much of my attention is diverted in many different directions at once toward the multiple demands of the surface world and toward my own chattering word-tooled mind.

What would it be like to free up this diverted attention from the confines of limited word-tools, and place it in the depth of Connectivity?

The tree I see from my window knows what to do without any mind-chatter pressures, without any word-tool demands from outside or inside itself. Its attention isn't pulled away from its core functioning. The tree is not distracted by word-tool *shoulds*, measures, or judgments. For the tree, there is no right or wrong, no good or bad. There is simply Being. Being in Connectivity.

Not distracted by a chattering mind or outside advisors, its attention forms *a unified sense of knowing and Being.*

What if I could use my attention to form a unified sense of knowing and Being, like that of the tree's? What would it feel like?

When I feel as if I'm flowing *with* life rather than against it, without resisting *what is*, and recognizing the limited nature of cognition as only one of many possible ways of knowing and communicating, then, like the tree, I sense a direct embracing of Connectivity.

When I'm fully aware and in Connectivity with my surroundings, my mind isn't dominating. The whole of me is present as the mind temporarily stops or slows its chattering. It's as if I have somehow weaved touching Source with using my mind as a limited tool. When I'm in this kind of flow state, I don't even notice my mind, just as I don't notice the functioning of my heart muscle, thyroid, pancreas, or the interactions of the trillions of cells in my body.

My mind becomes one of the crowd as just one of many tools that function for life. It no longer strains to overstep its nature.

Touching source, and allowing my whole self to use its many tools without resistance, feels like the *unified sense of knowing and Being* that the tree seems to have.

When I read the following, sourced from the writings of Frederick Buechner, it was as if a light has been shined on this type of "tree Being":

> God calls you to the place where your deep gladness and the world's deep hunger meet.[66]

Perhaps that's what a tree experiences. The tree's attention causes no resistance as its "deep gladness" meets with the "world's deep hunger".

My choices of where I place my attention can do the same for me. I've experienced just enough of this *unified sense of knowing and Being* to know that this book is where my attention is best placed – the place where my "deep gladness and the world's deep hunger meet". That place is me as A Whole of The Whole.

---

[66] Phillip Shepherd, *New Self, New World: Recovering Our Senses in the Twenty-First Century*, page 430 (Berkley California: North Atlantic Books, 2010).

Last Part: Addendum

More Words on Each Section as an Aid to Jumping to a Topic You May Enjoy Today

Introduction

It made sense to me that relationships, jobs, and stuff was primary to whether or not I was happy. But I began to discover that these "outside" happenings were not most important. I have begun to see that it's the inside that matters most to feeling grounded in life, and happy. When I am able to allow myself to Be with my surroundings, rather than trying to force them to satisfy me, I find that the answers are inside me, I find that I am the source.

Through the tension I caused myself by misusing words to judge, criticize, and blame, I discovered how limited conceptual thinking is. I began to call the symbols used for this thinking "word-tools". Viewing words as only tools, and coming to see how limited they are, helped me find a new, more-grounded place of Being.

This book was written as it flowed out, one section at a time. It's not linear as perhaps most books are. Once you get a feel for the limitations of word-tools, perhaps by reading through the first fifteen to twenty sections, you could skip around and read whatever section sounds interesting at the moment. Also, carrying a view of words as only approximations, I often grouped many words together to point to the same general idea-arena. With that in mind, I've listed terminology to show which words I've used as synonyms for the purpose of this book.

Lost in Concepts

A word is a symbolic tool created by human beings to indicate something we experience in reality. We generalize and say "All of these things we will call *dog*, all of those things we will call *ball*." A word is a this-not-that categorization that provides a name, a shortcut for communication. It represents, in symbolic form, what we experience. But a word does not carry the fullness of that experience; it holds only narrow slivers of the context from which it was drawn. Each word is a limited, inflexible tool that excludes far more than it includes.

Ten years before this book, it seemed I was almost 100% lost in concepts. Although familiar with where concepts come from, I didn't see them as a tool, I saw them as the only way to access reality. I believed all truth must be conceptual. If it couldn't be put into words, with logic to support it, it wasn't worth considering.

But I began to notice that there were so many different versions of

"The Truth" around me, and wondered why peoples' truths could be so seemingly oppositional. As this tense, stressed adult I call "me" became aware of how lost he was, and of the limits of the words he used every day, my life opened up to a feeling of peace and a joyful flow of living that seemed new and wonderful.

6. Feel Good Now   35

Using Feel Good Now as a motto helped me develop the ability to stand back from my thoughts and watch them. When I caught myself feeling less good, I could shift attention from what was making me feel bad to something that felt just a little better. I began to see other people, myself, and life differently; and I started enjoying it all so much more.

7. Objective Knowing   40

For most of my life I was committed to learning facts, being right, judging, and believing one truth for all people – I viewed these as *the* ways toward knowing what was real. I rejected everything non-objective, such as intuition, the knowing of my body, and the knowing that is inherent in nature.

Then I wondered: Does believing in "one truth for all" cause stress inside of me? I saw that it did. Eventually, I realized that my underlying state of tension was caused because I was rejecting much more than I was accepting. I was trapped inside the limits of word-tools. A word excludes everything except its one category. I excluded everything except what I viewed as Objective Knowing, which for me could be found only through word-tools.

8. The Tyranny of the Should   43

Establishing and following *shoulds*, in order to do the right thing, may appear to be the way to create "good" in the world. Reaching for ideals, and measuring one's value by their attainment, is a common part of growing up. But what if this approach backfires as it puts pressure to measure-up to an image above life itself? What if it feeds feelings of inadequacy more than it inspires right action?

Soon after I began shifting my attention inside myself to discover what I was actually feeling (using Feel Good Now), I realized that I could find flaws in anything and everything. I had trained my mind to constantly scan for problems so I could fix them, and being immersed in this approach to life, I had blinded myself to the stress it was causing inside. Then I realized that if I can find flaws anywhere and everywhere, I can also find positives in the same places. The difference was amazing! Awareness of this realization, along with practice in shifting my attention based on it, made a huge difference in how I felt about life.

Fifteen years before this book, I took a course on creating definitions from scratch. We didn't use dictionaries. Instead, we were required to pull definitions from real-life experiences. Prior to this course, I viewed a definition in the same way I viewed an object such as a tree or a rock. Trees were in my yard, rocks were in the garden, definitions were in the dictionary.

After this course, I began to view definitions as very different from trees and rocks. I saw them as *derived from* reality not *of* reality in the way trees and rocks are. Trees and rocks are at the base of reality, but words and definitions are only extractions. I discovered that definitions are derived from the reality of life experience, which came before words. With this course I began to see that words are not just out there as if they always were. Rather they are tools created by us for a specific and highly limited purpose.

As a well-educated person who studied philosophy for years, I thought I knew more than others. I felt superior to people whose knowledge didn't fit mine. I also felt invulnerable and viewed people who were feeling any kind of pain, especially emotional, as weak. I thought they had brought it on themselves by being lazy and stupid. Then I experienced a painful loss and life began to look different.

12. Posts in the Sand   54

I came to see and feel that viewing words as absolutes was keeping me stuck. Holding my words as absolutes more often led to destruction than to better living for all involved. I thought that there must be a better way. Coming to know words as limited, and as freeze-framed snapshots of the constant movement of life, I realized they are more like temporary placeholders than absolutistic truth-tellers. Most of my life, I had used words as posts in cement. Later I realized they are, at best, only posts in the sand.

13. Crazy Thoughts   59

I grew up in a house filled with blaming. Perhaps many of us did. I always wanted to stop the cycle of this negativity but didn't find a way out until my late 50s. I had a roommate who I had labeled as "messy". After internally churning my complaints about her for a few days, I was finally ready to mention it.

Huge surprise! As I was about to start talking she said something that brought to mind the affection and respect I felt for her and for us. Immediately, the thoughts and feelings of blame and complaint dissolved. This dissolution happened so quickly and effortlessly, I realized the unreality of my negative thoughts. That's when the name *crazy thoughts* popped-in to signify this kind of internal chatter. And then I was shocked to see how prevalent my crazy thoughts were hour after hour and every day.

14. Efficiency Monster   63

I am ruthless both with myself and others about being efficient.

After all, isn't life wasted when we aren't as efficient as possible? Don't we deserve to be blamed when we aren't efficient? Releasing the hold of this monster, with its constant pressure for perfection and blaming, has helped me view life differently.

I was an absolutist in my thinking about productivity and profit. But once I began to watch my Efficiency Monster in action, I realized that what is regarded as "wasting time" can be converted to "the enjoyment of living in the moment". The real waste of time comes when we respond to the pressure for perfection and blaming.

15. Overgeneralizing a Tool   67

I often get caught-up in taking word-tools too seriously. For example, when I make a plan, I feel as though I must complete it because it's an intention set in place by words. It's as if just putting it into words forms a "must-complete" commitment. For me, putting something into words creates false importance. As I continue to remind myself that words are only tools, I have gradually come to use words in ways that fit their limited nature, and to overgeneralize and misuse them less frequently.

16. Slowing Down and Opening Up   70

Slowing down as I move through seemingly insignificant activities has expanded my experience and enjoyment of life. For example, eating blueberries one at a time, instead of in small handfuls, opened me to seeing how my words had closed me off from enjoying softer sweeter ones as well as the firm, sour ones I had thought I liked best. As I more carefully watch the words I use to describe my experiences, I open up to a wider range of vibrant living and enjoyment.

17. Comparison is the Devil   72

I grew up among people who continuously wanted more – more stuff, more pleasure, more knowledge, and more skills and abilities.

And I became one of those people. I adopted the mindset that there is never enough now, always hoping there may be enough in the future.

When I started practicing Feel Good Now, I caught myself sliding down the slippery slope into these never enough, lack-finding comparisons. But lack is an imagined relationship, generated by comparing one bunch of word-symbols to another bunch of word-symbols. None of it is real. As symbols, all of it is imagined. Comparison is the devil because so many of us misuse comparison so much of the time. Well, at least I do.

18. Superiority   76

Each time I misuse words to judge, criticize, blame, evaluate, or place an identity on someone (myself included), it's as if I am stepping up to a place that's above the person and above reality. Words are tools that make that step-up possible, they make Superiority seem as if it were valid and real. But I've found that "thinking I own the truth" through words, just isn't so.

Watching myself judge others as stupid, incompetent, inferior, I've discovered that I use those derogatory words as an attempt to compensate for my own feelings of the same. Underneath it all, it's me who feels below. And that's why I try so often to compensate by stepping above.

19. Blaming Myself – Blaming Others   80

Previously I thought that when I blamed someone, my blame was a description of something real about that other person. That person is worthy of blame because of what they are or what they did. I simply gave a name to the blame worthiness, to the fault I had created, so that I and others could then respond appropriately.

But I began to notice that something happens inside of me just before I blame another. I noticed that when I blame someone else for anything, I have first internally blamed myself, most often for something completely unrelated. Seeing that blaming is an externalization of a feeling of inadequacy, usually connected to blaming myself first, sheds light on my view that any form of "blame" is not a valid way to use word-tools.

20. The Moocher Shortcut   85

A friend owes me money, and at times I could use the word *moocher* to describe her. What have I done? I've used a shortcut to distort life. I've been too hurried to view the situation in its wholeness by using enough words to describe it fully. I've misused word tools again forgetting that they don't carry enough information to justify that type of use. As noted many times in this book, I remind myself to *use words in such a way as to highlight the Connectivity from which they come, rather than the separations to which they lead.*

21. More-Than and Have-To   89

I am trapped-in, but gradually releasing myself from, the ultimatum that I always need to be progressing. I thought if I wasn't doing more-than and getting more-than, then I'd be going backward into less-than. My *more-than* pushed everything else to the side as irrelevant. If something didn't help me get more, then it was just in my way. But I began to sense something wrong here. I found that the foundation for living comes out of something deeper, not something more. It involves stepping away from my more-than and have-to ultimatum.

22. Goals Are for Losers   92

I was shocked when I first read this in a book by Dilbert cartoon creator Scott Adams. But then I began to understand that his idea about a system of action worked much better than setting sights on a must-reach end.

If I set a goal to finish this book by June 30, I create tension, a pretty good chance of failing, and a lot of negative energy. But if I realize goals are a product of word-tools, and that their this-not-that rigidity is damaging to positive energy, then I'm more apt to want a different kind of goal, for example "write at least four days each week and stop if you're not feeling good while doing it".

Words freeze a moment of life and trap it in an inflexible bucket. But life is continuously moving. It's too easy, at least for me, to stick with a goal as an absolute just because I decided to do it. That's why I've found it works better to allow any goal-like tool to move with life. Preconceived endpoints as measures of failure (or success) don't work because they don't fit the continuous movement of reality.

23. Categorizing Stops the Flow   95

My mind pulls me to put a word to everything. It wants to categorize my writing before I write it; and it wants to categorize a person I see before I even talk to them. Putting a word to something fakes me out into believing I really know it. But "knowing because I labeled" is seeing one frame from a movie, then using that frame to represent the whole movie. Word-tools freeze life. They pull a snapshot from a moving, changing whole of reality. When I quiet my categorizing, that's when I can open up to the flow of living.

24. Creating My Reality through Categories I Choose   99

Different conceptual groupings lead to different views of reality. When I forget that I choose where to point my attention, I fall into believing that objective facts determine where my attention lands and how I feel about it. I forget that I have choice in directing my attention to either negatives or positives. I choose the categories I attend to, then feed my mind with them, and that determines my experience of reality.

25. Little Me Superior Me   104

I've carried a feeling of being a "little me" from the time I was very young. Now I realize that to hold that feeling without challenge is like playing a role. As I let the feeling-label grab me, it's as if I put on a costume to act out a particular part in a play. It's still easy for me to "get small" in this way.

Again and again, I notice what appears to compensate for being small: feeling superior to other people or situations. If I make them seem even more-little than me, I feel bigger in some way. Feeling the free space of something more than the this-not-that labels of word-tools has helped me view "little me" and "superior me" as roles I play, not as my identity, not as what I Am.

26. Miss-Taking a Word for Reality   106

Word-tools cut out uniqueness in order to create the shortcut groupings we use to communicate. Actual differences held by reality are left out of the concept. The generalized differences between groupings are given prime importance even though those differences are artificial, created by us not held in reality.

I lose my sense of what's real when I take these differences between groupings (word-tools) too seriously. Every word-tool "nots-out" most of reality as it retains only the one boiled-down grouping it extracts from the whole of reality. Each word is a tool of exclusion. And based on how I use words, and how I see others use them, they easily become tools that lead to destruction.

27. I Have a Right! – Follow the Rules!   111

When drivers inconvenience me because they don't follow the traffic rules, I criticize them. I've often used *rights* and *rules* as clubs for beating up on people. And when I do that, it seems I am better than they are – I am superior. But what are rights and rules for? What is their ultimate purpose? Are they created for blaming? Forgetting their limitations, I've frequently used them as tools of blaming and punishment. Seeing this in myself, helped me realize that a person's right to Be, and life itself, is greater than anything created from word-tools.

28. Earners with Entitlement Attitudes   115

What happens when we realize that the concepts we created to point fingers at "those kinds of people" apply equally, or more so, to ourselves? For most of my life, I viewed "entitlement" as an attitude exclusive to poor people who clamored for handouts. Now I view it as just another form of Superiority that may be more prevalent in business circles than in the shelters where street people receive "handouts".

29. Conceptual Force   118

As I experienced brief glimmers of the non-cognitive, I came to question the usefulness of "motivational" concepts such as goals, outcomes, results, structure, and discipline. Considering these as important, urgent, and crucial created a lot of tension inside me.

But that tension was well hidden and I would have never noticed it without having opened up just enough to consider something more than logic, reason, and cognition; in other words, more than word-tools. Now I've seen that getting things done can flow with enjoyment and creativity, without any sign of the resistance caused by trying to *make* something happen by forcing it through these types of concepts.

30. "Facing Reality"   123

I often hear people say "I am only facing reality" when they are afraid about something that could happen in the future. When I do this, I notice my mind making me think that the future event is more certain than my state of being in this moment. Then I remind myself that this moment is the reality I can actually know. But when concepts seem more real than reality, I find myself viewing the thought "she is bad" as carrying as much reality as the observation "she is wearing a red shirt".

I misuse word-tools when I view judgments as real, as if they were just as believable as the here and now I sense right in front of me. And what's in front of me seems here-then-gone so quickly because all my attention is on mind chatter rather than on myself and my surroundings. When I face the reality that I don't know what I don't know, it helps me see that being so sure about the future is just another way to feed the illusion that I own the truth.

31. Synthetic Essentials   128

A few years before this book, I accidently stumbled onto a sentence I had written forty years prior while studying a book for a university course. It turned into one of many launch-points for beginning to sense that there is more to life than logic, reason, productivity, profit, and all the other word-tool products I've been so immersed in.

This sentence, combined with a definitions course I once took, planted a seed in me which became vital to this book. Part of the sentence included the words *cannot be comprehended in them*, which for me touched just lightly on the idea of a base, an origin, a source, that is in reality but can't be represented by word-tools. As a result, I've come to value *that which I cannot comprehend through concepts* as an inroad to a non-word kind of knowing.

32. Wow! I Don't Believe in Right/Wrong
Good/Bad Anymore!   135

This pop-in came to me as a severe shock. At first I thought it was a crazy thing to think, and yet, it stayed with me. As the days passed, I wondered "What about killing? How can I not believe in the wrongness of that? What about Hitler?" My previous reaction had always been "we need to kill these killers so they can't do that again".

But as the shock and surprise of this pop-in dissipated, I began to realize that my previous reaction carried the same destructive energy as those I'm calling wrong, bad, or evil. I also began to realize that taking action to change situations that seem destructive, doesn't require the negative energy of a judgment followed by a forceful counterattack. A punishment mindset is not required to stop destruction; simple non-reactive action works much better.

Actually, it is a killer's sense of being "right" that drives the killing. That "right" gets used as a word-tool cloaking device. If I then try to kill the killer because I'm "right", the back and forth never ends. As I loosened my embrace of right/wrong good/bad, I began to sense a feeling of oneness with people and gratitude toward life. This would not have been possible if I'd continued holding the widely accepted view that judging right/wrong good/bad are good for life.

33. We Choose Our Authorities 140

I hired a life coach and, after a year of beneficial sessions, got extremely angry at her. I thought it was due to her approach and expectations. But who chose to hire her? Who paid her? Isn't the person who hires and pays in charge of, or at least a partner in, the relationship?

I had stumbled into the word-tooled images of me as a little guy and her as the expert. I trapped both of us inside my interpretation of what a relationship with an expert is, all of it constructed using the highly limited shortcuts of word-tools. And many months after my burst of anger, I realized that her approach and expectations toward me was something I habitually used towards others. What I didn't like in her, was what I don't like in me.

Connectivity

34. A Brief Whisper of Connectivity   145

Toward the end of my marriage, just before my wife and I divorced, I was alone for a few months in California. Totally lost in concepts, I did not allow myself to contact friends because I thought I *should* put all my time into my philosophy studies and finding a job.

During this lonely time, there was one moment with a checkout clerk at a store that stayed with me. I didn't understand it at the time but it became what I later called a *marker*, something I remember repeatedly that seems to call for my attention. The moment with the store clerk was the first marker I remember allowing myself to be aware of, and it was a precursor for discovering Connectivity.

35. Life as Process Not Frozen Snapshots   147

Life moves, words freeze. Life is real and words are artificial symbols. A word pulls a sliver out of the movement of life and then pretends to "stand for" the reality it tries to represent. But a frozen snapshot cannot "stand-in-for" the movement of a process. It can only indicate. Word-tools pull us into believing we know the reality because we know the word. But actually, in reality, they can only point us in a general direction. To know life, we must fully experience its movement, not just create and memorize a name tag.

36. Vulnerability   149

I would have never thought I'd prefer feeling vulnerable over believing I was above it all by thinking I owned the truth. To my surprise, I discovered vulnerability felt better than superiority. Vulnerability brought a sense of steady groundedness that wasn't there for me when I felt superior. By vulnerability I do not mean a fearful cowering. I mean a sense of calm openness and acceptance where there is no need to fight, defend, or be right about an idea.

During a time of feeling loss when my wife and I divorced, this newfound treasure of vulnerability brought a little more peace and gratitude to my life.

Usually when I use the restroom at the coffee shop, I have the room to myself. But since it is not locked and has a stall and a urinal, sometimes I end up sharing with another. Then the battle ensues – not between me and whoever else is there, but inside me as I internally resist the situation. The resistance comes in the form of feeling that the other person is interfering with or slowing me down. But if I remind myself of the limits of word-tools and the reality of Connectivity, my feelings change.

One day, as my friend's dog was taking me for a walk, I noticed I was having silent conversations with him in my mind. Despite the beautiful nature surrounding us, most of my attention was taken up by mind chatter. But noticing can be a breakthrough. After this walk, I discovered conversations in my mind often and almost anywhere: in my car, standing at the sink washing dishes, in the shower, etc. Noticing I was having conversations with my friend's dog, opened up more noticing. I became more aware of frequently having talks in my mind with Beings of all kinds.

How can we become comfortable with not knowing? I never thought I could. But I discovered that not knowing is the source of knowing. And by recognizing the logic of honoring what I don't know, I came to feel its value, and then I came to realize a different kind of knowing: a wholistic kind of knowing that isn't filtered through the limiting screens of concepts.

40. I Use Absolutes to Blame   160

By looking inside myself, I've come to view absolutes as word-tool delusions. Most of my life, I've used them to blame, and to support my superiority over others rather than to contribute. I came to see I was putting blame above life itself by making it into an absolutely "right" and "true" thing to do. Yes, I actually thought I was doing "good" by blaming. But once I was able to remove some of the numbing effects of my word-tools, I could finally feel the tension in my body and mind caused by blaming. Then I knew it was not "right and true and good".

41. Next-Next-Next   163

I plague myself with the slightly frantic feeling of always imagining what I will do next. Whatever I'm doing, my mind is immersed in anticipation of something I'm not doing yet, but expect to do after this. It's a dis-ease I have, and once I noticed the tension it creates in my face and other parts of my body, I was able to watch for it. Surprised by how often I was in this state, I was then able to change my views about valuing multitasking and a constant drive to produce more and more and more. I finally became aware of the uselessness of always being there and never being here.

42. A Flow of Giving   168

As I eased my way out of the me-vs-them outlook, I found a new feeling to replace it: delight in the process of giving without expecting a specific response. The this-not-that of word-tools had always supported a tit-for-tat process of me giving to another person, hooked to a soft expectation of getting something back.

Once I began to sense the Connectivity I live within, which exposed the invalidity of my me-vs-them outlook, I also began to experience a pure outflow of good will. It has become enjoyable to sense this well-grounded benevolence because it no longer carries the barbed hook of thinking about what might come back.

I admit to occasionally noticing my surface self/ego sneak in when I give to another. But I also notice a lot of giving then forgetting. I don't intentionally forget. The memory of giving simply dissolves as I approach the next experience of life in Connectivity. And so, I watch my ego, and at the same time, I smile as I sense this outflow of good will gradually replacing my tit-for-tat score keeping and the me-vs-them viewpoint that supported it.

43. Disengaging Word-Tools to Engage with Life   171

I bumped into some friends at the coffee shop on a day I had planned to write. When they began talking about a funeral they just attended, I felt my word-tooled plan try to push its way to a place of superior importance. The subtleties of how my plan competed for attention became an experience that showed me that life is a process to be enjoyed, not a plan to be strictly observed.

44. Connectivity – What It Is and What It Is Not   173

Although useful for communication, word-tools are inadequate for gaining a full sense of Connectivity. Real connection with each other happens through Being with each other. But I am accustomed to connecting only through my concepts. It's as if my concepts are talking to the other person's concepts. Although these surface connections are all I've known for most of my life, it's been amazing to experience Connectivity as a Being-to-Being experience.

45. Energy of a Killer   179

When I lose my temper, I can feel the same kind of energy a killer allows. It's a kind of rage that can seem quietly deliberate because it's fueled not by emotion as we so often suppose, but by thoughts made up of word-tools. When I am following orders to kill an "enemy", whether emotion accompanies the process or not, those orders are first held in the form of words. When I lose my temper and yell at my sister, that negative energy is fueled by thinking that she is wrong and that I must make her see what's right. Although the actions are different, whether I'm yelling or killing, the energy I allow to flow through is the same.

46. Selectivity   183

I wondered how I could make choices without judgments of right/ wrong and good/bad. For a while I had no answer. Then I had an experience with a man in a store parking lot who asked me for money. Setting aside my usual tendency to reject interruptions because I was too busy with the urgency of the next thing I had planned to do, I experienced myself listening to him with full attention. I discovered a neutral, non-judgmental form of choosing that I call *selectivity*.

47. What's in a Pen?   187

Countless interconnections. When I expand my view by considering all that preceded my use of this pen, I sense something almost non-conceptual, as if I'm experiencing the limitations of the word *pen* itself. I see that my superior feeling of certainty about knowing this simple object is not warranted. When I bring to mind, the countless interconnections involved with a pen, my certainty ends and is replaced by honoring and gratitude.

48. Keeping Score   190

I created a lot of suffering for myself and others when I wasn't aware of my mind's continual scorekeeping through measurement, comparison, and judgment. I thought if I could quantify, measure, and track the score, then the meaning must be objectively true. Once I realized the inadequacy of our word-tools to represent people, situations, and life itself, then I began to see that words are not suited for evaluating wholes. Using a limited tool for something it's not suited for only brings damage. Happily, awareness leads to change, and now I realize that despite its prevalence, keeping score has very limited application in the world around us.

49. Come to the Moment   195

Catching myself in next-next-next works as a great signal to change my state of mind. I notice my slave-to-the-clock mode relentlessly driving me forward and realize I have forgotten "the now". The tension in my face and the rest of my body becomes obvious once I notice. Then the relief of sensing what's around me, right here now in this moment, brings a sense of peace. It's as if I had been trapped in a dark room of tension and then opened the door to a bright sunny day.

50. Connectivity Example   197

Seemingly insignificant experiences of being in the moment with another person have accumulated to create a sense of abundance around me. For much of my life, I had passed up Connectivity experiences because I had too much to do and my time was too important. Now that I've found the non-usury value of Connectivity experiences, I also sense a gratitude for living and a multitude of interconnections with everything.

I gave a tip to a man for plowing the snow in a commonly used throughway next to the house I rent. There was no need to tip him, I simply felt gratitude for the thorough job he always did. He then generously plowed our renters' private parking area free of charge. But, I realized that it was the Connectivity between me and this man that meant so much more than my tip or his generosity.

51. She Doesn't Know What I Know   199

I ran into a friend who didn't know what was meant by the word "concept". Forgetting that I hadn't known what a concept was even after finishing seven years of university, I heard my inner voice accusing my friend of being stupid. Happily I was aware enough to catch the thought, realize its insignificance, and see its distortion of reality. I reminded myself of the many thoughts and judgments I've seen for what they actually are: fuel for my ego rather than indicators of something true about the world.

52. Recognize the Negative Inside But Don't Feed It   202

Watching my thoughts has been a process of bringing awareness to something I never really noticed before. It was a fight inside of me that affected my experiences without me realizing the effects. It caused tension, yet I didn't notice the tension until I began to see how unserious the thoughts were. For most of my life, I had fed negatives without knowing it. As I practiced shifting away from negatives, I repeatedly discovered that there is no need for the inner tension, no need for the fighting inside my mind, once the negatives are brought to light and once I stop feeding them.

53. A Sense of Unfiltered Neutrality   207

At times I ask myself whether there have ever been moments when chatter wasn't dominating my mind. Have I ever experienced a quiet mind? If I address this question to my mind itself, it tries to tell me that quiet mind can't happen, that the nature of mind is always to be actively moving word-tools through it.

But when I look deeper, I realize that it's not true – I have experienced many moments when my mind was quiet, but I have misinterpreted those moments by overlaying word-tooled explanations on them. More often now, I notice the moments of realizing a quiet, untroubled mind, moments of mind-neutrality when I don't carry the judgmental tension of sifting what I experience through the filtering screens of cognitive labeling.

54. Disciplinary Inner Control System   210

Blaming and punishment have always been discouraging for me – they don't lead to long-lasting change. By sensing the Connectivity that surrounds me I also became aware that we are far more connected than we are separate. This vast interconnectivity I have come to experience has helped me see there is another way to nurture change: allowing ourselves to "grow out of" our unconscious actions. Attempting to change my damaging unconscious actions through blaming and punishment doesn't work, not long term. But allowing growth does. It ends the process of trying to stop destruction by using destruction.

55. Happy Tails – Watch Like a Puppy   216

I noticed something new the last time I babysat my friend's puppy – it was his warm approach and tail wagging with me and other people. I saw him respond naturally to his surroundings, without judgment or word-tool labeling, as he looked out at the world in a state of eager neutrality. If one person or thing in his environment didn't respond, he simply shifted his attention to something else, never running out of potential moments of engagement with the abundance of what surrounded him. Once I opened-up enough to allow experiences of Connectivity, I found this orientation in myself – a feeling of "wagging my tail" at the richness of Being that always surrounds me.

56. Lack and Longing   218

When I think of things that feel good, I often find they are in the past. I start feeling bad instead of good because I'm not experiencing those things today, this week, this month, or in this period of my life. I discovered that feeling "lack" is something I create through images that aren't real, supported by my misuse of word-tools. I make up story-based comparisons that are like fractions of loss: I had this then, but now I don't. It's one way I make myself feel bad by letting "what isn't" take precedence over "what is".

57. This Breath is Different   223

How can one breath be different from another? Doesn't each breath I take seem pretty much like the next? Yes, when I'm lost in concepts. But noticing the differences between this breath and that, this tree and that, this person and that, brings richness back to life experience. It helps transform the tense, stubborn separateness that word-tools support so well into a sense of lively Connectivity.

58. Traits and Characteristics Distort Reality   226

Depending on a handful of words to describe the "essence" of
a person has led me further away from knowing what is real. It
closes my mind to seeing the essence of the whole person. It gives
precedence to surface patterns as it ignores the whole-self Being
that is at the core of each one of us. Because the limitations of
word-tools don't allow the wide, open view that is necessary, they
close my mind to seeing what is really true about myself and about
other people. Traits and characteristics are a misuse of word-tools,
often acting as superiority fuel for a feeding the ego.

59. Fabrications vs Life and Nature   232

I drive down the street in my car and see buildings, fences,
billboards, windows, doors, bikes, and so many other manufactured
things. I call these fabrications – things assembled from parts,
formed into a whole by outside forces, I mean by we people who
put them together. When I was lost in concepts, I viewed myself as
one of these fabrications. But when I became more aware of the
limits of our word-tools, I also became more open to what makes
living organisms and nature different from the many things we
people manufacture.

60. Loving Is Better Than Being Loved   236

In the tit-for-tat world I see around me, I uncovered something
different that made me change my views about the importance of
always getting something back for what I gave. Feeling alone after
my second divorce helped. Coming out of my rigidly conceptual
mindset also helped. As I began to give just because I enjoyed
it, I found a new experience connected to letting love inside me
flow. Sounds like a song doesn't it? But, it didn't come from a
song, it came from me living life in a natural way rather than in the
restrictive word-tooled way I was so accustomed to.

61. Narrow In Order to Expand   239

Word-tools narrow the focus as they zero in on the one generalized grouping that excludes all else. In order to function as shortcuts for actual experience of what's real, they leave out uniqueness and Connectivity. These communication shorthands expand our lives when we are aware of the limitations. But when we forget the limitations, and pay no attention to the underlying, ultimate purpose of coming in contact with reality, words become tools of distortion and destruction.

62. Resistance, Force, and Heroism   242

It amazes me what I find inside when I'm able to dig deep at underlying conditioning. I've always worshiped heroes. I thought of them as people who fight against all odds to help, save, and make lives better. But once I began to sense Connectivity and to realize the flaws of the this-not-that separations to which word-tools lead, I began to notice that I generate resistance situations in order to "engage life". I noticed that I create military-like engagement so that I can show some form of what seems like intellectual heroism. It's just another way I find myself misusing word-tools to compensate for a deadness inside me that's initially caused by filtering life through word-tools rather than living it directly.

63. Connectivity With-All and With-In   247

Haunted all my life by the demands of an "ideal self", I began to uncover another way to live. As I broke through my judgments of other people, to see that there was more than just their surface characteristics, I began to do the same for me inside myself. I broke through many judgments of myself, and took them less seriously as I began to see a deeper self cradled in a sense of peaceful well-being. My relentless and critical *shoulds* dissipated to the point where I noticed entire days without beating myself down.

Seeing judgments of others as ultimately illusory helped me see judgments of myself in the same way. Opening up to feeling Connectivity with all that surrounds me, helped create the same within.

64. Bursting a Bubble   253

Embracing the words "she is so beautiful", about a girl who walked into the coffee shop, generated a separation inside me that set in mind a form of above-below positioning. It was as if the words placed a thick layer of insulation between me and her. This was followed by a sense of fear about the simple situation of being in a room with this girl.

But then something surprising happened. Minutes after putting the words "beautiful girl" in their proper place as symbols not to be taken seriously, I felt an immediate change that allowed me to relax enough to talk to her. Even though the words seem positive, they have the negative effect of boxing-in her, me, and the entire situation. That realization allowed me to transform the experience of viewing her as an object into an enjoyable relating between two human beings.

65. From Rigidity to Life – Chocolat the Movie   256

In this movie, we see people living life based on excluding and restricting – two functions that are embedded in our basic form of communication, our word-tools. Then we see the people loosen-up on clinging to their rigid beliefs and allowing life to flow in. Without explicitly stating it, the movie *Chocolat* shows people who come to see that life comes first, and that holding word-tools as absolutes restricts life and denies the Connectivity inherent in it.

66. Indirect Not Direct   259

Word-tools support my desire to make things happen, to force a preconceived outcome, to control life directly. But life continues to show that I don't have direct control; my control is indirect. If I step back for a wider than word-tool view, I see that growth happens as a process of nature, not an outcome from an instruction book. I sense that I am like a seed through which my life grows. If I stay in tune with my environment, aware of the multitude of interconnections it holds, I then have a beneficial influence on what happens. But if I try to force my growth, through some form of "single-caused", direct control, then I diminish my awareness of Connectivity and of the quality of what happens in my life.

67. My Stories about Their Stories about Me   266

Guessing what others think of me began as a child when I worried that my mom was angry or sad or happy because of something I did. But these thought-circles depend on holding-tight to a view of separateness. If she is separate and has authority, then it makes sense I'd be worried. As a child, I didn't know about Connectivity. I had zero awareness that all of us breathe the same air and that we are ultimately more alike than different.

Since the word-tools we use to communicate function as separators, it makes sense that we would have no clue about Connectivity. But once I sensed something more than what word-tools can carry, I not only saw a wider picture of the movement of life, I felt it in the reduced stress of my daily being.

68. Expanding Out of Conceptual Restriction   271

Coming to see the restrictiveness of the conceptual realm has helped me step back and take a more expansive viewpoint, and eventually to actually *feel* the expansiveness. I especially notice this when I quiet my mind during walks I take outside. Weaved with consciously watching the self-criticism that creeps up so often, I have experienced amazing walks. At first this use of my time seemed arbitrary and frivolous. But with a closer "look", I realized that it was my production-related *shoulds* that were arbitrary and frivolous.

69. A Goal Without Consequence   274

Most goals I've experienced are fueled by a threat, either of not receiving a reward or of receiving a punishment. Can a goal be fueled by something else? Can I allow my own growth without threatening myself with some negative consequence such as withdrawal of approval? I sense it can be done, but not through strict adherence to a word-tool way of viewing the world. It requires looking beyond our limited tools of communication and bringing back the reality of life that the tools give names to but can never fully represent.

70. What Mattered Then What Matters Now   279

In seeing everything only through conceptual filters, what mattered most was the differences between the groupings of concepts. Good versus bad, earners versus moochers, lazy versus hard-working – all are forms of one grouping against another. And I discovered that all are prejudices I didn't want to admit to.

I was unaware of what was actually important to me when I used concepts to put myself above others and above reality itself. Discovering the this-not-that nature of word-tools, along with a feeling of Connectivity with people and the rest of reality, shined a light on what was important to me deep down: it was the core goodness, the Being, and all the uniqueness I had been blinded to. Instead of using my conceptual groupings as tools, I had allowed them to use me.

71. Comprehensiveness – Parts and Wholes   284

I get so easily trapped in the *should* of making sure I make the right choice or the most all-encompassing assessment of a situation. It boils down to me feeling pressed to check every possible option or variable. I feel I must make sure I don't miss something important. It's a form of perfection I call *comprehensiveness*. Caught in the swirling flux of all the fabricated stuff around me contributes to my confusion.

I forget that the pieces we put together to create fabricated stuff pulls my attention away from the source of it all: nature. I forget that nature is moving and growing, and I forget that it is not the result of a manufacturing process. Realizing this has helped me acknowledge and trust the wholes of nature as I acknowledge and trust the vastness of what I don't know.

72. To Identify Is To Follow the Crowd   288

I thought I was unique in viewing myself as "quietly rebellious" and "intellectual". Identifying with these traits, I thought of myself as different from and better than others. I realized with surprise that I was actually the same as most people because the process of identifying *is* what most people do. Identifying is not only trapping myself into a view that is constricted by the very word-tools I use, it is also a form of following the crowd.

A Whole of The Whole

73. Against Word-Tools?   293

Sometimes I overreact and use the word *against* as if word-tools are bad or something I need to fight. But if I create this kind of resistance, my mind only holds tighter to them. Opening up to the hidden positives in life, including those that aren't logical, doesn't require me to fight with a tool. It seems like a fight only if I overuse word-tools and then blame myself for my misuse. Recognizing the tool, as part of a whole-self way of functioning – that's what I am *for*.

74. Kill It! It's Only a "Robot"   297

Words can mask our vision of what is real. In the movie *Automata*, men destroyed robots out of anger and misunderstanding. But these robots consistently took action that was more life sustaining and enhancing than that of the humans who killed them. The men who killed these robots were blinded by their own words – they were unable to see that by destroying what they called "machines", they were also destroying life itself.

75. Giving Up Absolute Importance   301

I still catch myself trying to force a result by assigning it the status of being absolutely important. Putting accomplishment of a goal above everything else seems to be the best way to make sure it gets done. But this type of clutching only constricts my own life flow. It closes me to tapping into life energy, which is made up of my own energy and the energies of all that surrounds me.

The heroism of absolute importance fuels my superiority. It creates an opposition that I then feel I need to put myself above or set myself against. But once I'm able to drop the restraints of making a string of limited symbols into an absolute, I see the reality of me using absolute importance to boost myself up in order to compensate for the inadequacy that arises from being disconnected from Source.

76. Panoramic Sensing   306

As a way of widening into a sense of Connectivity, I occasionally practice looking at one thing in front of me such as a tree, and then expanding my view to include things on either side of the tree, and then wider and wider until I feel I am taking in nearly one hundred and eighty degrees of my surroundings. If I can avoid naming, it quiets the mind just a little, and at times gives me a sense that I am surrounded by interconnected wholeness. It helps offset the feeling that all reality is just a bunch of separate "things" that were fabricated by sticking pieces together. It reminds me of a direct sense of knowing that doesn't require fabrication, neither of "stuff" or of word-tools.

77. A Different Kind of Knowing   309

I am gradually more able to distinguish mind-based orders, preferences, and judgments from sensing and realizations that come from a wider place. The fear, doubt, and pseudo problems springing from my narrow word-based functioning is dissipating. And trust in my whole-self is growing as I apply to a wider range of daily actions the distinction between the purely cognitive and a whole-self way of Being.

It's a trust that feels more secure than cognition, as if it embraces the whole span of the energies of reality. It carries a wide sense of Connectivity that seems more enduring. I repeatedly remind myself that the tools we know of as words are meant to point to reality not replace it. They are not meant for building elaborate structures made up of concepts pointing to other concepts that ignore the whole of reality from which they were extracted. They are not meant to bite the reality that fed them.

As I use this different kind of knowing to connect to the whole of what is real, I notice more and more that elaborate integrations I had loved so much were actually just food for my egoic superiority. I am now seeing that words that only point to other words most often sabotages their prime function of pointing to reality. The kind of knowing that connects directly with reality feels real and well grounded. It carries a sense of energetic potency that doesn't feed the illusion that I own the truth or that I am above or against anybody or anything in life.

78. Evaluation – A Misuse of Word-Tools   314

Almost all the evaluation and judgment that flows through my mind creates tension inside my body. I find it especially on my face, but also around my head, neck, and shoulders, and in my torso, legs, feet, and arms. Previously, I thought tension was part of doing right rather than wrong things in life, just as I thought that some stress was natural to the unquestionably necessary processes of evaluating and judging.

But as I began to sense Connectivity by breaking through my initial judgments, and realizing that reality held much more than words could address, I saw that my judging was more wrong than right. Before this my righteous judgments were so deeply buried under layers of word-tools that I was simply unaware. But as I exposed the true nature of my evaluations, as an attempt to make myself superior to life itself, I realized I could no longer take them seriously.

79. Pop-Ins   321

At the beginning of writing material for this book, I experienced unintended word combinations popping into mind for no apparent reason. With no specific plan or goal, I would write them down when they popped in. Then I would look at the words, and to my surprise they brought delight as if I were admiring someone else's words. I came to feel a sense of kinship with this, and eventually the words Arm-in-Arm popped in to name this sense of indescribable yet connected alignment.

80. Bad Deep Down   323

A friend I feel affection and admiration for told me there was something deep inside him that was bad. It surprised me, and it kept coming to mind for many months. Then another friend told me the same thing about herself. At first I thought I didn't carry any form of *bad deep down* in myself.

But as I continued to wonder, I found it. For me, it comes from following the crowd and betraying my deep-down uniqueness. Giving in to a cognitive pull to "walk someone else's world" has covered up the good that was always deep inside. So for me, bad deep down points to betraying the deep-down partnering that fits life as a whole and me as a Unique Expressor.

81. Being As The Payoff   327

Life works a little differently now that I've experienced watching my mind rather than being swallowed up by it. Now that I've been able to "know" Connectivity, there is a sense of Being that overshadows the need for payoffs in the surface world. I still want and enjoy the pleasures of a meal, feeling romantic, getting a new car, etc. But there is much less need to clutch onto them, less desperation to get and keep them. When I'm not ruled by word-tools and the separations to which they lead, I take actions toward these pleasures from a place where cause merges into the effect and the Being itself becomes the payoff.

82. A New Kind of Right   330

Gradually, as I broke-through my initial judgments of people and situations as being either good or bad, I began to see a deep goodness everywhere that nullifies the idea of blame. We don't need discipline, punishment, or any idea of needing to measure up to something; we need to allow ourselves to grow. As I allowed myself to grow into opening up, to see the goodness behind the surface of a person I blamed, I felt the life experience of Connectivity. I also felt the inadequacy of word-tools and more clearly realized the destructiveness of blame in any form.

This new kind of right has no blame. Its focus is the reality of

Connectivity and the highly limited nature of everything made up of word-tools, including "morality" which I had used for so long as both a club to beat people with (especially myself) and a stool to step up on so I could feel superior.

83. Creating a Mental It   335

My first understanding of the concept of identification came through studying objective philosophies. From that, I came to believe that to identify something, I had to be able to define it clearly in words. Then I discovered how limited words are and I began to feel a sense of tightness when I identified myself or others. Looking back, I had felt this tightness all my life but had never noticed it before.

Words freeze the motion of reality by excluding uniqueness and Connectivity in order to create a shortcut for communicating. This process of extracting from reality produces identifications that serve as boxes with definite boundaries. The this-not-that separation that results is like a mental "it". It is a sort of confinement because once formed and held in mind, it is closed to any new motion from reality.

It's as if once I create and hold an identification in mind, my world is darkened and I've walked away from life. The definite nature of our artificial symbol system, *word-tools*, chokes off the flow of receiving life as it happens. Happily, when I'm not completely dominated by one mental "it" or by a group of them, and when I'm able to see through the conditioning that leads to frequent misuse of word-tools, my life is vibrant and full of wonder.

84. Reason Is Faith   338

When I was born I did not know. What I then came to know arose from that state of not knowing. If I had not carried a sense of acknowledgment and honor for the vast unknown, how would I have learned anything? A newborn's openness is a sense of trust in what is, a sort of faith in Connectivity, that allows reasoning to develop.

But when I grew-up and became lost in concepts, I also lost sight of the source of my surface knowing, the source of reason and all thought. Losing the sense of Source, I used reason only in destructive ways. I had forgotten that life comes first, before reason, and before everything that comes from word-tools.

Now as I bring myself back to Connectivity with Source, it's as if there is a renewal, a re-dawning of life. Much of the time I am able to allow people and surroundings to Be as they are. Now I use reason as the derivative tool it is, aware that life and Source came first. And it's as if the ability to breathe fresh air is coming back after being trapped in a reason-only place that was suffocating to the flow of drawing on the energy of life.

85. Uniqueness and Connectivity   343

To use word-tools constructively rather than destructively, I must be aware of their limitations. What word-tools miss, what these shortcuts cannot hold, are uniqueness and Connectivity, which includes the continuous movement of the reality they are drawn from.

If we hadn't put ourselves on our word-tool high horses, above the whole of life that is Source to all, there wouldn't have been more than one hundred and fifty million deaths, caused by humans killing other humans in the twentieth century alone. Concepts without uniqueness and Connectivity are tools of destruction. But word-tools can contribute much to life when we use them with full awareness of their limits.

86. My Body "Talks" – Can I Receive Without Words?   351

I've begun to sense that listening to my body is something I can learn to do. Fully attending to the sensations of my skin and the tissues in my belly is one of the ways I've experienced that a noncognitive, wordless way of knowing is possible.

87. The Pull To Narrow My Awareness   355

I discovered a frequent "tug" to put a whole-self choice through the filtering of word-tools. The discovery made me more aware of my conditioned need to put words to everything, to name, explain, justify, and defend. It's a compulsion that keeps me in a small-minded and defensive place.

Lost in concepts this way, I don't trust myself in my surroundings. When I narrow my awareness, I naturally don't trust because I've vastly reduced the scope of what I'm allowing to flow through me; I've turned my back on Connectivity and on the whole of life, the reality that is not subject to word-tools.

88. You're Not Allowed to Touch Source   360

As a growing boy and a young man, I experienced sensing Source. But I rejected these moments of living as "silly, wasteful, and not real" because everything real had to fit my word-tooled social conditioning. The feeling of touching something more than the surface world around me was not allowed.

What I had missed is that I was simply so buried under layers of word structures that I couldn't allow the whole of my life to shine through. I had used word-tools to overshadow and restrict my own reality, as I disowned some of my deepest-felt life experiences.

89. A Beautiful Mind   365

I hear people say that down deep they feel they are losers, failures, or inadequate in some way. I have my own forms of this, one of which I eventually came to call "lonely guy". *Everyone else is out on a date, at the party, or with their families on weekends and holidays, but I'm not.*

In the movie *A Beautiful Mind*, the main character John interacts with three illusionary people who seem as real as everything else. Eventually John came to see them as the delusions they actually were.

I have come to see that John's unreal people are very much like the unrealities created by my crazy thoughts, and this includes my "lonely guy". In the same way John expressed affection for his imaginary people when he said goodbye to them, I can often view my thoughts with an affectionate lack of seriousness. As with a puppy or a very young child, I can accept them for what they are while at the same time not following where they may lead me.

On Christmas Day 2015, I received a gift I hadn't expected. It was the release from feeling bad whenever my lonely guy is present. During this day that I spent alone, it was as if I could see my lonely guy image across the space of my kitchen, and in that same moment I was not pulled in by him. It was surprising and delightful to experience being conscious of the image but not dragged down by it any time that day. And since then, the frequency of those bad lonely guy feelings has dropped to nearly zero.

Both of us, John in the movie and me in real life, stopped embracing our images, we ceased viewing them as if they were The Truth. As I see it, each of us disengaged from the heaviness of taking our word-tooled thoughts too seriously. And feeling released from that often present burden feels wonderful!

90. Unique Expressor   371

It was a surprise to me when the idea popped-in that traits and characteristics are damaging. Yet the surprise dissipated as I repeatedly found that life is better without thoughts that someone is good or bad, ugly or handsome, accomplished or a failure, or lazy or productive. These are all just tension-generating labels with nothing but the miniscule amount of information word-tools can carry. And most of the time I find my thoughts about people to be more an externalization of my inner life than a description of a person.

If these surface aspects of people and things are set aside, what then is left? I sense that the light that shines through every person comes from the same source in some way. So what's left of a human being after I've stripped away what I'm calling surface traits and characteristics? What am I seeing as I practice looking through the surface of a person to the Source that is the same in all of us?

I've come to sense an interaction. It's the delicate balance between where I choose to point my attention and the environment that nurtures the growth of my inner seed. The growth itself is what's unique. A growth that stems from the same source, but that expresses differently depending on my connection with that source. And that connection happens best by pointing my attention to the whole of what's real, not just to what I can express through the cognitive filters of my word-tools.

91. Openings Create More   375

Opening the door to realizing that I choose where I point my attention seemed to provide keys to further openings. These openings continue to appear as pop-ins and as a sense of being Arm-in-Arm with life movement. To illustrate how these further openings continue to lead to more openings, this section makes note of titles and concepts from many other sections in this book. Though not comprehensive or linear in its approach, it may serve as a connecting overview for some readers.

92. *Enjoying Knowing* Is Different from *Enjoying Knowing More Than*   378

My awareness of sensing pure joy in something *just because it is*, and for no other reason, was almost nonexistent until a few years before this book. But as I began to open up to more than my world of word-tools – more than the world of logic, reason, measurement, comparison, and profit – it was as if I'd tapped into a new way of being alive.

I have just begun to let go of the tension created by always comparing and measuring to see if I am gaining something from every activity. To enjoy moments of living *just for what they are* is something I'd always longed for in a vague way. I remember repeatedly looking back at a conversation or activity, thinking that I'd missed the full enjoyment of it. At those times, I didn't know why it was happening because I was so dominated by word-tooled thinking. But now I see that what I had missed was that I hadn't put full attention on it because I was always chasing some gain to compensate for feeling inadequate.

93. Admitting Frees Me from Appearing   383

All my life I've felt the pressure to fit, match, and comply with expectations. What my boss, spouse, or friends expect of me, how they think I should look or talk, all these form a messy pile of appearances. I end up being a role player interacting through expectations of appearances. And others interact with me through their own view of expected appearances.

Then I realized that words are tools of appearance, masqueraders that make it easy for me to do the same. Since they seem to represent reality but actually carry only the miniscule amount needed to form a name tag, they invite me to fake it whenever I'm not aware of their limits. They encourage me to put on a false front in order to make the right impression.

But to be the whole that I am is to realize something much more all-encompassing: admitting that words are only limited tools and that experiencing the whole of reality includes all types of knowing, not just the narrow cognitive knowing I cling to out of fear. Admitting to the limits of my words, thoughts, and emotions, and reminding myself that they are only tools, frees me from the pressures of straining to match predefined images that crowd-out the possibility of simply being myself. Through admitting, I open the door to Source and to the wonder of uniqueness and Connectivity that word-tools cannot carry.

94. Allow All of Life – Find Source   387

Even though I find value in shifting attention away from negatives and toward positives, I've discovered that rejecting negatives doesn't work. If I carry a feeling of negativity toward negatives with a view toward eliminating, outlawing, or casting them out, I strengthen and maintain them. If I want to release them, gentleness is required.

I am beginning to sense that I need to rely on my negatives in order to "look through" them to find positives. The negatives are like a stepping stone toward a deeper knowing. It is "by means of" them that I can grasp a "farther focus". On the other hand, when I believe in negatives as if they are objective endpoints, I close off full awareness of what's real.

Negatives are best viewed as transient veils to look through. When I take seriously any form of blaming, judgment, or criticism, I miss the chance to look through these short-lived energies toward realizing the deeper meaning that resides in Source.

95. Arm-in-Arm   394

There is a delicate interaction that I had no sense of when I was completely lost in concepts. It is a subtle, gentle partnership that I can sense only when I abandon my will to make things happen. When I experience Arm-in-Arm, it comes out of an open allowing of me in recognition and gratitude for all that surrounds me. It is a fragile kind of coming together, me with the whole of life.

When I turn on a light switch, light somehow shines on what was before engulfed in darkness. When I relax my Being, quiet my mind, and allow for the unknown, I somehow open a channel to a partnership that flows in ease with what was before engulfed in the stressful tension of hardship.

I don't know how electricity works to bring the light. And I don't know how an "allowing awareness of Being" works to bring a sense of Arm-in-Arm. I know only that they happen, and that they flow without resistance to bring whole-life experiences we can enjoy.

96. There Is No Controller   402

I've often thought that it is just part of reality for someone to be in charge. Parents, bosses, owners, religious leaders, scientists, government officials, and experts of all kind are everywhere. And they tend to put themselves above others as they function in their roles of authority. I thought I wanted to be one of them. But after discovering the tension and denial of the whole of life that being in charge carries with it, I found something better. The only time I want to be one of them is when I fall back into being lost in concepts for a bit.

Happily, falling into the word-bucket hole of being lost in concepts is temporary. I can always crawl out of it by bringing forth a wider awareness. This wider awareness is what leads to a sense of being Arm-in-Arm with reality rather than below it or above it.

I've tried to control reality by first putting myself above it through use of word-tools. Then came the other side of that coin: making up word-tool stories about reality being above me, about the universe being a boss that tells me what I should do, a boss whose advice is closed to options just like word-tools are. But I find that when I put word-tools and the stories I create with them in their place, a naturally occurring opening-up to options is allowed and I realize that ultimately there is no controller – not me, not anyone, and not anything else.

97. Grateful Being   405

Grateful Being started in my late 50s with an experience of feeling more loved than ever before. Over the years that followed, this new awareness of Being grew and became stronger after encountering feelings of deep Connectivity with friends and acquaintances. During these moments I felt as if a light-hearted sacredness were flowing up from the ground and through me, then across to the other person's eyes and back down through the ground.

Later I began to view this as a Source-to-Source experience that can undo the rigid hold of principles, beliefs, truths, and any other word-tool products. Grateful Being counteracts the clenching power of word-tools by allowing the momentary restoration of a noncognitive connection to life that we all first experienced as babies. I wonder how many of us had an experience like this later in life but then misinterpreted its deep meaning by trying to put words to it instead of simply allowing and embracing the wholeness it carried.

For me Grateful Being started with people, but now it applies to other natural beings such as trees and animals, and even to bugs and rocks. It carries a sense of gratitude for all of what is, and it feels really good whenever I'm in tune with it.

98. Noncognitive   410

Having been totally immersed in word-tools for most of my adult life, I was one who dismissed and even became hostile toward any view that couldn't be reasoned out through use of concepts. I rejected outright everything noncognitive without any consideration.

Then as I began to see how limited our words are, as I began to break through the walls of my word-based prejudices about real people in my world, something seemed to open up in me. A willingness to look further, an allowance of taking tiny steps outside my word-tooled rigidity. I began to sense that it was logical to look beyond logic, it was reasonable to look outside of the kind of reasoning that can only be expressed through the narrowed filtering of word-tools.

As I relaxed my rigid devotion to thinking I began to sense a wider span of life as if I were directly experiencing more of what is real in the world. I repeatedly saw the smallness of my use of word-tools to describe others, and this allowed a new kind of sensing, a way of looking through the surface to the deep source of each person I encountered. For me, all these were steps toward experiencing directly the value of what I don't know, and the noncognitive happenings of Connectivity, pop-ins, and Arm-in-Arm.

99. Where Did It Come From?   415

How do we bring awareness of ultimate sources into the forefront, and gain a sense of Being? Ten years ago, I would have replied, "Who cares? I just want to get more done, work more so I can provide for me and my family, do fun things, and buy more things."

I was far too busy to be concerned with ultimate sources. I had to deal with the needs of this day, the bills this month, the work situations here and now. I thought I was living in the now, but was totally unaware of my immersion in word-tools. And I didn't realize that most of the time I used words, I was pointing attention toward something negative or tension producing, such as judging people and situations as flawed in some way, or I was wishing the past were different, or worrying, planning, and stressing about what might happen next.

It's understandable that I was not aware. After all I was born into this world surrounded by fully formed buildings, comforts, and support systems that seemed to just be here without any origins. *Who needs to ask about origins? The stuff is here, let's use it.*

I finally discovered an inherent and hidden stress in being detached from ultimate sources. I gradually found ways to bring back my awareness of sensations, nature, earth, air, and sun. I finally was able to acknowledge gratefully where it all came from, and when I did, when I do, the hidden stress dissipates and is overridden by a sense of joyful playfulness that carries a sacred honoring along with it.

100. Does Life Respond?   421

I took life for granted, thinking I earned the right to take and to have, without any sense of gratitude for the air I wake up to every day and the earth and sun which constantly support my existence.

What if my relationship with life impacts the happenings in it? What if my taking life for granted works like taking another person for granted? Does a feeling of gratitude and acknowledgment of Connectivity create different happenings in my life?

101. Being Like a Tree   426

I feel pulled in so many directions by my chattering mind and by what seems to be an endless stream of advice and *shoulds* from outside. And there is tension, sometimes noticed, but much of the time hidden under the facade of claiming I am living a happy human life. While I'm living what I've been trained to think of as having a life, I've forgotten the silent calm stillness that resides underneath it. I've buried that peace under layer upon layer of the compulsion to respond to word structures and fabrications including the pull of our modern gadgets which take me in all directions at once and rarely acknowledge the ultimate Source of it all.

That is why I've fallen deeply in love with trees. Crazy, huh? Each day when I walk I look at trees, reminding myself of the possibility of having a quiet mind, with no words swarming around in it. One day as I looked out a window at the tree in front of my house, I felt its sense of non-cluttered being, its oneness with its surroundings, its quiet responsiveness.

It was as if, for one brief moment, I were feeling what the tree feels, a *unified sense of knowing and Being*. This book has helped me find moments of this silent calm stillness, and it has made my life full as I connect to my surroundings as A Whole of The Whole. I hope that you too may find the place where your "deep gladness and the world's deep hunger meet".

Reference List by Author

Adams, Scott. *How to Fail at Almost Everything and Still Win Big: Kind of the Story of My Life,* page 3 (New York: Portfolio/Penguin, 2013).

Brach, Tara. *Radical Acceptance: Embracing Your Life with the Heart of a Buddha*, audiobook read by Cassandra Campbell, Chapter 3, 10:20 (Tantor Audio, 2012); print format Chapter 1, page 9 (New York: Bantam, 2004).

Brach, Tara. *True Refuge: Finding Peace and Freedom in Your Own Awakened Heart,* page 151 (New York: Bantam Books, Reprint edition 2016).

Gladwell, Malcolm. *Blink: The Power of Thinking Without Thinking,* page 119 (New York: Little, Brown and Company, 2005).

Horney, Karen. *Neurosis and Human Growth: The Struggle Toward Self-Realization* (New York: W.W. Norton & Company, 1991).

Katie, Byron. *Your Inner Awakening: The Work of Byron Katie: Four Questions That Will Transform Your Life*, read by the author, Chapter 3, 26:57 (New York: Simon & Schuster Audio, 2006).

Meek, Esther Lightcap. *Longing to Know: A Philosophy of Knowledge for Ordinary People,* page 47 (Grand Rapids, MI: Brazos Press, 2003).

Post, Allison and Cavaliere, Stephen. *Unwinding the Belly: Healing with Gentle Touch* (Berkley, California: North Atlantic Books, 2003).

Schucman, Helen and Thetford, William N. (scribed and edited by), *A Course in Miracles: Text, Workbook for Students, Manual for Teachers,* Workbook for Students Lesson 5, page 6 (Omaha: Course in Miracles Society, 2012).

Shepherd, Phillip. *New Self, New World: Recovering Our Senses in the Twenty-First Century (*Berkley, CA: North Atlantic Books, 2010).

Simon, Tami. *Waking Up: Over 30 Perspectives on Spiritual Awakening - What Does It Really Mean?* Chapter 32, interview with Bentinho Massaro, 29:32 (Boulder, CO: Sounds True, 2015).

Tolle, Eckhart. *A New Earth, Awakening to Your Life's Purpose (*New York: Plume, 2005).

Tolle, Eckhart. An Evening with Eckhart Tolle; June 17, 2016; Denver, Colorado. (quote is also included in the announcement for the lecture accessed December 2, 2017 at https://www.soundstrue.com/store/eckhart-tolle-denver)

Tolle, Eckhart. *The Power of Now (*Novato, CA: New World Library and Namaste Publishing, 1999).

Trudeau, Kevin. *Your Wish is Your Command,* audio read by the author, cd 6, track 5, 01:59 (New York: Global Information Network, 2009).

Watts, Alan. *Out of Your Mind: Essential Listening from the Alan Watts Audio Archives, The Inevitable Ecstasy – This Is the Game (*track-section six) 07:59, (Boulder, CO: Sounds True, 2004).

Watts, Alan. *Tao: The Watercourse Way* (New York: Pantheon Books, 1975).

Watts, Alan. *The Wisdom of Insecurity* (New York: Vintage Books, 1951).

Whiteley, Jody. *Best Sleep Hypnosis Story Ever* (internet accessed November 3, 2017), https://www.youtube.com/watch?v=eu9RbDNaw-8, 7:26.

Winfrey, Oprah and Tolle, Eckhart. *A New Earth, Awakening to Your Life's Purpose: A Worldwide Web Event,* Chapter 7 (internet accessed October 16, 2017) https://www.youtube.com/watch?v=QwWgpEJxDI0 26:45

Other References Listed by Title
(Film Media and Miscellaneous)

A Beautiful Mind, directed by Ron Howard, written by Akiva Goldsman and Sylvia Nasar (Universal City, CA: Universal Pictures, 2002) DVD 2006.

Automata, directed by Gabe Ibáñez, written by Gabe Ibáñez, Igor Legarreta, and Javier S. Donate (Los Angeles: Millennium Entertainment, 2014) DVD.

Chocolat, directed by Lasse Hallström, written by Joanne Harris and Robert Nelson Jacobs, (Santa Monica, CA: Miramax, 2000) DVD.

(I Can't Get No) Satisfaction, by Mick Jagger and Keith Richards, track 7 on Rolling Stones American Release album *Out of Our Heads*, London Records, 1965.

Jenny's Wedding, directed by Mary Agnes Donoghue (Philadelphia, PA: PalmStar Media, 2015) DVD.

Remote Sensing, NASA Earth Observatory, internet accessed August 8, 2017 at https://earthobservatory.nasa.gov/Features/RemoteSensing/remote_02.php

Touched by an Angel, television series episode "Life Before Death", directed by Martha Mitchell (New York: CBS Productions, 13 February 2000).

Touched by an Angel, television series episode "The Big Bang", directed by Chuck Bowman (New York: CBS Productions, 25 November 1995).

Touched by an Angel, television series episode "The Violin Lesson", directed by Peter H. HuntNew York: CBS Productions, 22 December 1996).

War Dance, directed by Andrea Nix and Sean Fine, written by Andrea Nix Fine and Sean Fine (Atlanta: Velocity, 2007) DVD 2008. This film may also be found on the internet at https://www.youtube.com/watch?v=UATS5K9IZT0 (accessed October 20, 2017).

About Me, the Author

I'm a guy who went from being shy and unnoticed as a child, to a well-meaning but cruel-at-times believer of objective truths and rules; and now to a joyful being who can be lighthearted and playfully silly at times.

Earning a Master's Degree in Industrial Psychology seemed good when I finished it in 1980. As part of this, I enjoyed studying leadership and management. Being a manager in business, which included strategic development and data analysis, also seemed important and successful at the time.

But more important than all that thought-and-status-based stuff was choosing to take Latin dance classes after a divorce in 2008, and to read books from the field of positive psychology which later expanded to works of philosophy and spirituality. And, better than that was falling in love with nature: trees, other plants, sun, air, and earth. This appreciation, which grew during walks through the tree-lined neighborhoods between my home and coffee shops in the city, was accompanied by sheer enjoyment of the movement of, and stillness in, my body.

Best of all was discovering how to step aside from my thoughts and watch so I could see that they are not the absolute truths I had always taken them to be. Watching thoughts, rather than being controlled by them, allowed the uncovering of a more complete self able to flow freely with the interconnected whole that is reality.

This author is a guy who found joy in living by seeing through the masquerading truths of everyday tensions, regrets, worries, and a continual focus on what's next. Realizing these "truths" as the mental chatter they are, and then being able to set them aside, made room for other things to be conscious of such as a wholistic awareness of my body, the surroundings, and all their interconnectedness. I shifted away from the constraint of limited head-based stuff and opened up to the fullness of what is real in the world, a wider view of possibilities and appreciation for life.

The most essential thing to describe about me, this author, is the journey of taking steps away from functioning as a know-it-all who almost continually put himself above and against life, toward a sense of being that moves with ease and gratitude through a life that is abundant whenever I'm open enough to allow it.

Most of the time now, I am a guy who wishes the same for each person I encounter, and for those I don't encounter as well. I wish for each of you to find the same underlying sense of ease and gratitude, but in a way that is unique to you. I wish for every person a full and happy meeting of "your deep gladness" with "the world's deep hunger".